*W*oolf
*S*tudies
*A*nnual

Volume 25, 2019

Copyright © 2019 by
Pace University Press
41 Park Row, 15th Floor, Rm. 1510
New York, NY 10038

All rights reserved
Printed in the United States of America

ISSN: 1080-9317
ISBN: 978-1-935625-34-6

Member

Council of Editors of Learned Journals

☉ Paper used in this publication meets the minimum requirements of American National Standard for Information Sciences–Permanence of Paper for Printed Library Materials, ANSI Z39.48–1984

Editor

Mark Hussey — Pace University

Associate Editor

Vara Neverow — Southern Connecticut State University

Book Review Editor

Amanda Golden — New York Institute of Technology

Editorial Advisory Board

Tuzyline Allan	Baruch College, CUNY
Judith Allen	Kelly Writers House, University of Pennsylvania
Morris Beja	Academy Professor Emeritus, Ohio State University
Pamela L. Caughie	Loyola University Chicago
Kimberly Engdahl Coates	Bowling Green State University
Sarah Cole	Columbia University
Kristin Czarnecki	Georgetown College
Emily Dalgarno	Boston University (Emeritus)
Beth Rigel Daugherty	Otterbein University
Claire Davison	Université Paris III–Sorbonne Nouvelle
Jane de Gay	Leeds Trinity University
Erica Gene Delsandro	Bucknell University
Madelyn Detloff	Miami University
Jeanne Dubino	Appalachian State University
Jane Goldman	University of Glasgow
Elizabeth Willson Gordon	King's University, Canada
Leslie Kathleen Hankins	Cornell College
Alice Keane	Queens College, CUNY
Emily Kopley	Concordia University Library
Karen V. Kukil	Special Collections, Smith College
Michael Lackey	Distinguished McKnight University Professor, University of Minnesota, Morris
Jane Lilienfeld	Curator's Distinguished Professor of English, Lincoln University of Missouri
Maren Linett	Purdue University
Gill Lowe	University of Suffolk
Celia Marshik	Stony Brook University
Ann Martin	University of Saskatchewan
Gabrielle McIntire	Queen's University, Canada
Toni A. H. McNaron	University of Minnesota (Emerita)
Eleanor McNees	University of Denver
Jeanette McVicker	SUNY Fredonia
Jean Mills	John Jay College, CUNY
Patricia Moran	London City University

Editorial Advisory Board (continued)

Steven Putzel	Penn State Wilkes-Barre
Beth C. Rosenberg	University of Nevada, Las Vegas
Victoria Rosner	Columbia University
Derek Ryan	University of Kent
Randi Saloman	Wake Forest University
Bonnie Kime Scott	University of San Diego (Emerita)
Urmila Seshagiri	University of Tennessee
Drew Shannon	Mount St. Joseph University
Kathryn Simpson	Unaffiliated
Anna Snaith	King's College London
Helen Southworth	Clark Honors College, University of Oregon
Elisa Sparks	Clemson University (Emerita)
Peter Stansky	Stanford University
Alice Staveley	Stanford University
Diana L. Swanson	Northern Illinois University
Janine Utell	Widener University
Julie Vandivere	Bloomsburg University
Susan Wegener	Purdue University
Michael Whitworth	University of Oxford
Alice Wood	De Montfort University
John Young	Marshall University

Many thanks to readers for Volume 25 (in addition to the Editorial Board): Charles Armstrong (U of Agder), Emily Bloom (Columbia U), Christine Darrohn (U of Maine at Farmington), Benjamin Harvey (Mississippi SU), Maggie Humm (U of East London, Emerita), Brenda Helt (Independent Scholar), Erica Johnson (Pace U), Shawna Ross (Texas A&M U), Lorraine Sim (Western Sydney U)

Woolf Studies Annual is indexed in *Humanities International Complete, ABELL,* and the *MLA Bibliography.*

Contents

Woolf Studies Annual

Volume 25, 2019

	vii	Abbreviations

ARTICLES

Theodore Koulouris	1	Virginia Woolf's "Greek Notebook" (VS Greek and Latin Studies) An Annotated Transcription
Erica Gene Delsandro	73	No More Missed Connections: A Lesson in Transpersonal Feminism with Virginia Woolf, Audre Lorde, and Adrienne Rich
Diane F. Gillespie	97	Maps of Her Own: Virginia Woolf In and Beyond the Archives

GUIDE

	137	GUIDE to Library Special Collections

REVIEWS

Jane de Gay	159	*Orlando: A Biography* by Virginia Woolf, Suzanne Raitt and Ian Blyth, eds.
Elisa Kay Sparks	162	*The Handbook to the Bloomsbury Group*, Derek Ryan and Stephen Ross, eds.
Annalee Sellers	165	*Woolf's Ambiguities: Tonal Modernism, Narrative Strategy, Feminist Precursors* by Molly Hite

Margaret Greaves	169	*Modernist Physics: Waves, Particles, and Relativities in the Writings of Virginia Woolf and D. H. Lawrence* by Rachel Crossland
Suzanne Hobson	172	*Virginia Woolf and Christian Culture* by Jane de Gay
Cristina Carluccio	175	*Trans-Woolf. Thinking Across Borders,* Claire Davison and Anne-Marie Smith-Di Biasio, eds.
Derek Ryan	178	*Sentencing Orlando: Virginia Woolf and the Morphology of the Modernist Sentence,* Elsa Högberg and Amy Bromley, eds.
Elisa Kay Sparks	181	*Walking Virginia Woolf's London: An Investigation into Literary Geography* by Lisbeth Larsson
Jeff Rosen	183	*Virginia Woolf's Influential Forebears: Julia Margaret Cameron, Anny Thackeray Ritchie and Julia Prinsep Stephen* by Marion Dell
Kelly Walsh	186	*Virginia Woolf and Being-in-the-world* by Emma Simone
Amber Pouliot	190	*Homes and Haunts: Touring Writers' Shrines and Countries* by Alison Booth
Drew Patrick Shannon	193	*Virginia Woolf: The War Without, the War Within: Her Final Diaries & the Diaries She Read* by Barbara Lounsberry
	197	Notes on Contributors
	198	Submission Guidelines

Abbreviations

AHH	*A Haunted House*
AROO	*A Room of One's Own*
BP	*Books and Portraits*
BTA	*Between the Acts*
CDB	*The Captain's Death Bed and Other Essays*
CE	*Collected Essays* (4 vols.)
CR1	*The Common Reader*
CR2	*The Common Reader, Second Series*
CSF	*The Complete Shorter Fiction*
D	*The Diary of Virginia Woolf* (5 vols.)
DM	*The Death of the Moth and Other Essays*
E	*The Essays of Virginia Woolf* (6 vols.)
F	*Flush*
FR	*Freshwater*
GR	*Granite & Rainbow: Essays*
JR	*Jacob's Room*
L	*The Letters of Virginia Woolf* (6 vols.)
M	*The Moment and Other Essays*
MEL	*Melymbrosia*
MOB	*Moments of Being*
MT	*Monday or Tuesday*
MD	*Mrs. Dalloway*
ND	*Night and Day*
O	*Orlando*
PA	*A Passionate Apprentice*
RF	*Roger Fry: A Biography*
TG	*Three Guineas*
TTL	*To the Lighthouse*
TW	*The Waves*
TY	*The Years*
VO	*The Voyage Out*

Virginia Woolf's "Greek Notebook" (VS Greek and Latin Studies) An Annotated Transcription
Theodore Koulouris

Introduction

    The following is an annotated transcription of Virginia Woolf's "Greek Notebook." I first heard about this manuscript from Angeliki Spiropoulou sometime in the late 1990s, just before I commenced my DPhil research on Woolf and the Greeks at the University of Sussex. Spiropoulou, who was then working on "On Not Knowing Greek" (1925) for an essay exploring Woolf's critique of authority,[1] told me that there was this "Greek Notebook" in the University library, which contained Woolf's analyses and translations of several Greek texts. It was then that I decided to capitalize on this rare opportunity and transcribe the notebook for my own work. There was a moment of surprise when I entered "Virginia Woolf's Greek Notebook" in the library catalogue because the search yielded no results. Surprise turned into confusion and confusion into embarrassment when I asked one of the librarians for the manuscript. Alas, it seemed that the so-called "Greek Notebook" did not exist. "VS, Greek and Latin Studies,"[2] as the "Greek Notebook" is formally known, is one of Virginia Woolf's reading notebooks. It contains her notes on a number of ancient Greek and Latin texts that she read between 1907 and 1909 (see table of contents below). Until 2013, the manuscript, which forms part of the *Monks House Papers*, was housed in the Manuscripts Section of the University of Sussex Library. In 2013, most of the Sussex Library special collections were moved to The Keep, a new, state of the art center for archives—a few minutes' walk from the Sussex University campus.[3] Oblivious at the time to the benign yet rather violent appropriation I was exerting on a document whose author had died sixty-odd years earlier, I kept referring to the manuscript as the "Greek Notebook" despite the appearance in it of Juvenal and Virgil. The purpose of this transcription

---

[1] Angeliki Spiropoulou, "'On Not Knowing Greek:' Virginia Woolf's Spatial Critique of Authority," *Interdisciplinary Literary Studies*, 4.1, Fall 2002, pp. 1-19. Apart from Greek, this notebook contains Woolf's commentary on three of Juvenal's *Satires* and on Virgil's *Georgic IV*. Both works, nevertheless, demonstrate an interest in Greek mythology (Virgil) and an interest in the general socio-cultural influence of Greece (Juvenal, *Satire VI*).
[2] The new reference number of this manuscript at The Keep is SxMS-18/A/21.
[3] See www.thekeep.info/about_us/.

is to provide scholars and students of Woolf's work with a glimpse of, and an insight into, her early engagement with Greek and Latin letters. The first iteration of this transcription was produced during the course of my DPhil research and was appended to my thesis, "Virginia Woolf: Hellenism, Greekness and Loss" (Sussex, 2005). The new, complete transcription will constitute an invaluable resource not only for scholars working on Woolf and the classics, but also for scholars working in the following areas: her intellectual and literary influences at large; the development of her early feminist thinking and the conditions of women's higher education in Victorian and post-Victorian Britain; Woolf's narrative style and her modernist textual aesthetics; her relationship with western philosophy and intellectual history; the influences of Greece and Rome on modernism and British letters in general; and, of course, it would be of great help to scholars working on Woolf as a (not so common) *reader*; for it is an indubitable fact that in this manuscript the reader will not encounter Virginia Woolf, the towering figure of British modernism, but Virginia Stephen, a young female reader of texts at the threshold of her career as a woman of letters.

The "Greek Notebook" (GN), then, is a quarter-leather reading notebook, which bears a marbled hard cover on the front and a soft cover on the back. It is 7 inches wide and 8.7 inches long. On the inside of the front cover, on the top-left hand side, it bears a label which reads "Parkins & Gotto, Oxford Street, London, Wholesale & Retail."[4] The document bears covering notes by Quentin Bell, Woolf's nephew, and by his wife, Anne Olivier Bell; also, it contains a small note by Leonard Woolf written on the back of a loose calendar page dated "Sept. 15 1955"; under the date, this page also contains a quotation from John Keats: "I am certain of nothing but of the holiness of the heart's affection, and the truth of imagination."[5] The notes by the aforementioned individuals do not constitute part of the notebook itself, but of the packaging when the manuscript—one of the many that comprise the *Monks House Papers*—was passed to the University of Sussex.[6]

---

[4] Parkins and Gotto established a high quality retail outlet at 2 Hanway Street, Oxford Street, in the 1840s. See www.hamptonantiques.co.uk/index.pl?id=2900.

[5] The whole quotation reads, "I am certain of nothing but of the holiness of the Heart's affections, and the truth of Imagination. What the Imagination seizes as Beauty must be Truth—whether it existed before or not,—for I have the same idea of all our passions as of Love: they are all, in their sublime, creative of essential Beauty" (From a letter to Benjamin Bailey, 22 November 1817). H. Buxton Forman, ed., *The Complete Works of John Keats, Vol IV*, Glasgow: Gowars & Gray, 1901, 46).

[6] Fiona Courage (Sussex University /The Keep) informs me that the collection came to Sussex via the artist Trekkie Parsons (1902-1995), who became Leonard Woolf's companion after Virginia's death in 1941. Upon Leonard's death in 1969, the house and its contents were left to Parsons who in turn presented everything to the University of Sussex. In time, the house was passed to the National Trust, while the papers formed part of the Sussex University Library's Special Collections.

Woolf's handwriting in the GN is elegant and free-flowing; it bears witness to her intellectual genealogy and evinces her ancestors' special relationship with the act of writing. To be sure, Woolf was very serious about all aspects of writing. In another notebook, she writes:

> This book has now got to be a kind of testing ground, where I come to test my new pens. I have made the most heroic resolution to change my ideas of calligraphy in conformance with those of my family, which are more generally accepted by the world as the correct ones. (*PA* 416)

As with the *Diary,* Woolf prefers to write by means of a dipping-pen and ink. We know that because there are ink-stains on the verso of almost every page of the manuscript. Whenever she runs out of ink or there is a problem—say, with a defective pen—she resorts to using a soft pencil. The table of contents is all written in black ink with a neat hand. Pages 1-10 are numbered in blue ink—pages 8-10 are blank, but pre-numbered. Pages 11-84 are numbered in blue ink—pages 76-84 are completely blank but for page 79, which contains a short note. Page 1 and up until the first half of page 15 are written in black ink; after that, and up until page 21, Woolf is writing in pencil. The first four lines of the second paragraph on page 15 are written in pencil, but written over again in somewhat faint ink, only for Woolf to resume in pencil. When it comes to dating, the entries in the GN are simple and read thus: the first entry, Juvenal's *Satires,* is dated "Dec. 1st 1907." The *Odyssey* starts "(Feb. 27th [19]08)" and finishes "15th May [1908]." Then, A.W. Verrall's introduction to *Ion* and Woolf's own commentary on the play are dated "May 18th [1908]," and p. 50 suggests she finished on "5th June [19]08." The *Symposium* finishes on 15th July [19]08, whereas Virgil's *Georgic IV* is dated "28th July [1908]." *Ajax* begins "Dec 7th [1908]," while *The Frogs* "Jan. 11th: [19]09." Lastly, Plato's *Phaedrus* is dated "25th May [1909]."

Woolf has a very particular way of writing; for instance, her diaries and letters are full of abbreviations, nicknames, euphemisms and other idiosyncrasies, all of which coalesce to make the text decidedly Woolfian. Luckily, similar idiosyncrasies are present in the GN, albeit in a different way. For instance, she tends not to write Greek names in their entirety; she would write "Odysseus" or "Socrates" the first time, but the second and subsequent times she would just write "O" or "So:." However, this tendency is not a standard practice. When it comes to the *Symposium* for instance, there are a few Greek names such as Aristodemous or Alcibiades—names definitely more complex to the non-Greek eye and ear—which she renders in full. What I can say with certainty is that Woolf is decidedly *not* consistent in her writing in the GN. Her spelling is good throughout.

The text itself is very intriguing. The reader may notice that she is vacillating between the ancient text and her mother-tongue; between her own attempts at translation and whatever official translations she might have been using; between the *logos* of the original text and the images created in her head; between the reality of Greek as a language, an intellectual heritage and a culture, and the reality instilled in her by external determinants such as the role of Greek in Victorian and Edwardian Britain; between the "glory that was Greece" in British Victorian and Edwardian imagination and the reality—that is, the ramshackle state of Greece in the 1910s, a reality that Woolf herself experienced during her first trip there in 1906, a year before commencing work in the GN. All this had, to a certain extent, tempered her ability to absorb and render such texts with the objectivity that a strictly scholarly approach in the 1910s would require—and I, for one, am most thankful for that. The commentary she produced, therefore, is neither a strictly philological approach nor a simple, amateurish play at "serious" literature. It is an honest production, a serious, painstaking rendering of several canonical texts that she, I gather, considered central to structuring a grounded life in literature. As we shall see, her text evinces a number of emotions, easily perceived by the reader, emotions generated through identification, alienation, catharsis and mental as well as psychical elevation. This is a central property of the GN. In my view, the aforementioned vacillation gives rise to anomalous syntax and, to a certain extent, grammatical inconsistency. Sometimes she seems to be carried away by the syntax of the original text to the extent that she produces irregular sentence patterns—a form of *glossolalia*, whose constitutive elements are separated only by an ampersand or a dash, thereby preventing the reader from clearly distinguishing, as Olivier Bell remarks, "whether a single mark made at speed is intended as a comma, a full stop, or a dash; or [whether] two marks as a colon or a semi-colon" (*D*1 xii).

Indeed, the element that most hampered my approach was Woolf's handwriting which, at times, makes the text illegible; scores of colleagues who have also worked in the archives would attest to the veracity of this statement. Mindful of the speed of her writing, it is surprising that she has not crossed out many words or sentences. That said, whenever she has crossed out something I am providing, if possible, both the abandoned and the sustained version. Generally, I have promoted the special dynamic of this notebook by aiming at maintaining Woolf's esoteric approach to these texts. By esoteric, I mean her insistence on probing deeply into the text whilst seeming to be dismissive; forgetful; at times, even reductive. Another problem I had to cope with whilst working on this text was an insurmountable (at the beginning) desire to draw parallels between the manuscript and Woolf's life and work. Of course, one could argue that this is the goal of all archival research. However, due to the fact that the GN is hardly an established text in Woolf studies, I initially approached it with certain preconceptions generated by my own reading of other texts, either by or on Woolf. For instance, while I was transcribing the first passages of her commentary on the *Odyssey*, I found myself wondering why Woolf had chosen not to comment on passages that I, as a student of Woolf's work, thought that she would have felt compelled to do so. To give an example, keeping in mind Woolf's lifelong struggle against patriarchy, I found her skipping Calypso's speech against the Gods rather peculiar.[7] In other words, I was pre-empting the manuscript, a text written between 1907 and 1909, of all its potential because I wanted to discover qualities, both personal and textual, that Woolf developed, and became famous for, later on in life. It was not until I succeeded in ridding my approach of all spasmodic glances at her *whole* life and work that I discovered the wonderfully charming as well as potentially powerful interventions that this manuscript could make in Woolf studies.

Nonetheless, there are a few points that warrant a degree of scrutiny. We may ask, for instance, to what extent did her readings in this notebook influence her own creative work? Also, why did she choose to comment on Juvenal's *Satires* over, for instance, a text by Aeschylus? In addition, why did she read texts such as the *Symposium* when it is certain that the brotherhood of aristocratic, intellectual men glorified by Plato as the most pertinent means towards the crystallization of the "ideal" form of love, would only serve to remind her that she was, at least between 1907 and 1909, a female amateur in a society of men? Before approaching these questions, I should say that Woolf started Greek lessons with Dr. George Warr in the late 1890s.[8] By her own admission, Greek was her "daily bread and a keen delight" (*L2* 35); she found, she adds, that to her "immense pride" she really enjoyed, not only admired, Sophocles (*L2* 42-43). Greek constituted her intellectual mainstay during the "seven unhappy years" between 1897, when her half-sister Stella Duckworth died, and 1904, when Leslie Stephen died and the Stephen children moved to Gordon Square, Bloomsbury. However, although Woolf generally

---

[7] See *Odyssey*, V, 129-130.

[8] Woolf's relationship with university education is a much-debated issue and cannot be analysed in any substantial way here. In my *Hellenism and Loss in the Work of Virginia Woolf* (Ashgate, 2011), I followed received knowledge and worked on the understanding that Woolf had not received any formal higher education. However, the extraordinary revelations by Anna Snaith and Christine Kenyon Jones (2010) suggest that not only was Woolf's study at King's College extended, but that it "brought her in direct contact with some of the early reformers of women's higher education" (Kenyon Jones and Snaith 1-2). Though it was unfortunate that my book was in press when this very important study was published, Kenyon Jones and Snaith acknowledge that it is very curious indeed that Woolf herself did not draw on her own university experience (ibid., 40). If I were to hazard a guess as to why this was the case, I would say that her silence does not suggest lack of candor, but rather a committed socio-political stance against an educational asymmetry that militated against women. To be sure, and no matter how serious, noble and innovative women's higher education was in post-1860s "Ladies' Departments," it was not recognized as formal—in other words, it did not lead to a degree. Therefore, for the purposes of this introduction, I have maintained the general tenor of my original approach with this qualification: although Woolf *did* go to university, her understanding of her experience at King's College was that that it was "informal."

enjoyed all her readings, it was predominantly her engagement with Greek that, in my view, made her realize the gendered asymmetry between men and women of letters. Leaving aside incidents such as the one involving George Duckworth, Lady Carnarvon, Mrs. Popham of Littlecote and an eighteen-year-old Woolf lecturing them on Platonic values (*MOB* 174), Woolf found out very early that the study of Greek was a man's business, a business to which only a select few were invited.

Despite her fascination with Greek, Woolf begins this notebook with Juvenal's *Satires*. She translates the first lines of the first satire freely: whereas Juvenal writes "s*emper ego auditor tantum*" (must I always be the listener?),[9] Woolf translates "He writes—why not I too?" She clearly marks, therefore, her position against the time-honored British philological tradition: for her, neither the text nor the "truths" it contains are sacred any longer. More importantly, though, the choice of words, "He writes—why not I too," evinces an overflowing desire to partake of a cultural heritage but, at the same time, to exercise her intellectual right to intervene on that heritage with a view to building a personal textual aesthetics. I should note here that she does not translate "They write" or "Everybody writes"; she rather boldly declares "He [a man] writes—why not I [a woman] too," thereby explicitly gendering the asymmetry of the *right* to write. I do not read the above as a mere complaint, for that would indicate passivity and submission. Rather, I read it as a serious indictment of British classical education which, still in the early twentieth century, seemed to exist for the exclusive benefit of (aristocratic) men. Be that as it may, and since neither I nor Brenda Silver (in *RN*) are sure which edition of the *Satires* Woolf was using, it is really remarkable that she produced such a lengthy summary given Juvenal's biting social commentary and multiple references to his contemporaries (especially in *Satire III*). It is also of interest that she reserved her most sustained commentary for *Satire III*—Juvenal's most caustic yet pretty xenophobic indictment of Roman reality in the first century AD—and *Satire VI*—on the surface, probably one of the most overtly misogynistic literary works of classical antiquity.[10] This is surprising especially if we keep in mind how quick Woolf was to indict Homer's treatment of Penelope in the *Odyssey*.[11]

By far, Woolf's most sustained engagement in this manuscript is with Homer's text. One could argue that this is due to the length of the text itself, but, interestingly, Homer's narrative devices have not gone unnoticed by Woolf. For instance, the ways in which Homer breaks up the narrative in order to intensify, as and when

---

[9] Peter Green translates this as "Must I *always* be stuck in the audience [?]," (Juvenal, *The Sixteen Satires*, Trans. Peter Green, London: Penguin Books, 1998, 3). Green's emphasis.
[10] Susanna H. Braund argues that in contrast with earlier works—those of Stobaeus or Semonides of Amorgos—*Satire VI* maintains a rather favorable view of women; see "Juvenal— Misogynist or Misogamist?" *The Journal of Roman Studies*, 82, 1992, pp.72-73.
[11] Whilst reading Book XVI of the *Odyssey*, she appears angered by the way in which Penelope is perennially depicted as suspicious just because she is a woman: "They [men] treat her with suspicion always; the blameless woman!" (GN 29).

needed, Odysseus' story, are singled out by Woolf and commented upon: "[t]his," she writes in the GN, "seems to me a most ingenious device for you could not have all the story at once, but broken in pieces like this it is more audible; & made more intense by the feeling of the audience"(GN 23). Further, in her short story "The Journal of Mistress Joan Martyn" (*CSF* 33-62), written in 1906—a year before she commenced work on the GN—there is a willful resurrection of Woolf's Homeric readings of the 1890s.[12] By interweaving a story (Miss Rosamond Merridew, the female investigator of old English manuscripts) within a second story (Rosamond Merridew visiting Mr. Martyn whose ancestress's journal she sets out to review), and from there, the second story within a third (the actual journal of Joan Martyn), Woolf echoes a multi-layered, Homeric narrative which Erich Auerbach discusses at length in "Odysseus' Scar" (Auerbach 3-23). Homer's resonance does not stop there. In reviewing the journal, Miss Merridew discovers that Joan Martyn has been reading the story of Helen and of "the fair town of Troy" and, underscoring the importance of the text, she remarks

> … for though we none of us know where those places are, we see very well what they must have been like; and we can weep for the sufferings of the soldiers, and picture to ourselves the stately woman herself, who must have been, I think, something like my mother … "It must have been in Cornwall," said Sir John, "where King Arthur lived with his knights." (*CSF* 46-47)

Furthermore, showing that she is entirely aware of the ways in which the Homeric epics survived before being committed to writing, Woolf employs the figure of the roaming bard, Richard, who, in a veritably Homeric fashion, roams England selling his books and telling stories, and who, subsequently, is cordially invited to dinner at Mistress Joan Martyn's house:

> My daughter tells me Sir that you come from foreign parts, and can sing. We are but country people: and therefore I fear very little acquainted with the tales of other parts. But we are ready to listen. Sing us something of your land; and then, if you will, you shall sit down to meat with us, and we will gladly hear news of the country. (*CSF* 55)

If we juxtapose Woolf's text with Homer's own depiction of Odysseus in Alcinous' palace in which the minstrel, Demodocus, sings of the story of Troy leading to

---

[12] See Susan M. Squier and Louise A. DeSalvo, "Virginia Woolf's 'The Journal of Mistress Joan Martyn'," *Twentieth Century Literature*, 25 (3/4), 1979, pp. 237-269. Woolf first heard about Homer from Thoby (*MOB* 125). In M. G. Holleyman's catalogue of the books Woolf inherited from her father, there are three books on Homer, including the *Odyssey* in two volumes, and both of Homer's epics in Greek (see Koulouris 42).

Odysseus' revealing his identity and the subsequent freeing-up of the narrative towards his eventual return to Ithaca (*Odyssey*, XIII), we may conclude that Homer's influence on Woolf's early work was of tremendous importance; not only did it provide Woolf's early writing with fruitful parallel narrative lines—Richard, the bard in "Joan Martyn," Demodocus in the *Odyssey*—but also because it highlighted the importance of narrative structure and story-telling.

The *Symposium*, one of Plato's most famous dialogues, was also central to the development of Woolf's thinking in the first decade of the twentieth century. Leaving aside the nature of the "dinner-party"—a habitual occurrence at 46 Gordon Square and a central mode of philosophical investigation that strengthened the ties of friendship among the members of the Bloomsbury Group—the structure of the *Symposium*—the carving out of the theme of conversation, the pluralism and diversity of its treatises, the syncretism with which the treatises contribute to the crystallization of a certain concept (here, love)—contains elements mirrored in Woolf's own narrative properties in later life. In *The Waves*, for instance, she renders the dramatic soliloquies of six different people in order to reveal the way in which their minds work—to discover, as fully as it may be possible, some notion of existence or identity. It is important to note that with the *Symposium* we have perhaps the beginning of the Western philosophical canon in so far as this dialogue establishes principles of investigation and methodology that have since punctuated the intellectual development of the so-called West. We have the choice of a set topic; the necessary plurality of approaches to that topic; the required clarity with which these approaches (should) succeed one another; the exposition of ideas based on reason (*logos*), and we also have the intervention of the metaphysical, or intuitive, element as exemplified by Aristophanes in his use of mythology (*muthos*). Woolf is aware of these principles; she, nevertheless, challenges their currency and expands their value in her own work. Plato's elusive idealities are mirrored in Woolf's own committed textual search for an idea of "self" which, nevertheless, remains continually deferred. This is a sustained characteristic of Woolf's textual poetics. And although attributing her lifelong struggle against patriarchy *only* to her Greek study would be facile and inaccurate, the fact that in the GN she underscores Homer's unfair treatment of Penelope and highlights the general prejudice against Creusa in Euripides' *Ion*, bears testament to the importance of her Greek readings in the formation of her early feminist thinking. There is no doubt that the GN was a serious engagement for Woolf between 1907 and 1909. One has but to read her commentary on the *Ion* and Sophocles' *Ajax* to understand her determination to produce a good piece of work. In the *Ajax*, for instance, she has produced a close, almost line-by-line, translation in addition to her overall analysis of the play and of R. C. Jebb's introduction (GN 67-70). It is this tremendous amount of dogged devotion to reading these texts that enabled her to conclude on the *Ajax*: "In these choruses I can see now & then, the inimitable style, a music of words—transcending meaning" (GN 72).

However, the GN should not be thought of as a first-class piece of scholarly work; then again, it was never meant as one. In my view, it ought to be thought of as a private affair intended to remain private for ever. Woolf's own note on page 79—"Read over again, Jan. 1917; an interval of nearly ten years"—suggests (though it does not prove) that Woolf must have had but one look at it after she finished it in 1909.[13] Perhaps the GN was used as a commonplace book, in which Woolf had jotted down a few ideas on the classics ready for use either in the company of her Bloomsbury friends, or in her novels and essays, festooned as they are with Greek references. After all, its contents are neither straightforward translations nor straightforward analyses or summaries; rather—as perhaps is the case with the entirety of Woolf's output—the answer lies somewhere in the middle, in the interstices of philology and social commentary, and/or of literature and philosophy. Perhaps, and this is how I choose to look at it, this notebook constituted a *memento mori*, poignant reminder of her brother Thoby, who died immediately after their first trip to Greece in 1906. It was, after all, from him that she first heard about the Greeks.[14] Indeed, we should keep in mind that by the time Woolf started this notebook in 1907 she had already lost four members of her immediate family. If we consider the enthusiasm with which she renders Odysseus' descent to Hades in Book XI of the *Odyssey* (GN 19), or her rendering in Latin of a similar passage in Virgil's *Georgic* (GN 60, verso), we can understand one way in which her deep, multi-faceted as well as lifelong interest in loss, memory and mourning has, to a considerable extent, its textual roots in this document. In particular, her longing to crystallize a poetics of loss is evident in the closing paragraph to her commentary on the *Odyssey*, worth quoting in full:

> This is a characteristic ending; as though the voice, simply, had finished speaking, the sun having set, & it being time for bed. But there is also a great sense of that the drama is completed; we are relieved of all anxiety about the future by the knowledge of what must happen to Odysseus—that he is to travel, & meet death, the easiest way, by sea. The scene dies out, as a landscape in the evening. (GN 41)

---

[13] Brenda Silver writes that "[p]ages 9-10 are blank, indicating perhaps that Woolf meant to go on with her notes on Juvenal" (*Virginia Woolf's Reading Notebooks*, New Jersey: Princeton UP, 1983, 166).

[14] *MOB*, 125. Woolf started this notebook in December 1907, thirteen months after Thoby's death. The Stephen children and Violet Dickinson, a close family friend, travelled to Greece in September 1906; they had visited a number of places and had been there for about a month before Thoby had to return to England on October 14. When the rest returned on November 1, they found him seriously ill with high fever and diarrhoea. Thoby Stephen died on November 20, 1906.

The relief Woolf underlines here—the one provided by the realization that the drama has come to an appropriate conclusion—tempers the significatory currency of the words "ending," "finished" and "set," and operates to elucidate mourning as an ethical stance of a life that is thought of, after all, *also* as a drama in need of completion. In adopting a textual poetics of loss undergirded by mourning not as a linear, therapeutic process to be rid of but as an indivisible part of life, Woolf sets the foundations of a lifelong textual experimentation with loss and memory.

Note on the Text

I have already mentioned that Woolf's handwriting was, at times, very hard to read. Lacunae are denoted by means of three-dot ellipses [...]. Whenever I have not been able to decipher more than one word, I mark this by brackets and a number—for instance, [3]—to indicate the number of illegible words. Lacunae of one or more sentences are marked with a four-dot ellipsis in bold type. When I have been uncertain of a particular word or phrase, I render this by inserting a question mark—[?]—or I opt for a potential alternative. In the event of anomalous syntax obscuring meaning, I provide clarification in brackets or in a footnote. It should be understood that everything appearing in brackets [__] is my intervention, but everything in parentheses (__) is Woolf's. When Woolf seems to be quoting from the original I give a bibliographic reference in a footnote, whenever possible; in such instances, I maintain the standard bibliographic classification of ancient texts—for instance (*Symposium*, 197c) or (*Odyssey*, XXIII, 123). This is because it has not been possible to locate every reference text or translation that Woolf was using. Therefore, using the standard bibliographic referencing for ancient texts will enable the reader to locate a passage of interest more easily. At times, Woolf seems to have written a phrase or passage in bold; as I cannot be sure whether this was intentional or whether it was merely a case of having freshly dipped her pen in ink, I only render in bold those parts that I think were important. This is done either by using italics or a footnote. In some cases, Woolf uses "wd," "shd" and "cd" instead of "would," "should" and "could"; I have maintained this in my transcription. However, whenever she uses just "wh" for "which" I have given the whole word in brackets to aid readability: "wh.[ich]." Greek names are mostly rendered phonetically or directly transliterated; for instance, she would write "Lestrygonia" instead of "Laestrygonia," or "Menelaos" instead of "Menelaus." Another famous feature of Woolf's personal writing, the use of ampersand as her predominant conjunction instead of "and," is also maintained in my transcription. I have also maintained Woolf's famous (if not notorious) tendency to omit apostrophes in contractions and possessives. These features do not hinder the reader's ability to follow the text in all its complex qualities as a referential work. It is a rather easy piece to follow, but only once the reader has grown accustomed to its idiosyncrasies.

I have maintained Woolf's pagination throughout. The page numbers of the manuscript are given in bold type followed by the text they contain: for instance, **GN1**, **GN2** and so on. Whenever Woolf has written on the verso of a page, this is rendered thus: **GN22 Verso**. In order to provide the reader with a feel of the notebook I have, as much as possible, rendered a diplomatic transcription of the manuscript. Finally, as far as my overall interventions are concerned, the reader should understand that I am not a professional classicist; therefore, my annotations, translations, or comments on Woolf's own translations are those of a native speaker of Greek and, as far as the classics are concerned, an amateur who has, nevertheless, received formal instruction in ancient Greek and Latin as part of his schooling. Lastly, given my background and interests, my annotations on the Greek texts are more substantial than on the texts by Juvenal and Virgil.

I would like to thank the following individuals for their help and support; first, members of the faculty at Sussex when I was researching my DPhil (2000-2004): Alistair Davies, my supervisor, guided me expertly and supported me through scholarly and personal problems, while Laura Marcus, Norman Vance, Lindsay Smith, and Elena Gualtieri offered me advice at the early stages of this project. I would also like to express my deep gratitude to Elizabeth (Bet) Inglis, the then head-librarian at Special Collections, University of Sussex, who prepared a copy of the manuscript for me, many years ago, thereby saving me innumerable trips to the library; also, my thanks to Rose Lock and Fiona Courage (University of Sussex / The Keep) for their help whenever I visited the archives. My thanks also to Adèle Cassigneul and Simon Goldhill for promptly helping me whenever I asked, and to Angeliki Spiropoulou, from whom, to paraphrase Woolf, *I first heard* about the "Greek Notebook." I should also thank the Society of Authors, representatives of the Literary Estate of Virginia Woolf, for granting me permission to transcribe and reproduce pictures of the manuscript. I would also like to thank Karen Humble, not only for her help with the transcription but also for her support and encouragement. Finally, I would like to thank Beth Daugherty, who suggested I consider publishing this transcription, and Mark Hussey and the editorial board for accommodating this important resource in *Woolf Studies Annual*.

Works Cited

Auerbach, Erich. *Mimesis: The Representation of Reality in Western Literature.* translated by Willard R. Trask, Princeton UP, 1974, 3-23.

Kenyon-Jones, Christine and Anna Snaith. "Tilting at Universities: Virginia Woolf at King's College London." *Woolf Studies Annual*, vol. 16, 2010, pp. 1-44.

Koulouris, Theodore. *Hellenism and Loss in the Work of Virginia Woolf.* Ashgate, 2011.

Silver, Brenda R. *Virginia Woolf's Reading Notebooks.* Princeton, 1983.

Spiropoulou, Angeliki. "'On Not Knowing Greek': Virginia Woolf's Spatial Critique of Authority." *Interdisciplinary Literary Studies* vol. 4, no.1, 2002, pp. 1-19.

Woolf, Virginia, *The Complete Shorter Fiction.* Edited by Susan K. Dick, Harcourt, 1989.

———. *The Diary of Virginia Woolf.* 5 Vols. Edited by Anne Olivier Bell and Andrew McNeillie, Penguin Books, 1977-1985.

———. "The Greek Notebook" (VS Greek and Latin Studies) ms. [SxMS-18/A/21] The Keep, Sussex, UK.

———. *The Letters of Virginia Woolf,* 6 Vols. Edited by Nigel Nicolson and Joanne Trautmann, Harcourt Brace Jovanovich, 1977-1982.

——— *Moments of Being.* Edited by Jeanne Schulkind, Harcourt Brace & Company, 1985.

——— *A Passionate Apprentice: The Early Journals.* Edited by Mitchell A. Leaska, Hogarth, 1992.

Monks House Papers
Virginia Stephen: Greek and Latin Studies
(MH/A.21)

GN Cover Page i

V[irginia]. S[tephen]. Greek & Latin Studies. 1907-1909[15]
"dated: Dec. 1st 1909"[16]
"note: Read over again Jan.1917"[17]

GN Cover Page ii

Translation, analyses & notes on Juvenal, Plato, Virgil [...].[18]

The golden June rising from dirt, from dried earth, & the midges staining the sky, making a net, a veil, slowly, dreamily: gilding shop windows staining faces, & turning the pavement to beaten brass.[19]

[GN Table of Contents]

The *Satires* of Juvenal[20]

Satire I. Page   I. The reason for writing satire.
Satire 3 "   2. Why a man may not live in Rome.
Satire 6 "   7. On Woman.

The *Odyssey* of Homer[21]   11

---

[15] Quentin Bell's note.
[16] Anne Olivier Bell's note.
[17] Olivier Bell's note; my thanks to Elizabeth Inglis for this information.
[18] This is the note by Leonard Woolf. It is written on the verso of a loose wall-calendar page. There is another sign after this that looks like an ampersand followed by "others." Unfortunately, the sign, whether it is an abbreviation or a mere scribble, is not clear.
[19] This is a note by Woolf on a blue piece of paper laid in loose between pages 78 and 79. I give the transcription of the note here as I do not think that its having been placed between those pages was intentional or significant.
[20] There is no indication of which edition of Juvenal's satires Woolf was using.
[21] Again, there is no indication of which edition of the *Iliad* Woolf used here.

Books 1, 2, 3, 4.	11
Books 5, 6.	12
Books 6, 7.	13
Books 7, 8.	14
Book 9	16
Book 10	17
Book 11	19
Book 12	22
Book 13	24
Book 14	24
Book 15	27
Book 16	29
Book 17	31
Book 18	33
Book 19	34
Book 20	35
Book 21	36
Book 22	37
Book 23	38
Book 24	39
Ion of Euripides[22]	42
Symposium [Plato][23]	53
4th Georgic [Virgil][24]	60
~~Frogs of Aristophanes~~	~~62~~
Ajax: Sophocles.[25]	62
The Frogs [Aristophanes][26]	74
The Phaedrus [Plato][27] 77	

---

[22] According to Brenda Silver (168), Woolf was using the 1890 edition with a translation and notes by A. W. Verrall, (Cambridge: Cambridge UP, 1890).
[23] No indication as to which edition Woolf was using.
[24] As above.
[25] According to Silver (*RN* 168), Woolf was using Richard Claverhouse Jebb's *Sophocles: The Plays and Fragments. The Ajax* (Cambridge: Cambridge UP, 1896).
[26] Woolf was using Aristophanes, *The Frogs*, "Greek text revised with a Translation, Introduction and Commentary by Benjamin Bickley Rogers. Bell, 1902" (Silver, 169).
[27] Uncertain edition.

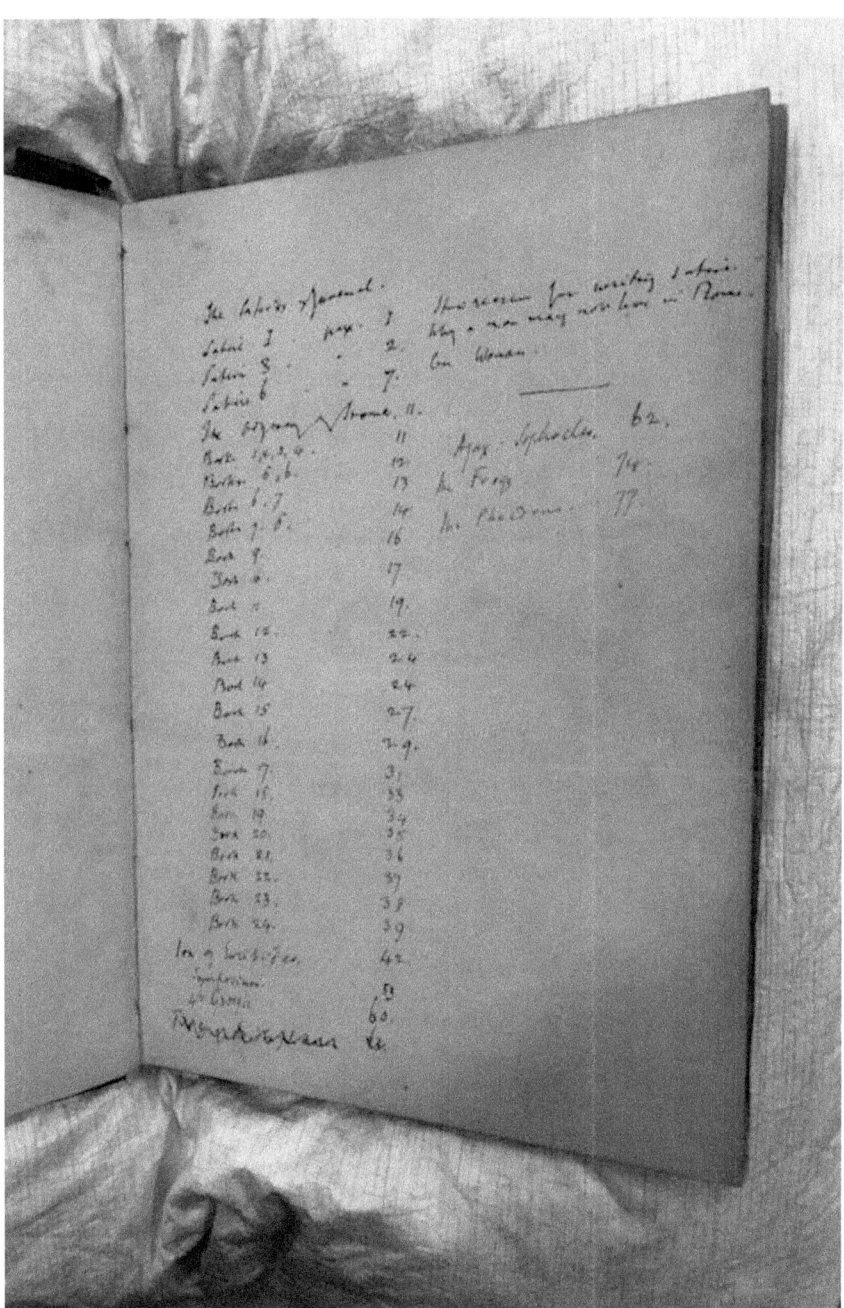
GN1

GN1[28]

Juvenal

Dec. 1st 1907.

Satire I

He writes—why not I too? I have reasons for choosing Satire. Vices flaunt themselves everywhere. They bark in a medley. Noble & low lowly crowd alike for the scanty dole distributed by the rich; Wealth [3] no temple, though it is the divinity [that is, wealth] most worshipped in our age. After trudging [?] all day after their dole the poor clients are refused dinner at the table of the patron, who feasts on a whole boar [by] himself or takes a whole peacock to the bath—& often suffers for it. For the rich die suddenly, without wills, & such deaths are applauded not mourned. My friends however, bid me beware of the enmity of the living, & advise me to write once more about the old mythologies which cannot possibly interest anyone now. So I will see what entertainment the noble dead of the past generation have to offer.

GN2

Satire 3

I must commend, though I regret, the decision of my friend to move from Rome to Cumae. No place can be so desolate, but that it is not preferable to the dread of fires, of falling roofs and reciting poets. But while his move went on we went together to those groves where the Jews encamp, & descended into the valley & artificial caves of Egeria. How much more vivid would be "the spirit of the stream" if only there were grass banks & no marble sides!
Then Umbricius spoke: There is no place in Rome for honesty, or reward for labour. Day by day that little goes. So let us depart, while we may to Cumae. Let only those live, & in Rome, who are capable of all contracts, of their banter of men. The old trumpeters, even, of the swollen cheeks, have become millionaires, & all is in their power—What should I do in Rome? I neither lie, nor star tell, nor act [as a] procurer. No one shall be a thief at my behest. I am no better than a cripple. Presents given or taken, make secret compacts. He will be dear to Verres, when he has reason to fear [2] all the gold that the Tagus washes over with the sand will [retract?] you for loss of sleep, for the [3] of your friends.

---

[28] I am using the Peter Green translation (1967) in the Penguin Classics edition. Juvenal, *The Sixteen Satires*, trans. Peter Green, London, 1998. All annotations and clarifications pertaining to the Latin text and Rome's history are sourced from his introduction and/or notes.

GN3

III cont.
How I will speak of that […] that […] in prime favour with us. I cannot endure a Rome turned Greek. Still, there others, Asiatic scum, who are worse. You hear their music & meet their prostitutes. [....] They worm themselves into great families, swift, daring, glib of speech, eloquent. They are infinitely versatile. [They] know all the […] of grammarian[s], […] & so on. Yet, I fly their purple cloaks. Why should he[29] always have precedence of me, who was born here by the wind that brings [2] & cotton. I was nourished on hard Sabine nut. They flatter, & it goes down; we are not believed. So, [is] there any better actor than a Greek? Comedy is in their bones. They laugh with you, & cry with you -but [they] do not grieve. Ah, he is beyond us in his sympathies and his perceptions, as swift and as true. And as we have for when true Greeks […] to some of their crime. How the "stoic" killed Bareas, his pupil. The old man killed the young. Rome is no place for me; Protogenes & his friends live there, & […] their friends alone. For directly [2] the poison dropped into his ear by some such friend, then I have the word to move on, the times of my long servitude (Juvenal was a poor man & writes from the point of view of a client) are gone for working. There is working simpler than to drop a client.

GN4

Yet I wont lay the blame entirely on all the Greeks. What service do the poor render, and what do they deserve, who run through the streets early [or only?] to snatch the dole of some rich widow? A rich slave takes the wall (work? walk?) of a free born man. Suppose some great man of old were to return & ask—what does he pay his slaves—how does he live, would not the answer be—he is honoured in proportion to his money bags. A poor man has cause to think that he can ignore the gods who ignore him. The cruellest part of poverty is that it makes men ridiculous. If the beggar take his seat by the bastard, or the young fencing master, nor push for a chair with the knights![30] What son in law can succeed who cannot equal his brides dowry? How soon will those [who] succeed in life whose means are narrow.[31] At Rome the struggle is worst. They will not dine off earthenware there, though that is good enough for the Marsix [Marsos] & Sabella. There is a

---

[29] Denoting a Greek or someone from Asia.
[30] Lines 53-60. Peter Green translates this as follows: "'You! Get out of those front-row seats ... You ought to be ashamed—your incomes are far too meagre. ... Make way for some pander's son and heir, spawned in an unknown brothel; yield your place to the offspring of that natty auctioneer with the trainer's son and the ring-fighter's brat applauding beside him'" (18).
[31] Would we be justified in arguing that the emergence of Woolf's materialist thought, especially concerning women's professional prospects in *AROO*, may be located somewhere here?

large part of Italy in which people only wear a white toga at death. There is […] at the […] play & the orchestra & the people [?] wear[s] the same clothes. Why is it in Rome then—where everything costs money. You must pay for a free mans smile[s] while he valishes benefits on his slaves.

GN5

190

What fear is there in the country of the tall of roof or wall? The mayors of Rome are always at work. & there is a fire & the cry is for water. The poor who own nothing lose that nothing. "In time, poor Cordus nothing had to boast, & yet poor Cordus all that nothing lost."[32] But when a noble house is burnt Rex is mourning, & all his friends bring contribution[s] to repair his loss—till some say that he set fire to his house on purpose. If you could only leave Rome you could have a plot of your own ground in the country, your [?] sole property. Some die in Rome for lack of sleep and others from indigestion. Drovers stand cursing in the streets. Rich men of course pass through the city quickly, upborne in their litters; where they can read or draw the curtains—sleep; the poor clients [?] struggle along in the crowd, doles are given, & slaves […] work. "Drunk [?] kitchener" & fire.[33] The free are carried on wagons, & if the wheel breaks some wretch is crushed beneath. And the slaves at home make ready while their master crosses the sticks nor has a farthing to pay his fare. (if it is the master would he not have more? & if the slave why prepare for him?) But […] again the dangers of her [Rome?] night— Every open window may be your death.[34] Ruffians

GN6

abroad who will not sleep without their brawl. Time [2] to get clear of the rich man with his guard of footmen—but they will stop you, bully you, beat you till your ribs crack. Then bail you to the bar for beating them. And some of you stay at home & lock the doors, & all the shops are barred, soldiers come into some and sack the place. All our iron is spent in making fetters and shackles; no ploughs or hoes are made. Happy were our ancestors who could contain all their prisoners in one gaol. Well these are all causes why I should leave Rome; & the muleteer beckons. Remember me when you in despair too retire to Aquinam. I will come & listen to your satires.

[32] Line 208.
[33] Lines 245-250.
[34] Line 270.

GN7

Second Book. Satire 6

Modesty still dwelled on Earth when Saturn reigned; & a cave did for house, or man made him[self] a bed with the beasts of the mountains. That is [?] strange to you, Cynthia, or Lesbia, whose tender eyes are moistened by a sparrow's death. Their woman gave such to hefty babies, & fed on acorns. Men lived otherwise then, when sun & earth were new;[35] born of oak they were, & had no human parents. Some few ~~of~~ traces of Chastity remained [...], when Jove was young. But Astraea and Chastity fled the earth together. The crime [?] of the marriage bed is of ancient birth. The age of silver beheld it. And yet your marriage settlements [?] are making ready; Are you mad to take a wife? What fury has bitten you? ~~Can you not~~ Why marry when there are ropes to hang yourself with, high windows open, & a bridge [that] stretches on before you?[36]

How ridiculous to observe the Julian law, & beget an heir.[37] You will lose the sweet gifts of legacy [...]. If you seek the ancient virtue of Chastity in a wife, you are mistaken [?]. Where will you find such a wife [?]. Look at Heppia, who followed the gladiator

GN8

across the seas, spreading there rumours of Romes vice, & left her husband, & sis, & all her comfortable luxury.

---

[35] Having been dethroned by Jupiter (Zeus), Saturn (Cronos) returned to earth escorted by Pudicitia (Chastity) and Astraea (Justice). Jupiter's coming ushered in a complex way of life, and men and women became spoilt by vice and luxuries. Juvenal describes Rome's gradual decay, a decay in which the Greek influence played a major role. According to the satirist, Greece was instrumental in emasculating Rome's men and, especially in this satire, in corrupting its women. Woolf has not extended her commentary that far.

[36] Juvenal means that it is far better to kill oneself than marry a woman. Judging from Woolf's rendition, I believe that she captured this quite adequately.

[37] *Lex Iulia*, passed by Augustus in 18 BC, was replaced by *Lex Papia Poppaea* in 9 AD. This law favoured large families by limiting the inheritance that unmarried citizens could hand down.

GN11

(Feb. 27th [19]08)

Odyssey[38]

"[Begun in Greece, 1906- and the first four books were read there - so I only give a summary of them]."[39]

Book 1

Council of Gods. Poseidon absent.[40] Pallas[41] demands, successfully, the return of Odysseus. She appears to Telemachus[42] & advises him to complain to the wooers, & then goes in search of his father to Pylos & Sparta.[43]

Book 2

Telemachus complains in vain, & goes to Pylos by night; & his reception there.

---

[38] It should be noted that Woolf read, and kept notes on, the *Odyssey* at least twice in her life (the other time was in preparation for her essay "On Not Knowing Greek," which she included in *The Common Reader* (1925); she did not, however, demonstrate the same preference for the *Iliad*. This may be due to a variety of reasons, a fair number of which are explored, albeit not directly in relation to Woolf, in Vanda Zajko's "Homer and *Ulysses*" (Robert Fowler ed., *The Cambridge Companion to Homer*, Cambridge: Cambridge UP, 2004, 311-323). Discussing the reception of the Homeric epics by Victorian and modernist intellectuals and artists, Zajko argues that the *Odyssey* was much more of a modernist text than the *Iliad* (311). Particularly in relation to Woolf in 1908, it would be pertinent to suggest that the masculine heroics and the gore of the *Iliad* might not have been entirely to her liking: "and Pallas Athena guided the spear to the nose next to the eye, and it cut on through the white teeth ... through the tongue's base ... underneath the jawbone" (*Iliad*, V, 290-293).

[39] During Woolf's first trip to Greece in 1906. In preparation for *The Common Reader* (see note 30), Woolf reread Books I-VI. These notes are in the Berg Collection at the New York Public Library (Reel 13).

[40] God of the sea.

[41] Athena [or Athene] Pallas, Goddess of wisdom.

[42] Telemachus, son to Odysseus and Penelope, grandson to Laertes, Odysseus' father.

[43] The kingdoms of Nestor and Menelaus respectively were situated around the southernmost point of the Peloponnese peninsula and still retain the same names. As many youths now know since the release of the feature film *300* (2006), Sparta was also known as Lacedaemon, hence the Greek letter /Λ/ on their shields.

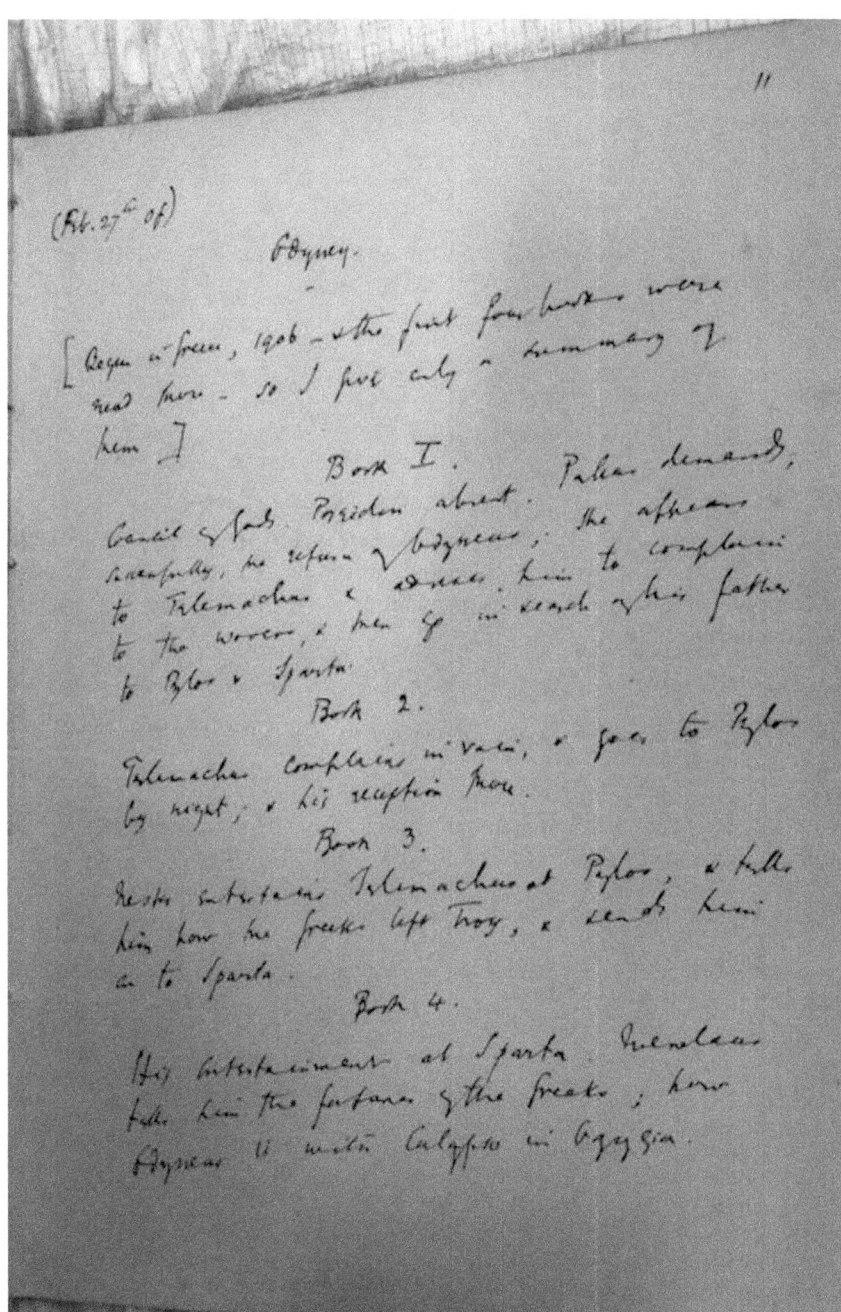

(Feb. 27th 04)

Odyssey.

[Begun in Greek, 1906 — the first four books were read there — so I give only a summary of them]

Book I.

Council of Gods. Poseidon absent. Pallas demands, successfully, the return of Odysseus; she appears to Telemachus & advises him to complain to the wooers, & then go in search of his father to Pylos & Sparta.

Book 2.

Telemachus complains in vain, & goes to Pylos by night, & his reception there.

Book 3.

Nestor entertains Telemachus at Pylos, & tells him how the Greeks left Troy, & sends him on to Sparta.

Book 4.

His entertainment at Sparta. Menelaus tells him the fortunes of the Greeks; how Odysseus is with Calypso in Ogygia.

Book 3

Nestor[44] entertains Telemachus at Pylos, & tells him how the Greeks left Troy, & sends him on to Sparta.

Book 4

His entertainment [Telemachus"] at Sparta. Menelaus[45] tells him the futures of the Greeks; how Odysseus is with Calypso in Ogygia.[46]

GN12

Book 5

Gods in council command Calypso by Hermes[47] to send away O. on a raft of trees & Poseidon scatters his raft off the coast of Pheacia; Ino[48] helps him ashore, & he sleeps on dry leaves till day light. There is a beautiful description here of the cave of Calypso. All romance in this poem; as bright as day, & yet remote, & moving with freedom of state.

Book 6

O. is woken by the voices of Nausicaa & the maidens, who have washed their clothes by the river brink, & are playing at ball.[49] He starts out naked, N[ausicaa] speaks to him as the Gods gave her courage. She takes him back to the city of the Pheacians to ask her father's help. This is perhaps the most beautiful book, so far: N[ausicaa]: exquisite truth & modesty, & the wondrous setting of the scene.

Also you see very clearly the look of the town, with its shipbuilding yard, & the Temple of Poseidon in the midst, & the palace with the great hall, in which the mistress sat,

---

[44] King of Pylos, the wisest and most respected of the Greeks at Troy.
[45] King of Sparta, Agamemnon's brother and Helen's husband.
[46] Demi-Goddess who lived on the island of Ogygia. Holding Odysseus in a state of captivity, she was ordered by the Gods to send him back to Ithaca.
[47] The messenger of the Gods, protector of travellers and tradesmen.
[48] Ino, a sub-deity.
[49] Nausicaa, daughter to Alcinous and Arete, Princess of Phaeacia. Phaeacia is thought to be modern-day Corfu.

GN13

spinning her purple yarn, in the firelight. Also, there is a meadow & a fountain sacred to Athene where O. sits. 183-185 Ideal of Marriage- "There is nothing better or nobler than this, when a man & [a] woman possess a house & are of one mind. ~~Much pain~~ Disastrous are they to their foes & a joy to their well-wishers, but their own hearts know it best ["].

Book 7

Athene in disguise leads O. to the palace. The honour done to Arete, wife of Alcinous, how she is honoured by the men, & [is] allowed to comfort their quarrels, honoured too of her husband & children. A long (58-88) description of the palace—golden hounds, a blue frieze, tapestries; golden figures holding torches; women "restless as the leaves of the poplar tree" weaving. The vineyard 124, a beautiful description. O. goes in to pray; they seat him in a silver chair, & decide how they meet next day & [2] his escort. He explains to Arete how he comes, her clothes & tells part of the story. [Alcinous]: "It was not right of my daughter not to bring you with her."

GN14

Would that I had you for a son in law. [He] offers to take him to any part he may wish, even as far as Euboea;[50] which is the furthest island our people have ever seen; yet they rowed there & back in one day without distress. They make him a bed there & he sleeps.

Book 8

O. goes down among the Pheacians, & is invited to join their contest, & one [Euryalus] taunts him, upon which he hurls a coit [discus][51] further than every other, & offers to meet them in any sport but wrestling, for which his fast has afflicted him. A boastful, muscular creature, like a great schoolboy; and yet shrewd; he will not fight, for instance, with with his host for that would be foolish.[52] Alcinous

---

[50] The second largest island in Greece, north-east of Athens.
[51] Woolf has clearly written "coit," but in the Greek text it is clearly stated that Odysseus hurled a discus—"δισκον" (*Odyssey*, VIII, 186).
[52] Woolf does not condone Odysseus' boastfulness.

bids him take note of all their excellences[53] that he may tell of them at home,[54] & calls the blind singer Demodocus.[55] This story of the games is not as beautiful as the other,[56] but probably a true picture of what happened. As Demodocus was blind, may it not be that his office of singer was his, as by right; & so the blindness marked bards became,

GN15

transferred to […] himself. The story of Ares & Aphrodite, & how they were found out by Hephestus in bed together. And Aphrodite went to Cyprus, & was anointed with immortal oils, & was ornamented by the Graces.[57] The end of the song.
    414 "May you never miss the sword"—*a regular form of acceptance?*[58]
Nausicaa, dowered with beauty by the Gods beholds him coming from the bath in his splendour, & bids him have memory of her in far lands; for she saved his life.
    480 For the Muse[59] loves singers, & asks men to honour [their] poem.
Demodocus sings the story of Troy, & O. weeps, & Alcinous bids the singing stop, for the stranger is at bother. Metaphor of the woman who weeps over her husband slain defending his city & children, & she is taken prisoner, & wastes her cheeks in wailing / weeping[?]. Even so, O. weeps—a noble, but large image. Then Alcinous bids O. reveal himself, his travels, & the habits of the peoples he has seen. A real fresh sense of the new […] ambient world. Why does he weep when the tale of Troy is told? Did he lose a father, or a friend, loved as a brother?

---

[53] Alcinous prides himself on the athletic and naval prowess of the Phaeacians (236-255) after Odysseus' boastful exposition of his own physical and mental superiority.
[54] Meaning when he (Odysseus) goes back to Ithaca.
[55] Demodocus, the minstrel, sang the torments of the Greeks at Troy.
[56] Meaning Homer's description of Alcinous' palace in Book VII.
[57] "Graces" (*Gratiae*) is the Latin name for the Greek Χαριτες (*Charites*): deities, daughters of Zeus and Eurynome or Hera; they were three: Euphrosyne, Thalia, and Aglaea.
[58] Woolf is clearly not impressed by Odysseus' behaviour in this Book.
[59] The nine Muses were Goddesses, daughters of Zeus and Mnemosyne, the Goddess of memory. More than likely, the one implied here must be Calliope, the Muse of epic poetry. Depictions of her often involve her holding a parchment scroll or a tablet. The rest of them were: Clio, Muse of history; Erato, Muse of love poetry; Euterpe, Muse of music and lyric poetry; Melpomene, Muse of tragedy; Polyhymnia (or Polymnia), Muse of hymns; Terpsichore, Muse of dance; Thalia, Muse of comedy; and Urania (the Heavenly One), Muse of astronomy.

GN16

Book 9

Odysseus tells the story of his adventures. How he came to the land of the Lotus eaters—95. how a man forgets all, who tastes of the Lotus—110. The painless [?] land of the Cyclop[e]s—This is precisely like an Elizabethan voyager writing of his travels. Then they go to an island near by—where are these clouds- where they see Polyphemous, by his cave with his herds.[60] They go in & await his return. He comes back, & milks his flocks, & then, getting guileful answers [by Odysseus], kills some of the men for his supper. And they cannot kill him, for fear of being left imprisoned in the great cave with the door closed "as a quiver with the lid on" (313) what is the lid of a quiver?[61] A wonderful description (371-402) of the blinding of the Cyclops with a green olive stake, burnt & sharpened, which they turn in his eye socket. There are certain simple metaphors, drawn from the processes of life, as for instance "the boring of a ship's beam with a drill," which are more effective than any others. At the same time, the technical words are many. The eye hissed like hot steel plunged in water to temper it. Immense vividness & strength of description. Probably this was what the audience loved. Like the Bible only more sinuous. Then they hid themselves under the flock, & fan [?] out of the cave in the morning. This is precisely like a traditional fairy tale of a man's great cunning in emergency. Imagine how the children wd have liked the dreadful plight Odysseus was in, with the giant sitting in the

GN17

doorway, & no possible way of escape it seems! But then the hero sees the withies, in which P.[olyphemous] sleeps, & uses them to bind himself to the ram. Also, there is the childish game of the Cyclopes, who come as Po[lyphemous] summons, & when they hear that he is tormented by Noman,[62] leave him to Zeus, who alone can suffer disease. I don't care so much for these ingenuities myself—spirited as they are.[63]

---

[60] Polyphemous was the strongest and most malicious of all the Cyclopes.
[61] The door was a large rock that only Polyphemous could move.
[62] At the beginning of this incident, Polyphemous asked Odysseus what his name was, to which the latter answered "No-man." Following his blinding then, when the other Cyclopes asked Polyphemous who had hurt him, he answered that, in effect, "No-man" had hurt him.
[63] We cannot be sure why this did not please Woolf. We may be justified in surmising, however, that perhaps it reminded her of the early Bloomsbury gatherings at 46 Gordon Square. In a letter to Violet Dickinson (1 October 1905), she expresses her dislike of her brother's university friends, the "Cambridge youths," who "occasionally escape to a corner and chuckle over a Latin joke" (*L1* 208). Perhaps this specific pun reminded Woolf of her position vis-à-vis the Cambridge "double-firsts."

Book 10

And they come to the Aeolian Isle,[64] where lives the man with the charge of all the winds. He entertains them, & gives them winds securely fastened by a silver thong in a wallet to blow them home. They are actually in sight of their own land, when Odysseus lies down to sleep; & while he sleeps his men murmur, & complain that he has brought home booty for himself. And they look to see what it is that he has in the wallet, & the winds burst out, & drive them back again to the Aeolian Isle. But they meet no kind men there, & make their way again in melancholy. Then they come to Lystrygonia,[65] where the way of day 7 nights are so close together that a sleepless man may earn a double wage as keeper of sheep & kine. But they are destroyed here by the gigantic race, & fly once more. They reach the island of Aya,[66] & O. from a high top, sees smoke among the

GN18

oakwoods. He kills a stag & carries him back to his company; & after they have [been] fed [he] tells them how they must adventure, & discover who it is there among the trees. A company is charged to [4] of the palace, Circe,[67] who sits singing a sweet song, & weaving at her loom while great lions & wolves, enchanted by her, roam […], & come fawning about the strangers as a dog, who expects food from his master's […]. Odysseus goes himself to rescue his companions, & he is met by Hermes, in the likeness of a man, who warns him, & gives him a drug, & tells him how he may make favour [?] with the Goddess. There is a plant, black of root but milk white of bloom, which men cannot pluck, but the Gods ~~can~~ who can do all things, can give it them. This was [a] charm against Circe's tools. He has [a] speech with her, & they lie together. But he will not eat till his comrades are free. Then he brings ~~others~~ his comrades to the feasting & they stay there at ease for a year. At last the men murmur, & he bids Circe let them go. Go to Hades & dread [?] Persephone & ask of them [the dead] your way, she [Circe] says. And they depart readily. Elpenor, waking & hearing them go, falls from the roof, & dies. But they set sail. This is a perfect, romantic narrative. A swift succession of
events, all beautiful in themselves. [2] no incident is over elaborated. The flower plucked. All […] with perfect order. Leaves [?] with [?] a broken ending.

---

[64] Where Aeolus, God of the Winds, lived; probably one of the Aeolian islands in the Tyrrhenian Sea north of Sicily.
[65] It should be "Laestrygonia."
[66] It should be "Aeaea."
[67] Circe was a sorceress who beguiled Odysseus' comrades and turned them into pigs. Woolf has omitted this here. This is what Hermes sought to protect Odysseus from.

GN19

Book 11

They sail to the bounds of [the] ocean, where the Cimmerian (sic) live in perpetual darkness. They come to the appointed land. Here they do as Circe bid them. O. cuts a trench, & they slaughter cattle. [...] souls alike "weak races of the dead" cluster around, but O. will not let them touch the blood, until Teiresias[68] has spoken. *Beautiful, beautiful!*[69]
Brides & unwedded boys, & toil worn old men, & joyous[70] girls freshly acquainted with grief come to him—(this is Virgil's famous passage. I suppose not here so elaborate).[71] And Elpenor who fell from the roof and killed himself begs burial of his body.[72] Will they lay his oar on [?] the tomb. After O.'s mother finally Teiresias speaks. He bids O. go on his way only take care when they come to the flocks of the sun[73] not to molest them or their return will be toilsome. Then, when he has greeted his wife & child,[74] he may go on adventuring further till he comes to a land where the men do not know the sea. And he must carry his oar with him. And when he meets one who says "what is that winnowing fan you have with you." Then he must make sacrifice. And he will die in old age very peacefully. "All this lies on the knees of the Gods," says O. & begs to speak with his mother. She tells him that all is well at home; but his father, for sorrow at his absence, lies in dirt by the chimney corner in the winter, & in summer makes him[self] a bed from the leaves in the garden. She died of longing for her son. Then all the wives & daughters

---

[68] Teiresias (or Tiresias), the seer, is a very prominent figure in Greek mythology, especially in the Theban circle.
[69] My emphasis. Woolf appears to be fascinated by the kingdom of Hades.
[70] "παρθενικαι τ' αταλαι νεοπενθεα θυμον εχουσαι" (11.39). Murray translates this as: "tender maidens with hearts yet new to sorrow..." (*The Odyssey*, 2 vols. trans. A. T. Murray, London: William Heinemann, 1931, [I, 389]).
[71] Probably Virgil's *Aeneid* (VI, 221-322). In that specific passage Aeneas, very much like Odysseus, sees many of the souls or ghosts of the Greco-Roman world ascend from Hades at his summons. However, Woolf may also be referring to Virgil's *Georgic IV*, which she analyses a bit later in this manuscript (see GN 60 Verso). See Book X (*GN*, 18).
[72] Elpenor, a figure of sloth in the *Odyssey*, had fallen asleep on Circe's roof; he died after waking up suddenly and falling from it.
[73] It should have been Helios Hyperion. *Helios* is the Greek word for "sun."
[74] Penelope and Telemachus in Ithaca.

GN20

of heroes approach & speak to him. A long bit follows with some brief genealogy & mythology. "If I were to tell you all, the night would pass."[75] Here then there is a break very skilfully interrupting the monotonous piece of the story.[76]

They listen spellbound in the shadowy (σκιοεντα)[77] halls & Arete promises gifts. So he would stay for a full year, & gain consideration from the people of Ithaca." *Is this a kind of traditional psychology?*[78]
He begins again—how the ghost of Agamemnon comes, & tells him his story; how Clytaemnestra killed him without giving him time to see his son.[79] Trust not your wife with all your mind, or she will betray you—Lo—your wife, good Penelope, is discreet & true. But Clytaemnestra would not even close my eyes or shut my mouth. Women, C[lytaemnestra] & Helen, have been fatal to the sons of Atreus.[80] Then, Achilles, a prince even among the dead, addresses him. But he would rather serve a poor man & hind[81] on earth than rule all the nation of the dead. They all ask news, then O. in fear lest Persephone should send him the Gorgons head (what is that myth?)[82] goes back to his ships. Achilles asks news of Peleus[83], & Odysseus tells him of the valiant deeds of his son, Neoptolemus,[84] so that he went with great strides across the meadow, pleased at heart. Then he saw Ajax, still grieving & wrathful for the

---

[75] Murray translates this as "there is a time for many words and there is time for sleep" (Murray, I, 413).
[76] Indeed, if not for this break Odysseus' narration in this Book would have gone uninterrupted for 335 lines.
[77] Woolf's parenthesis; σκιοεντα is "shadowy" in ancient Greek.
[78] Woolf's emphasis.
[79] Clytaemnestra (or Clytemnestra) was Agamemnon's wife and Iphigenia's mother; with the help of her lover, Aegisthus, she killed the Achaean chieftain straight after his return from Troy (see Aeschylus's famous tragedy *Agamemnon*, the first play of the *Oresteia* trilogy).
[80] Mythical king, father of Agamemnon and Menelaus.
[81] Here, Woolf translates the Greek "βουλοιμην κ' επαρουρος εϖν θητευεμεν αλλω, ανδρι παρ' ακληρω" (I would rather live a poor man / peasant who has little in the service of another); she uses the archaic English word "hind": a farm steward or a peasant.
[82] From the myth of Perseus, son of Zeus and Danae. His step-father dared him go and fetch Medusa's (or Gorgon's) head which, once looked at, turned one into stone.
[83] Peleus, a mortal, was Achilles' father; his mother was Thetis, a demi-Goddess.
[84] Neoptolemus, Achilles' son, had excelled in battle against the Trojans.

GN21

loss of arms.[85] And he would not even now speak to Odysseus, & great is the pity. 565. Then he came back, & would have spoken, but O. saw many others—a curious touch. He saw Minos, Orion,[86] chasing wild beasts, & Tantalus standing in water, & whenever he made to drink it, it was sucked up, & the earth parched. & there were fruity trees all round him with [?] taunted / taunting [?] pears & olives at his feet, & a wind whirled them out of his hands;[87] & Sisyphos for ever rolling his stone. & there was Hercules faffing alone among the dead. His hand was at his bow, always on alert as though to shoot. & he wore a wondrous golden girdle […][88] with beasts. He had been sent to bring back the Hound of Hell.[89] But, at last, Odysseus turned, & went in fear that Persephone[90] should send him the Gorgons head.

GN22

Book 12

They set sail from the river Oceanus, & reach the isle of Circe. She comes to them at once, fairly dressed, with food, & they eat. Then, she takes O. aside with her & questions him; & tells him of his future. He will come to two great rocks—one so steep that the birds of Zeus cannot [1] ambrosia & all ships are destroyed. **The sirens come before he comes to the rocks.**[91] On the other side there are two pinnacles, one lofty, & the other low. In the lofty one there is a great cave, in which

---

[85] Ajax, the celebrated king of Salamis, was second only to Achilles in courage and somatic might. Odysseus had a feud with him over Achilles' armour in the *Iliad*—see Sophocles' *Ajax* in this manuscript.

[86] Minos and Orion were judges of the underworld and second only to Pluto.

[87] Tantalus and Sisyphus were mythical figures punished by the Gods. Tantalus' torment in Hades was to be eternally hungry and thirsty; exquisite foods hung over his head only to disappear every time he tried to reach them, while the river in which he stood would dry up whenever he tried to drink its water—hence the English verb "to tantalize." Sisyphus' torment, on the other hand, was to roll a rock to an unreachable summit for all eternity.

[88] The illegible word looks like "charred" or "carved," but I cannot be certain. The meaning is that Hercules was wearing a golden belt, on which wild animals were depicted or, indeed, carved.

[89] Cerberus was a three-headed dog/monster guarding Hades. One of Hercules' labors was to descend to Hades and bring back Cerberus.

[90] Demeter's daughter, abducted by Pluto/Hades in order to become his wife. The Gods took pity on Demeter, the Goddess of harvest and vegetation, and decided that Persephone would be spending six months with her mother and six months with her husband, Pluto/Hades.

[91] I have highlighted this sentence because Woolf has written it on the side as a note.

Scylla dwells, up to her middle in water. But some of her 12 heads crane out of the chasm, & sweep the water for dolphins & dog fish, & she will pluck men from their ships & devour them. In the other cave rock there is Charybdis, who sucks out water & in again.

And here the sirens live & sing. If you hear them you are destroyed. They sail on, & put wax in their ears, all but O. who listens bound tight to a mast. Lovely are the voices, reaching out to him, "Come hither, Come hither"—but to that he would gain? Pain; but his comrades row on. There is exquisite romance in this, & in all the small properties of the scene: the bright calm when the waters flow white beneath the oars. The honey sweet wax, broken from great cakes, & warmed in the hands. ~~Then they come to the island where there are the immortal sheep of the God of Sun.~~

After this follow their adventures in due order.

GN22 Verso

"Dancing ground of Dawn! Dancing ground of Nymphs!"

GN23

Charybdis[92]

First they come to Scylla, a great monster who sucks in bitter sea & belches it forth;[93] & then there is Scylla with the many heads foraging. She plucks ~~two~~ several men out of the boat as a fisher letting down his bait with the ox horn at the end of it, draws up fish and casts them on the rock. This was the bitterest sight of all. Then there is the island where the Sun pastures his fat flocks.[94] Here they are stated by the winds; & the men who are always grumbling against O. kill the oxen in his absence in defiance of the Gods. They make a great sacrifice of flesh to appease them carting bright oak leaves in the flames in default of barley, and water for wine; Next they set sail and are destroyed; for the Sun[95] has asked vengeance—so says O. with great regard for likelihood, Calypso told me, who heard it from Hermes.[96] He alone survives astride the keel. He is washed back to Scylla, but manages to

---

[92] It appears that Woolf in this instance gives an overview of this particular book and then decides to describe each scene/adventure.

[93] Woolf has mistaken the identities of the monsters in this sentence; it was Charybdis who sucked the sea-water.

[94] The island of Thrinacia where Helios kept his sheep and oxen.

[95] Meaning Helios Hyperion.

[96] Odysseus' narration at this point switches back to his audience on the isle of Alcinous. Woolf, most interestingly, notices the shift in temporality from past to present.

escape in the evening when the lawgiver comes back to supper.⁹⁷ ~~Dancing~~⁹⁸ After this he comes to the island of Calypso—but I have not to repeat a plain story! This seems to me a most ingenious device for you could not have all the story at once, but broken in pieces like this it is more audible; & made more intense by the feeling of the audience in the shadowy halls.

GN23 Verso

A beautiful image of the ships going, like four [?] male horses leaping over the plain.⁹⁹

Book 14[100]

GN24

Book 13

The Pheacians send him on his way, in a boat rowed by their men, & laden with gold & precious staffs. He is fast asleep, in a sleep most like to death, in the stern. They land him, still sleeping, on the coast of Ithaca, & leave him there with his wealth piled beside him. On their way back they are confounded to the depths of the sea by a great rock;[101] & the Pheacians watching in the harbour see them disappear. The Sun threatened, else, to shine among the dead. O. wakes, nor knows where he is, for Athena has changed the land. She appears [to him] like a boy, & he questions her & tells her a long story of feigned wanderings—at which, changing her disguise, she smiles. Odysseus, you are crafty as ever. She bids him slay the suitors & makes him like a worn old man. He recognises the land & the cave where of old he did sacrifice to the nymphs—promises years of offerings if they will befriend him.

Book 14

Athena goes, & O. makes his way to the swineherds hut. He has built, with his own hands, a courtyard unknown to Penelope. He has driven stakes round it &

---

[97] Woolf's translation here is rather free; she translates πατηρ ανδρων τε θεων ("the father of Gods and men") simply as "the lawgiver."
[98] GN 22 Verso.
[99] Perhaps Woolf means *Odyssey*, XII, 405-425.
[100] Woolf has confused which Book comes next; she has rendered Book XIII and XIV under the same header.
[101] In the original text, Poseidon turned the ship into a great rock and rooted it in the bottom of the sea.

made a number of [pig]sties. He has trained several big dogs who fly at O. The swineherd[102] sends them off, & makes O. come inside. All strangers & beggars are from Zeus. They lunch, & the swineherd tells him his sorrows, how he has to herd swine for the suitors, who eat

GN25

his fatted swine, & his master is away "with nothing to eat"![103] He tells over all his masters possessions in the temper of one loyal & boastful old retainer. O. asks of his master; at wh.[ich] Eumaeus [the swineherd] breaks out, shrewd & angry—"No you dont."[104] Beggars come here with tales of him, & make my proud mistress cry—& earn a clothing by their lies. You are at the same game. He loves his master more than [his] mother & father. Even though he is away. Yes, he is dead, a dry skeleton, a food for fishes, or beneath the sand. Odysseus then tells him a long ingenious fiction about his wanderings—how he was son of a rich man and a slave woman—had been at Troy—& wandered in Egypt—where he was taken prisoner, & almost sold for a slave. But fate rescued him, & threw him on the shore of Ithaca. In his wanderings he had come about a man who had entertained Odysseus, & O. had left there a vast treasure though for ten benefactions, & had gone to ask the counsel of the oak at Dodona.[105] He [Odysseus] was about to set off home. But the swineherd wont believe this, & bids him leave off his lying. O. offers to wager, but the swineherd [...] by his oath, & [...] to say [?] the rich [?] of treating as stranger ill. "What sort of home showed I love among men?" The swine are driven in, & they kill [a boar] & make sacrifice. O. has the long back as his is guests portion.

GN26

Then it comes on to rain with the South wind & O. wishes to know whether the swineherd will give him his own cloak. He tells therefore a little story about himself & Odysseus under the walls of Troy. They lay out in a thicket one cold night & the snow [?] froze on their shields, & he alone had no cloak. So he went to Odysseus, who sent a man with a message to Agamemnon. O.: "so I took his purple cloak & lay happy." The good swineherd says for this night Odysseus shall have a cloak though

---

[102] Eumaeus.
[103] What Woolf does not clarify here is that Eumaeus has not realized that the stranger was, in fact, Odysseus, his master.
[104] Odysseus asked whether he knew his master.
[105] After Delphi, the most important oracle in Greek mythology.

they have but one apiece. And he gives him one, & O. lies before the fire on a bed made of goat skins. The rest of the men lie by him, but the swineherd is not happy far from his swine, so he takes a great a great cloak & a spear to defend him from dogs & men & his [...] by the hens in a cave so that he is sheltered from the wind. This is a ~~very~~ careful study of the old mans character, & his surliness, & shrewdness, & his foolish & obstinate, but beautiful loyalty to his master. It is the nearest approach to drawing on individual character yet; but [it] is, I suppose, a typical picture too. These were the characteristics of the old family servant. His hospitality is perpetually insisted upon.
End of B. 14

GN27

Book 15

Athena goes to Telemachus who is with Menelaus in Lacedaemon; & finds him awake sorrowing for his father. She bids him home, for his mother is courted and may yield. Her heart is the heart of a woman, all her thought will be for her husband & his welfare she will not remember the dead husband. Is this good psychology or only a dramatic phrase brought in to heighten the effect of Penelope's loyalty? Menelaos makes the young men feast, & loads them with gifts in the usual way, and then they start. All this gold, stored in treasure houses, remind me of Mycenae.[106] Helen brings out a [em]broidered robe, shining like a star, and gives [it] him (Telemachus) as fruit of her hands to give to his wife one day. As they start an eagle swoops across the chariot chasing a tame goose—omen of the descent of Odysseus upon the suitors. Helen interprets it. An old man tries to stray / scare [?] him. They put to sea. A descendant of Melampus, the seer, begs to be taken on his way—here is told the story of Melampus as there is some lack of incident. Then we visit the swineherd again. ~~He~~ Odysseus asks him news of the father & mother of O.: one is dead [Odysseus' mother], & one [his father] lives in grief. Indeed I

---

[106] Here is the most direct link between this notebook and Woolf's first visit to Greece in September 1906. She wrote in her journal about Mycenae: "... Mycenae, my next attempt, I might leave a blank page. Where does the place begin—where stop—where does it not gather on its way? There was never a sight, I think less manageable; it travels through the chambers of the brain, wakes old memories & imaginations; forecasts a remote future; retells a remote past ... The imagination does assert again & again, as you walk, that the place is crowded & compact ... But the tremendous stones are not to be ignored, & the two lions, which guard the gate, do still admit you to something august which is beyond. I tremble to write of the classics ... but the taste of Homer was in my mouth" (*PA* 331).The lions mentioned above were made out of stone and still exist at the front of the so-called Agamemnon's tomb at Mycenae.

would hear the gentle words of my mistress now. "she is beset by suitors." My old mistress treated me very nobly. "What was your stay then." And as there nights are very long, & sleep is

GN28

burdensome, the swineherd stretches his legs, & tells O. He was the son of a king; but the Phoenicians came to the island, with boats full of trinkets. How there was a Phoenician woman in the house, & one of the sailors seduced her, & offered to take her home with them. She consented & promised to carry off her masters son, that they might sell him & requite themselves. So the child, (that is E.) was caught up as he played in the courtyard, & a Phoenician sailor kept his mother busy with a golden necklace, strung with amber beads. She fingered it, & gazed at it. Well, they vagabond away to Phoenicia & suddenly Artemis[107] struck the woman, who fell like a seagull in the hold, & was dropped overboard to feed the seals—Is this the just punishment? And Eumaeus was sold to Odysseus.[108] Then they slept. Meanwhile, Telemachus landed, & was once more shown a torment: an eagle with a dove.

Charming story of the Phoenician woman.

GN29

Book 16

Telemachus goes to the door, & the dogs fawn in him, & do not bark. Eumaeus knows him, & falls on his neck. Odysseus makes way for him; but T. is gentle & lordly, & a seat is strewn for him on the floor. The herdsman tells him of Penelope. They treat her with suspicion always; the blameless woman![109] Then Eumaeus goes to tell her of her sons arrival & goes to Laertes too. And Athena stands in the doorway like a beautiful woman invisible to T. She changes his [that is, Odysseus'] shape, & he returns to the hut like a god. "Are you a god?" asks T & cries for help. "No god, but your father" & O. weeps, who had before entertained his fears. But T. like a crafty Greek will not be convinced, for no mortal man could change so from age to youth in a minute. But he is convinced; & they kiss & weep, & take counsel for the killing of the suitors. O. is for falling on them at once; T. reminds him that they are many; but the Gods will help. Meanwhile, none is to know that O.

---

[107] Artemis, Apollo's sister, was the Goddess of the forests and hunting.
[108] That is, to Odysseus' parents.
[109] Woolf is exasperated by this affront to Penelope's loyalty.

is returned, but T. is to hide all the arms in a corner of the house, under the pretext that they may hurt each other.[110] At a signal the fight is to begin. How the suitors saw the ship of T. brought up to the town—a boat carried on men's shoulders, & took counsel. Should they kill him? One said no.

GN30

And Penelope stepped down from her gleaming main [?] chamber, & reproached them with their evil thoughts. And one stood up & denied them [the accusations] utterly. He had been helped by Odysseus, but yet he lied.[111] The swineherd came back in the evening having given his message to Penelope, & O. was once more changed to an old man. They eat together. T. did not dare […] at the swineherd, but smiled at his father. These books have nothing so beautiful as the earlier ones; but still there is always some beautiful detail, as the picture of the goddess standing at the door.

GN31

Book 17

In the morning T. goes off to the town to see his mother; & tells Eumaeus to take O. to the fields & finally to the town, where he may beg for bread & water. T. f[inally] reaches his home, & stands his spear against the doorway. His old nurse [Euryclea] is laying the seats in the hall with skins: she falls on his neck, & other serving women come running. Then Penelope herself descends, like[ened?] to Aphrodite, & holds him in her arms—& questions him. But he bids her wash & make herself fair, & offer hecatombs[112] to the gods; then he goes to the market place where the suitors are plotting disaster in their hearts, though so fair of speech. He sits apart from them, & talks to the stranger, the seer, who had come with him. They return to the hall, & wash & feast, & Penelope sits beside them, plying her fine threads, & asks T. of his adventures. He tells her briefly. The suitors outside are carting weight & otherwise enjoying themselves, until the herald bids them sup. One metaphor here is good: how a stag lays his fawns to sleep in a lions den in the thicket, & the lions returns & slaughters them—so Odysseus re: [omission]. Curious metaphor; large & conventional. Meanwhile O, bent like an old man,

---

[110] The pretext is that the suitors may hurt themselves in their drunken brawls.
[111] The insolent suitor is Antinous or Antinoos (*Odyssey*, XVI, 417-425).
[112] Public sacrifices for the Gods.

GN32

is led up to the door to beg. He meets Argos,[113] who lays back his ears & wags his tail but is too old to move. O. wipes away a tear. Then Argos dies. A curious little story. A dog [was], of course, a valuable beast in those days—personified. O. goes in & feeds. Antinous[114] rebukes him, & flings a stool at him. T. "sneezes": P. saw the sneeze & […] on her words[?], predicting [the] downfall of [the] suitors.[115]

GN33

Book 18

O. gets into [a] quarrel with another old beggar, a privileged kind of messenger, who asks him to fight. And O. throws off his cloak, & shows strong limbs, & maltreats the old ruffian while the suitors laugh. This is the usual kind of humour. Penelope […] she will come among the suitors—Athena sends her to sleep & beautifies her, until she is white as sawn ivory. "Oh would that I might die now easily & suffer no longer."[116] She then has [a] talk with Telemachus, & reminds him of his father's injunction to her -to stay at home till he [Telemachus] was a grown man, & then to marry whom she wished. Now the time is come, & she will marry the suitor who brings the richest gifts. Odysseus smiles overhearing this, for he knows that his wife has other councils in her mind, & yet has the wit to profit. The suitors bring their gifts. P. withdraws to her chamber, & O. bade her maidens follow her, & he would [give] light the suitors in the hall. The women laughed at him, but he threatened [them], & they obeyed. Athena, however, [is] determined that O. should suffer fully,[117] & […] bitter words against him. Eurymachus taunts him.[118] Finally, the wooers depart, & T. & O. are left in the hall.

---

[113] On embarking on the war against Troy, Odysseus left his dog, Argos, behind.
[114] Antinous was the most notable of the suitors; he was also the cruelest and the most impudent.
[115] Since Telemachus sneezed while she spoke, Penelope took this as an omen and predicted the downfall of the suitors.
[116] *Odyssey*, XVIII, 201-205.
[117] So that his wrath would be greater.
[118] Eurymachus was one of the suitors.

GN34

Book 19

T. is bidden to hide the arms in another [?] chamber "to be out of the smoke."[119] P. comes down, & sits in the hall to question O. of her husband.[120] She tells him how she has beguiled the suitors with her weaving which she wrought by day & undid by night. But how she had to finish it. O. tells his fate. He describes O. exactly. He answers her that O. is near at hand. P. welcomes his words & bids her women wash & anoint him. He will only supper & the old nurse to approach him. She uncovers his scar & knows him. [The] story of the scar is told between her seeing it, & exclaiming. [He] got it when visiting Autolycous, his mother's father, & hunting boars.[121] Autolycous outdid all men in thievery & swearing. O. signs to her not to reveal him. P. then talks to him & ~~asks~~ tells him a dream she has had of geese & an eagle. She likens herself, in a beautiful passage, to the brown [?] bright nightingale, always mourning.[122] The Gates of dreams; of horn & ivory. The ivory dreams are untrue; the horn [dreams] are true.[123] She is to set the contest of shooting to the wooers; will marry the one who shoots best. They sleep.

GN35

Book 20

Odysseus sleeps in the forecourt on [a] fleece, [...] & hides. Penelope wakes & makes prayer to Artemis either to slay her, or that the winds may sweep her away as they swept the daughter of Pandareus. A beautiful little passage. O. hears her, & wakes. He prays to Zeus for a sign. And a woman who is grinding at the mill prays that the suitors may have eaten their last feast. Then Euryclea wakes, & sets all the servants stirring. They sweep, & wipe all the tables with sponges. T. rises & gradually the whole place is at astir. Herds are driven in. The herdsman speaks, & O. answers him with a prophecy of his own return. Then a great feast is made on

---

[119] The smoke from the fireplace.
[120] Penelope cannot recognize her husband as he, helped by Athena, has assumed the guise of an old man.
[121] This is one of the most famous passages in the *Odyssey*, XIX, 384-505.
[122] Penelope recounts the myth of Philomela who had been turned into a nightingale (*Odyssey*, XIX, 518).
[123] *Odyssey*, XIX, 562-565: Analyzing her own dream, Penelope here says that there are two kinds of dreams: dreams that pass through the gates of sawn ivory tend to prove to be lies whereas those that pass through the gates of horn tend to come true.

the shady hill of Apollo. O. feasts with the rest. He is reviled by the suitors. One flings an oxen leg at him, but it misses him. The stranger[124] rises & prophesies that doom is on them. The court is full of ghosts travelling to the underworld. This is in the spirit of a malediction in the Old Testament. They laugh at him. P. listens. Meanwhile the Goddess & the man[125] are making ready a bitterer feast.

GN36

Book 21

P: beheld [?] her of the great bow of O. laid by in an upper chamber with his treasures. She fetches it & declares that she will marry the man who can shoot with it through a hole in an iron wedge. They try. T fails. Wax is brought out & they anoint themselves.[126] All fail. O. meets the herdsman & the swineherd & asks them if they would protect O. should he come. He asks for the bow, which is finally at the command of P., & T. gives [it to] him. The suitors revile him. He strings it as easily as a flute player fits another chord to his instrument, and its sings in his ears like a swallow. He shoots, & hits every mark. Then bids Telemachus make ready the feast.[127]

GN37

Book 22

"Now in this trial, ended at last."[128] The slaughter of the wooers begins. They recognise their fate, but try to make terms [?]. One finds the way to the room where the arms are stored; but is caught there, & [is] slung up to the door to die miserably. Athene turned all the arms of the wooers away, & O. was unscathed. Two were spared, who had been enforced by the wooers. The [...] were slain. ~~Then O. stood~~ & lay like a fish taken from the sea & laid in the sunlight.[129] Then O. stood over them like a lion, all bloodstained with the blood of an ox. The old nurse is sent for, & would cry out with joy when she sees the [slain] suitors, but O. tells her (a fine touch, if the old woman would be reticent) not to boast in the presence of the

---

[124] Meaning Odysseus.
[125] Meaning Odysseus again.
[126] In fact, they use wax to loosen the stiffness of the bow.
[127] "The feast" is probably used sarcastically.
[128] *Odyssey*, XXII, 5-8.
[129] *Odyssey*, XII, 384-385. The slain suitors were lying like fish pulled out of the sea by the fisherman.

dead. He bids her send for the women who have been insolent & faithless, 12 out of 50; they are made to heap the dead in the courtyard - & then O. & Telemachus kill them [the insolent maids], with no clean death for their sin was foul. They are strung up in a row like thrushes in a snare. This is one of the most vivid of the pictures. They wiggled their feet for a while "ου τι μαλα δην."[130]

GN38

Book 23

The old nurse goes to Penelope & wakes her with news that her husband has returned. She will not believe it at first, but at length she bestirs herself, in order to see the dead & the man who killed them. Does she pretend? She cannot make up her mind how to welcome him: she finds him standing by a pillar with his eyes downcast for he wonders what his wife will say to him. She knows him not in his rage. ~~Tele~~ Then he speaks and calls her hand. And Telemachus upbraids her; (for P:[enelope] never meets with very generous treatment in spite of her suffering and loyalty). But she is grown sceptical of happiness & will not believe. Then O. dresses and is [...] with beauty. Still she hesitates. Then he asks to sleep, & she [Penelope] bids the old nurse bring out a couch. At this, as she had planned, he bursts forth & tells her how he [had] made himself a bedchamber building it from [?] a stout olive tree; & the tree became the bedpart; & he made a bed & inlaid it & it cannot be moved. Then P[enelope] knows him & falls on his neck. They go off to their chamber, & Athene stays the dawn while they talk. He tells her how he must travel till he comes to a people who know not the sea, in fulfilment of the prophecy. At dawn, he & Telemachus set forth to the home of Laertes, the dark covering them.[131]

GN38 Verso

The 23rd Book of the

---

[130] "But not for very long" (*Odyssey*, XXII, 473).
[131] The dawn having broken, Athena cast darkness over them. Woolf stops her translation here quite abruptly.

GN39

Book 24

Hermes takes the souls of the wooers to the underworld. They gibber like bats awakened in a vast cave by the fall of one of them which distracts them, & they fly in a chain cling each to each. They pass through the land of drams to the field of Asphodel. There Achilles & Agamemnon hold speech together. Why is this thought in again?[132] Achilles asks how Agamemnon came by his end seeing that the gods protected him through the war. Agamemnon tells Achilles how after his death [Achilles' death] he was honoured. His mother [Achilles' mother, Thetis], rose from the sea, & the muses raised a deathless strain & no man could keep from tears. Then they burnt him, & took his bones & set them in a golden jar with the bones of Patroclus; & they were buried beneath a great mound over the Hellespont, which men may see when they are out at sea. Games are held there always, far [?] greater than those at which you have […] been, at the death of some great king. But my fate was more harsh—" [sic] Then they see the souls of the suitors draw near, & question them. And Automedon tells their story. After which Agamemnon exclaims, Blessed is Penelope who waited for her lord faithfully. How unlike Clytaemnystra whose story shall be sung among men, & shall be a reproach to women for ever, even to the upright.

GN40

While the ghosts talk thus, O. & T[elemachus] go across the fields to the house of Laertes. They find that all his servants are out in the vineyard planting a new hedge, & they discover him with his head bent digging out the root of a tree. O. wonders whether to greet him directly or to make trial of him—a device [?], as usual, to prolong the scene. He tells him that he is a stranger seeking Ithaca, about Odysseus, who was his friend over the years. Laertes makes lament; & O. then pry [?] [tries?] him no more but embraces him. "A sign!" asks L[aertes], & O. gives him the usual one of the scar, but not in detail, which would lead to too much repetition. This time he tells over certain trees which L:[aertes] had given him when he was a boy. L[aertes] is convinced, & they embrace, & they make ready a feast. All this is very beautiful, as the descriptions always are. The old man in his farm, with his vineyards all around him, bent & faltered, but like a king. Love that the Greeks must have had of recognition scenes! They are always long drawn out.

---

[132] Woolf seems surprised by this repetition—see Book XI. Agamemnon recounts some incidents after Achilles' death.

They feast with Laertes and his servants; ~~then O.~~ but meanwhile the rumour of the death of the suitors has gone abroad, & the people make lament & go unto the halls & carry out the dead. Some they bury and some they send in fishing boats to their own lands. Eupeithes makes lament for his son, Antinous, the first to die, & incites the people to kill Odysseus. He tells them all the waste of men & ships

GN41

that Odysseus had caused; others try to dissuade; but they will not listen, but take arms, & go out to the house of Laertes. O. hears them coming & goes out with the servants, armed, to meet them. Athena has word from Zeus to let Odysseus rule & to compose peace between them. First they fight. O. urging on his son to preserve the honour of his house, & the old father exclaiming "How am I happy—when son & Grandson contend in valour!" Suddenly a bolt falls before the feet of Athena who stay[s] [the battle, & sends the men back into the city. She lays her oaths upon the combatants, & with sacrifice, "like to Mentor in shape & voice."[133]

End of *Odyssey*

15th May. [19]08

This is a characteristic ending; as though the voice, simply, had finished speaking, the sun having set, & it being time for bed. But there is also a great sense ~~of~~ that the drama is completed; we are relieved of all anxiety about the future by the knowledge of what must happen to Odysseus—that he is to travel, & meet death, the easiest way, by sea. The scene dies out, as a landscape in the evening.

---

[133] "Μεντορι ειδομενη ημεν δεμας ηδε και αυδην"—"Like Mentor in sight and voice" (*Odyssey*, XXIV, 548).

GN42

May 18th [1908]

Ion of Euripides

—

A.W. Verrall[134]

Prologue spoken by Hermes. He tells how Creusa once was ravished by Apollo, & hid the son born to her in a cradle with snakes, as in the tradition in her family. Hermes was sent by his brother [Apollo] to ~~lay~~ take the child & place it in the Temple of Apollo at Delphi. A priestess found it, & had pity in it. The child grew up, & served in the temple as keeper of the treasure, without knowledge of his parents. But now, Creusa having married a man, Xuthos, & they having no children, the two are coming in pilgrimage to the shrine of Apollo to pray for offspring. This has been contrived by the God, who plans to present Ion to them, without telling them his parentage. Then the boy will recognise his mother, & receive his due. This is spoken as prologue:
Ion comes out of the temple with a band of Delphians, who are occupied about the shrine. Ion sings, while he brushes the portals with laurel twigs, & washes them clean. A lovely strain, beautiful in its suggestion of the sight. May [?] welcomed by the untrodden heights of Parnassus,

GN42 Verso

Sarcasm about rich offerings necessary.

The confusion here is that Creusa says she comes to pray for children for <u>herself</u>; but the main point of her plea is for the other woman, whose story she brings in incidentally, & leaving Ion, who was betrayed by Apollo, & on whose behalf she is there, to ask where the child [Ion] is, alive or dead.

---

[134] Here, I have used the same edition as the one used by Woolf: Euripides, *The Ion*, trans. and intro. A. W. Verrall, Cambridge University Press, 1890. Therefore, whenever I reference Verrall instead of Euripides, I refer to the former's clarificatory notes to the translation.

GN43

Ion, who has neither father nor mother, is occupied always in tending the altars from which he draws his life; cleaning them, garlanding them, & scaring away the impious birds.
Chorus sings, consisting of the handmaidens of Creusa. They walk round the Temple, & admire the scenes painted on the walls; various myths are represented. Ion comes out, & asks their business. *They may not enter unless they bring rich offering of sheep. Is this sarcasm?*[135] Creusa appears, alone, & Ion remarks that she has the look of a well born person. She tells him that she comes from Athens, & her father was Erechtheus. Then Ion puts her through a very inquisitive examination, like a curious child.[136] Is the myth true, which says that her father was born of the earth [Gaea]—& so on. She grows impatient. She tells him her errand—that she comes on behalf of a childless mother; to pray to Apollo for children. Ion then tells his story, how he is *fatherless & motherless*; & he has no clue to help him in his search. Creusa says that she knows a woman who is in the same condition, seeking her child. She does not give her own name, but, by speaking of the husband who lags behind, implies that she is the woman herself. The story is too disgraceful to be owned [up to]. But a woman married with Phoebus—Ion cries aloud—who left her, with her son. She spared him, & has heard nothing of him since. Perhaps wild beasts devoured him. Or perhaps, says Ion, the God has him

GN43 Verso

God rendered simply as a great man, king for example, who sins like other men, but has the power to conceal his sins; & of course they would be doubly disgraceful. X. Natural thoughts upon the importance [?] / impertinence [?] of the Gods.

GN44

under his own protection. The weakness of her cause is, as Ion points out, that Phoebus will scarcely reveal his own sin. Nobody, he says, can possibly ask the God such a question—he [Phoebus] would at once wreak vengeance on him. Xuthus arrives. Creusa begs [Ion] *that nothing of what she says may be repeated to him; since good & bad women are equally disliked.*[137] Xuthus has brought word from

---

[135] Woolf's emphasis in bold type.
[136] Given that this addition ("like a curious child") is Woolf's, we can surmise that she foreshadows the revelation that Ion is indeed Creusa's son.
[137] This is also in bold type (*Ion*, 399-400).

Trophonius, that they shall not return home childless. Then he enters to make sacrifice. Ion is left to himself, & tries to think no move of Creusa & her story. *What is she to him?*[138] Yet, the God must be warned. A God to betray a girl, & leave her with his child, & let *the child perish!*[139] An unjust man is punished—How can those who set the law sin against it? Apollo, or Poseidon or Zeus, should pay the penalty & that would leave their Temples empty. Man then only imitates the doings of his superiors, & it is not fair to blame ~~her~~ him (435-450).[140] This is very remarkable, & ~~outspoken~~ much is outspoken here in the plainest way that the commentators hint at. Is this the whole motive of the play—to test some crude old myth nationally?

450. The chorus sings a hymn of invocation to Athena & Artemis to be present at the shrine of Apollo, & pray [to] him that a child may be born to the House of Erechtheus.[141] The blessing of children—how it is incomparably greater than wealth—O Athens what thy cliff hath seen![142] First, it has seen maidens dancing to the pipe of Pan:[143] it has also seen the ravishment of a girl by a God, & the desertion of the child, there on those very steps, as in bitterness against her marriage.[144]

GN45

508.
Xuthus comes out of the temple & straight away embraces Ion, as his son.[145] The boy demands reasons for this outburst. The God had told X[uthus] that the first man he met would be his son. But how is it possible? He had had no intercourse with women since his marriage. But before in his youth—still how should the child have come here? (for X[uthus] was a stranger). Then he confesses that he did come once to the Bacchic rites at Delphi, & was introduced to certain women, who gave him their favours; & in that moment, *no doubt, Ion was begotten.*[146] So he is as the son

---

[138] Woolf's emphasis in bold type.

[139] Again, Woolf's emphasis.

[140] These (437-450) are Ion's thoughts. Verrall translates this (437-450) as follows: "To force a maid and then abandon! ... what justice then that ye, who set the law to mortal man, should sin against the law? ... Thou Poseidon, or the king of heaven [Zeus]...To quit the fines would leave your temples empty .... then just it is to blame not imitative man, but them whose taste instructs our admiration what to ape" (Verrall 41).

[141] According to the legend, Erectheus was the first king of Athens.

[142] Probably *Ion*, 494.

[143] Pan was a goat-like deity, famous for playing the pipes and notorious for his lusting after nymphs.

[144] "Bitterness" is used here to render the "πικρων γαμων υβριν" (*Ion*, 505-506).

[145] According to the prophecy received by Xuthus, his son was the first man he would lay eyes on after exiting the temple; hence "straight away."

[146] This also seems to be in bold type.

"Greek Notebook" *Koulouris* 45

of a God—is that because Bacchus was supposed to be the inspirer of the amour? Ion wishes that he knew his mother—His father joins him, but in his joy is optimistic about everything. Anyhow Ion shall come back ~~to~~ with him to Athens, & there he will be treated with respect because he is rich, which will make men forget the stain of his birth. At this Ion winces—a sensitive, fare (sic) minded, & clearsighted boy. He says that to begin with his presence will be a constant sting to his stepmother, who will see herself slighted in every attention paid to him by his father; & then if he attempts to enter public life, poor men will revile him. The silent-wise who take no part in government (& correspond, according to V[errall], to our "the cultured") will wonder at his efforts to rise, & the other men, who do practise, will envy him if he gets any place.[147] Give me ease, mediocrity, such as I have enjoyed here, in my innocence, a faithful servant of the God. This throws a curious light upon the cultured class, who despise action; & is a subtle consideration of the domestic situation, unexpected in an ancient book.

GN46

650.
Xuthus says that he is going to have a feast here, to which all Ions friends are to come, & he is to say good bye to them. The plan now is that Ion shall be taken to Athens, as a guest to whom Xuthus would show the sights of ~~Athens~~ the town. By degrees, Creusa will accept him as the heir. Ion agrees, with strangely little difficulty, remembering his long argument, just spoken. He says that he may discover his mother, the one flaw in his happiness, & that she may prove to be an Athenian, for no stranger can ever have the right of free speech.
The Chorus sing; doubting this curious oracle, which brings sorrow on their mistress. They invoke the heights of Parnassus where Bacchus dances with flaming vine branches at night, to prevent Ion from ever reaching Athens. For he would bring destruction on the city.
Creusa comes out, with an old servant, who was as a son to her father, & is therefore as a father to herself. She asks the chorus what news Xuthus has brought from the God. They have been forbidden on pain of death to tell her the truth.
The chorus, after a moment of hesitation, tell her how her husband has been blessed with a son, wh.[ile] she is left childless. She wails. The chorus blame Xuthus, for he should have asked her wish. Then they unravel/reiterate [?] the plot—Xuthus has

---

[147] Quoting from the same note as Woolf: "598 ... σοφοι σιγωσι : 'are in their wisdom silent,' σοφια (culture) being the watch-word and mark of that educated class, averse from politics and devoted to self-improvement, which was just beginning to be important" (Verrall 54). I believe that Woolf here agrees, as I do, with Verrall, in so far that "culture" is more appropriate in this context than "wisdom."

had an intrigue with a slave woman, & they have sent the child to live at Delphi, & now that he [the son] is old enough to share in his fathers property, they claim him. The old slave the bursts out with a wild plan to

GN46 Verso

Then Creusa tells them of the disgraceful conduct of the God. They say nothing in blame of him—at once they take practical steps against Xuthus & Ion.

GN47

840.
enter the Temple while Xuthus is feasting with his son, & to kill them both. Creusa must act a womans part—that is, she must poison or kill the husband & child. He [the old slave], in gratitude bound, will help. For the shame of being a slave is in the name; a slave in all other vestments, if he is worthy, may be as good as any man. Another characteristic phrase for from Euripides. Creusa bursts out, addressing herself to the (sic) Zeus—Athena—The time has come. "O soul; how shall I keep silence any longer?"[148] She turns to Apollo, the singer of sweet melodies, & denounces him, beneath the open sky. She tells the story of her ravishment, turning away from the chorus, to the Temple. He came to her, with gold in his hair, as she was picking flowers to wear, & ravished her in the cave. "A false[,] false ravisher thou art!" At the end of this outburst the old slave questions her, not having heard all aright. She tells him the story in detail again; dwelling on each point of it. How she brought forth the child quite alone, & left it there [in the cave], for its father [Apollo] to care for it. But the birds snatched it, & it has grown up in Hades. The slave is amazed, & says how could you have [left] you son?—& it is even stranger that the god should have endured it— "Ah "If thou hadst seen the child stretching out his hands to me!."[149] This is a lovely exclamation. She will not argue his charge of cruelty. One line shows how unutterably she had felt it. Nothing abides. The slave exhorts her to kill either Xuthus or his son. She has an old tenderness for her husband, but will gladly kill Ion. She then tells how she comes

---

[148] Verrall translates this (859) as "Tell me, my heart, how can I hold my peace?" (Verrall 73).
[149] Verrall 81.

GN48

possessed of two magic drops of blood, one that kills—one that cures. She will give the slave the fatal drop. He shall mix it in Ion's wine, as he sits at the feast; she is careful to insist that one else shall take it. All her anger seems to be with Ion, not with her husband. [The] Slave says that scruples of right are all very well if you are prosperous, but they stand in the way of ones enemies.[150]
The chorus sing to Einodia, mistress of Hell.[151] One of Creusa's servants dashes in, in a state of agitation. She [Creusa] has been sentenced to death by stoning. He tells the story, at length, in the way of messengers. Ion framed a wondrous tent for the feast, with embroideries on the walls, statues at the entrance (the [?] purpose of this description of the pomp of Delphi). They sit at meat, & the old slave appears & makes them laugh by his officious desire to serve them. At last the time for drinking is come, & he serves Ion. But, just as Ion is to taste, a slave speaks ill-omened words, & Ion, skilled in rites, pours his bowl on the ground, & bids the others too. The doves [from the temple] come & sip the remains. All the doves are unharmed, save only the dove who sips from Ion's cup. She [the bird] reels & flutters, & finally "her rosy feet" stiffen. Ion attacks the old man, & bids him reveal the name of the poisoner. At length he confesses. She [Creusa] is condemned unanimously to die by being thrown from a rock.
Creusa (where has she been?) comes in, in flight, & casts herself upon the altar, by the advice of the chorus. She is pursued by Ion who reaches her; they then enter into a curious dispute, each upbraiding the other, hints at meaning. Very dark & tense—but expounded by E:[ripides] perhaps with too great ingenuity: difficult point of psychology:

GN48 Verso

Ion still cannot believe the story against the God—[he] goes back to their old story point again—how there must be some mistake. Even when she assures him of the truth of it, he is not convinced. The Athena has to appear in order to silence, & [as?] by violence, all his doubt.

---

[150] Verrall translates this (1045-1047) as follows: "scruples of right look well, and prosperous folk may prize them: but at war, and when you need to wound a foe, there is no rule against" (87).
[151] Verrall explains that Einodia is another name of Hekate, "identified with Kore, daughter of Demeter" (86).

GN49

Xuthus, she says, has no right to give what is not his, for as an alien he cannot inherit. Then, if ambition such as Xuthus," may not meet with reward, what cause have you to fear mine? says Ion. She hints darkly that she clings to the altar, so that the wrong doer may suffer wrong. The god wd be defiled if her blood were spilt there. Ion exclaims that there should be two altars, one for the pure, and another for the impure.

The Pythian priestess comes out, carrying the cradle in which she found Ion & gives it to him, as he is going away. He proposes to offer it up at the altar (to the delight of the priests! Says V[errall]) Creusa looks at it, & bursts out "Oh my Ion" She then describes the clothes & ornaments inside accurately so that Ion is convinced at last, & they embrace.[152] Then she tells how Apollo is his father. They sing short songs [?] of joy.

Then he [Ion] has a doubt, & takes his mother aside. Perhaps this story of the god is only invented to save his name & her reputation: she answers him that it is not so, & gives him an explanation by Apollo's late conduct in giving him to Xuthus as a son. Ion says the answer does not satisfy him. At this moment Athena appears. She says she has been sent by Apollo to explain matters. He will not come himself, for fear of reproaches. He had planned this scheme for the benefit of Ion. He had meant to reveal the truth after a time. She then goes on to ~~dese~~ recount the future of Ion, & of Creusa & the husband.

GN49 Verso

When Ion says he believes her, as he believed the story before, it may merely be a polite way of saying that he still finds it incredible. Otherwise he must contradict himself.

GN50

They are all to found great families, & to colonise new lands, which will carry their names to remote ages. "Well hath Apollo done in all."[153] How [to] keep this secret, so that Xuthus may be at ease, & you [that is, Creusa] are happy in your possessions. Ion answers that he believes her. Indeed, he believed the story when he

---

[152] Woolf's emphasis: she has written this excerpt in bold type.
[153] This is exactly the same translation as Verrall's (129). We cannot help but assume that Woolf is being sarcastic here.

"Greek Notebook" *Koulouris* 49

heard it before. Creusa blames Apollo, for giving her back her child.[154] Athena says the Gods are always strong in the end. She leads them to Athens. To [?] seat Creusa in her ancient honour. The chorus meanwhile: "Let him whose house is disputed worship Heaven; virtue is rewarded; evil damned; Justice cometh in the end."[155] 5th June [19]08.

GN51

The chief puzzle in the play, of course, is—what view did Euripides take of the conduct of Apollo? It is fairly obvious that he saw all the objections that any rationalist could now urge; he puts them into Ions mouth, when he says that the gods are judged by one law & men by another (c 300) 435. During the first part of the play it seems clear that Euripides has taken a gross old myth, & is treating it as though it were a fine story to be examined critically. Towards the end though [when] the action continues to be repulsive, the comment is silent. All Ion says is that he cannot believe it; &, if we like, we may imagine that he is still in the end, incredible that a god should act so, and be so leniently judged. All judgement of Apollo is implied; he says he will not come himself, for fear of reproach; but no comment is made on this; Athena sumps up the situation.—"Apollo has done well in all things." Was it impossible for Euripides to carry the play to its natural end? Which would have been, surely, to confront Apollo with Creusa, & to make some one, say Xuthus, judge of their share of guilt? Athena is merely a compromise. No one will be satisfied with the arrangement. But to have written the obvious end would have been a bolder act than any—his [Euripides"] boldness is very marked in various passages already. The outburst of Ion, against the gods; the slaves remark that a slave is as good as a free man, except in name, & the sentence about women "how women, both good & bad, are lumped together by men & condemned."[156] But all this is very crude commentary, upon an

GN52

unsatisfactory play. There are some beautiful lines and choruses; but on the whole you have the impression that the play was written to give shape to these strange situations—not to indulge in poetry. He was interested in the question; he puts it

---

[154] In fact, Creusa retracts her initial outburst against Apollo. Perhaps Woolf wants to make a point here.
[155] *Ion*, 1619-1622.
[156] *Ion*, 399-400.

in the most pertinent way; he refrains from a definite answer. But he shows the working of his mind, plainly, & a tremendous problem. In order perhaps to leave the outline of the questions clear, he has stated them very plainly, almost prosaically, as a lawyer putting a case.

GN52 Verso

εραστος = beloved
εραστης = a lover
εραω = to love
η ερωμενη = the beloved woman
ερατος = beloved[157]
προβαλλω = put forward

[The above appears on the verso of p. 52 and refers to the *Symposium* that follows].

GN53

Plato. *Symposium*[158]

Socrates & Aristodemus walk to Agathon's. Their talk is very colloquial, as per Euripides;[159] with all the half contradictions & repetitions, which the ordinary person uses in talk; & they are not happily rendered by Jowett;[160] who must smooth them into capacious lines, in the 18th Century model. Plato is often abrupt. This is a charming opening; in spite of the awkwardness of the form—a repetition after some years, of what someone else had told the speaker. But it is very natural &

---

[157] All these words have their root in the verb εραω/ερω—to be in love, to desire someone. Woolf has probably jotted these words in ancient Greek on the verso of page 52 to remind herself of their meaning whilst reading the *Symposium*.

[158] The protagonists in the *Symposium* are as follows: Apollodorus and an unnamed friend to whom the former narrates what had been narrated to him in the first place by Aristodemus. Thus, Apollodorus was not present at the dinner-party. Those present were: Aristodemus, a disciple of Socrates; Agathon, a dramatist; Socrates; Phaedrus, a dinner-party habitué and literary man; Pausanias, historian and Agathon's lover; Eryximachus, a doctor; Aristophanes, the comedian; and Alcibiades, Athenian General, famous for his good looks and rather wanton lifestyle.

[159] That is, in a colloquial, everyday language, not the exalted poetry of, say, Aeschylus (177a).

[160] Benjamin Jowett (1817-1893), British educator and Greek scholar; I cannot be sure which edition Woolf was using.

easy; the politest & best society in the world. Agathon makes his servants treat us as "though we were your guests"; they have no orders. Pleasant relationship. ~~Eryximachus~~ Phaedrus began, & sang the traits of love, loudly, but indiscriminately. He traced its mythology, & discovered it to the first of gods, but for some reason the least praised. Then he went on to name some of its triumphs. How it makes men suffer more than any other passion; for a man would rather die a thousand times than appear disgraced in the eyes of the loved one. Women also are inspired by the god: Alcestis[161] showed greater love for her husband than his own parents did; Achilles was even more heroic, for he killed Hector knowing that he must die himself as he did so. And this was after the death of the man for whom he did it.[162] Love, then, would make a perfect state, for men, under its influence, would be heroes.[163]

Then Pausanias spoke. The substance of his arguments was that L:[ove?] should discriminate. There are different kinds of love. In the manner of Plato he sketches a myth; that there are two kinds of Eros & two Aphrodites; one is pure Heavenly, the other "πανδημος,"[164] public—common.

GN54

The heavenly one was born without any female strain in its parentage; & is thus the love of men for men, which is a higher & more intellectual love than the love for women or for boys. *But the love of young boys has brought the practice into discredit;*[165] & it is thought disgraceful in many states. In barbarous places especially, it is censored; for the strength of such friendship[s] is dangerous to tyrannies. In some countries, like Boeotia, the people let it flourish ~~for~~ because they are too stupid & lazy to express any argument against it. In Athens the custom is difficult to understand: the utmost honour—licence is given to a lover; but at the same time, parents begin to discredit the practice, & male loves are periled. The only thing to decide whether such a love is good or bad lies in the nature of the love itself. In Athens, we discriminate, rightly, between swift[166] attachments, which are physical, or adulterate, in some way, & the lasting love, which is purely good. When love & lovers meet together with the same object of profiting & conferring profit,

---

[161] According to the legend, Alcestis offered to die in her husband's stead.
[162] She means Achilles' companion, Patroclus.
[163] This is in bold type.
[164] Παν meaning "whole," and δημος "public."
[165] Woolf's emphasis.
[166] "Brief" would be a bit more accurate here.

of the highest kind, the union is impeccable. A Deception, if it comes in, are (sic) who is nobly fruitful, is a no blame.[167]

Eryximachus, who was a doctor, agrees with Pausanias that there are two loves; he finds them in the bodies of all creatures. It is the doctors art to unite them harmoniously, or to suppress one, & incite the other.[168] It is the same in music; you take notes, which disagreed once, & reconcile them. But in theory this is simple, for love has no double nature; it cares no more for a high note than for a low one. But in practice, in education, which is the correct performance of airs already compared is difficult. All science & art, even the art of divination have to do with the discrimination between good & bad loves, their marriage, a proper composition.

GN55

Aristophanes speaks & invents a myth of the human race. There were 3 sexes, man, born of the sun, woman of the earth, & man woman, of the moon, a mixture of both. (They tried to destroy the gods, &)[169] They were round, & whirled about, double the size of men. They tried to destroy the gods, & were in consequence cut in half; & went seeking their halves. The man who was good man seeks men, & so does the pure woman; the man-woman seeks women, & the woman-man seeks men. They would have died had not Zeus made it possible for the man to beget children on the woman. They are always desiring to find the whole, & desire always something more than they can ever get, unless indeed they were melted into one.[170] As things are, it is happiest to be able to indulge poor love; therefore, let none flout him, or he will quarter them.

Agathon speaks; so far the gifts of love have been praised, but not the god himself. I will praise love—First he is delicate, for he lives only in the tenderest places, the souls of men, & will never stay when he finds them hard. Then he is the most beautiful, for he lives on flowers in flowery places, & directly they wither & fade he is gone. Then he is courageous, for he mastered Ares himself, & honoured him with love. Then he is temperate, for he is master of all the pleasures, their superior

---

[167] Unfortunately, it is hard to convey any meaning out of this sentence, but I gather it constitutes Woolf's opinion on the immediately preceding sentence by Pausanias.

[168] Eryximachus, a doctor, holds that in curing diseases and whatever is unsound in a lover's body, the doctor ultimately gratifies and exalts the duality apropos of love since he restores the body's natural balance.

[169] Woolf's parenthesis; according to Aristophanes, Zeus thought that hermaphrodites, owing to their double nature, constituted a threat.

[170] Aristophanes here elaborates his viewpoint with mythical hyperbole; he claims that in the perpetual longing for wholeness the two halves would not refuse Hephaestus' suggestion to melt and weld them into one.

& conqueror. Then he is wise, for he is himself the fount of all poetry, the maker of poetry. Every lover, be he never so faultless, becomes a poet. All craftsmen & artists, so long as they know not love, are impotent. He is the youngest & fairest of the Gods, who loves the young, & will never consort with the aged.[171] He is the source of all knowledge of fair things in the Gods, for before he was born they were constrained by necessity. But the hideous creatures of whom Aristophanes has spoken were born before his day. He [Love] can have no intercourse with what is ugly, so that his love always produces beautiful things.

GN55 Verso

Socrates: Love is the desire for something we have not got. It is, as A[gathon] has said, the desire for beauty & good. Therefore it [Love] cannot be good & beautiful in itself.[172] This was shown me by Diotima.[173] I will repeat what she told me. I was mistaken to say that if Love was without good therefore it was worthless. For there is always a mean. "A learned man is between a wise man & an ignorant man."[174] She told me a myth to account for the nature of Love. Porus lay drunk asleep, as one of the gods, & Penia came & lay with him.[175] Their child was Eros who has the inventiveness & fecundity of his father, the neediness & nakedness of his mother.
[Love is] Interpreted between gods & men.
All artists are touched by him.
What good does Love do to men?
Love the love of what?
[The] Love of particular people.
Love cannot be for ugliness.
Must be for beauty.[176]

---

[171] This is in bold type although this might have been entirely accidental.

[172] Here Socrates deconstructs the panegyric speeches of his fellow revelers. He commences his own speech by arguing that to the extent that people are in need of what they do not possess, Love, being in constant need of beauty and goodness, cannot be beautiful or good in itself. Woolf here has grasped this argument.

[173] Elaborating on his argument, Socrates uses a conversation he supposedly had with Diotima, a woman from Mantineia, a town north of Sparta in Peloponnesus (*Symposium*, 202a). Diotima was thought to be a prophetess.

[174] *Symposium*, 202a.

[175] *Symposium*, 203b. Poros or Porus (lit. "way" or "resource"—hence, a-*poria*, which means impasse) was the son of Metis (cunning). The myth is that when Aphrodite was born, the Gods had a feast, after which Poros fell in a drunken stupor. Then Penia (Poverty)—here, Woolf has Greekified the term by using the Greek /n/ (v)—lay with him and had a child. Therefore, Love is linked with Aphrodite—because he was conceived on the day of her divine birth (203b-c).

[176] These are several maxims that Socrates underscores as central in Diotima's treatise on Love.

Love is for the possession by oneself of beauty eternally.
Love is the name given to a whole class of things.
Love is for beauty both of body & soul. It is the passion to create, wh[ich] can only be done when you [?] find beauty.[177]
A truly instructed lover will go on, from better bodies [?], loving bodies. Then love till he gets finally a glimpse of absolute beauty, which is more beautiful than any other vessel in which it takes lodging.[178]

GN56

lays[179]
He [Love] brings "peace ~~to~~ on men, calm on the sea, stillness on the winds, sleep & rest on the unhappy."[180]

Socrates speaks, & first drives Agathon to admit that, as love is the desire for something which we have not, it cannot be itself either beauty or good; but is the desire for the eternal possession of them. He quotes Diotima, the prophetess, who had accounted for the diverse nature of love, by his origin [?]—the child of Penia & Porus (Plenty).[181]
What is the use of such love? asks Socrates. What does a man get by his love of beauty? Let us at present talk of "good" for it is easier: he [the lover] gets happiness. The desire of good is common to all men; but not the desire of love. One part of love is separated from the rest & receives the name of the whole. Only some creators are called poets; yet all creators are poets.[182] Only one class of people ~~are~~ is called lovers. What are they seeking? Some say they seek their missing half; but this is not true, because a man will cut off his hand if he is better without it. There is nothing that men love but the good. Love is the everlasting possession of the good. What is the manner of their pursuit? Love is only birth in beauty, whether of body or soul. All mature people desire to bring forth in beauty. When they see beauty,

---

[177] This sentence is scribbled on the side of the main text on the same page.
[178] Woolf has grasped here the gist of Plato's theory regarding the ideal form of love in that it is separate from the individual lover (*Symposium*, 198d-212c, especially 211a).
[179] "Lays" is superscripted over "brings."
[180] Woolf goes back on herself now; this is spoken by Agathon (*Symposium*, 197c).
[181] Woolf translates "resource" as "plenty."
[182] Woolf here follows Socrates' argument in relation to the differentiation of love from its objects of affection or from lovers; to illustrate this, he makes use of the Greek noun ποιησις (*poesis*) from the verb ποιεω–ω, which literally means "to create," hence the name for the poet—that is, the "creator." Furthermore, he argues that while many men "create" few may be called "poets" (*Symposium*, 205e).

~~they~~ which is harmonious with the divine & immortality, they, desiring immortality, produce ~~beauty~~ when they see ugliness they are contained [?]. Birth is the only form of immortality we have, & we have said that men desire eternal beauty. What is the reason of this love in animals, who do not reason? as in men? The mortal nature is seeking immortality[.] The body is always changing; a new birth is no more than the change & continuation of the old body. This is true also of the soul. Knowledge is recollection; re-birth.

GN57

The love of children, then, is the love of immortality. All these noble actions of Alcestis, Achilles & so on, have been done with a view to fame, immortality. Those whose bodies alone are creative, take women, & beget children. Some men have creative souls. They create wisdom & virtue. Such a man wanders about till he can find a beautiful soul with whom to produce the beauty with which his soul is laden. Who would not leave Homers children & Hesiods children rather than mortal children? [183]

The way of the highest love is something like this: He [the lover] should learn to have the beauty in one form first; then he will perceive that all beauty is related, & he will love the beauty in all forms equally. Then he will love the beauty of the mind above all others. Personal beauty is only a trifle. Then he will love the beauty of the sciences—he will contemplate the whole sea of beauty, until at last the vision is revealed to him of a single science, which is the science of beauty everywhere. At last he will gaze on [at?] pure beauty, which underlies all the forms of beauty, & is stable, & immortal. He must use the beauties of earth as steps with which to mount to the supreme beauty. This is the life which it most befits a man to live, in the contemplation of absolute beauty. He will bring forth not images of beauty, but the realities. He will be immortal, if any man may.

So

Diotima spoke; I believed her, & always teach that to affirm this end there is no better helper than Love. Wherefore I praise love always.

Socrates stops, & a noise is heard outside. Alcibiades comes in, drunk. He sits down, & suddenly sees Socrates.

---

[183] It is not entirely clear in Woolf's text, but Socrates here argues that the intellectual progeny of Homer and Hesiod is immortal.

GN58

You pursue me everywhere, he [Socrates] says, & are jealous if I praise anyone else. You always draw all the beauty in the company to you. Socrates explains that since Alcibiades has been in love with him, his conduct is impossible, so exacting is he. "Protect me Eryximachus!" This is a strange little scene, rather wild, & held in earnest. Alcibiades who is [in?] love is [?] passionate, few [?] are to feel. Then when told to praise love, he says he can only praise one person, Socrates. He takes a great gulp of wine & begins. Socrates is like one of those images of Silenus, which are always grotesque;[184] open them, & you find the figure of a god inside. So Socrates will always speak in rude language, often repeating himself. But, like Marsyas, the flute player,[185] he is a great charmer. Your words bring tears to my eyes. ~~He is~~ You are like a Syren (sic); when I hear you I repent of my past, & implore to stay with you; I tear myself away, lured by the applause of the people. I found such beauty in him [Socrates], that I resolved to trade up [?] all [?] my youth & lovers [?] & make him reveal himself to me, as to his beloved. One night I offered him all that I had, if he would be my lover. My beauty was great, but his virtue was greater. He laughed his odd laugh, & said, "Then I shall be the lover!" I said no more, but crept under his cloak. There I lay, with this wonderful master in my arms all night long, & would you believe me?—I left him in the morning, as though I had slept with a father or an elder brother. Then I will tell you how he went with me on the expedition to Potidaea.[186] He could go in [?] bare […], when we all shivered. He stood once all day & all night in thought—we watched him—when the dawn broke, he went away. I met him walking with another unarmed, on foot, in the […] of […][187]

GN59

the battle of Delium.[188] But he was calm, & unavailable as ever; as he is in the street of Athens.

---

[184] Silenus was part of Dionysus' entourage and was depicted as a figure of uncouth exterior; he could, nevertheless, be wise in his drunkenness.

[185] Marsyas, a Satyr, was also part of Dionysus' entourage; according to the legend, he challenged Apollo to a flute-playing contest; not only did he lose the contest, but Apollo flayed him as a punishment.

[186] 432-430 BC.

[187] Here, Alcibiades praises Socrates by saying that during the expedition on Potidaea he proved himself valiant. He also suffered hunger and thirst and braved the bitter cold (219e-220d).

[188] 424 BC.

Such is Socrates—unlike any other. But this is the way he has treated me, & I bid you, Agathon, "be on your guard."[189]
All this story of yours, said Socrates, is only to hide the end of it: you want to separate me from Agathon. Come here Agathon, & let me praise you.
"Ah, its the usual way—said Alcibiades—Socrates always puts the young & beautiful to his side.
Revellers broke in here; [...] them all to drink, & Aristodemous slept. When he woke at cock crow, he saw Socrates, Aristophanes & Agathon still awake; Socrates was telling them that the genius of comedy was the same as the genius of tragedy. They were so sleepy, that they could not to argue with him. Socrates put them all to sleep, & went, followed by Aristodemus. At the Lyceum he took a bath, & passed the day as usual. At night he went to his own home.
The speech of Socrates is one of the most beautiful I have read.[190] This is an entire expression of something often hinted at in the dialogue. He raises you [?][191] more swiftly and simply than usual—with his logic clothing[192]—to the utmost heights—good that it should ever have been written!
Alcibiades makes the most curious speech of any, in character, as though on a stage. He is half brutal, half in fear, a moving sight. He depends [defers?], like some unruly sea, on [to?] the potency of the moon, which is Socrates. He feels all Socrates' grandeur. He wishes the man dead sometimes—such is the conflict he [Socrates] raises in the bodies of his followers.
The end is almost tragic, for Socrates is alone in all, not to be moved, & acts with a kind of ~~delicate~~ chill irony [?], which must have maddened. There is an excellent phrase or two at the end, to finish off the picture, of the Athenian supper party, sleeping after their divine discourse, while the voice of S.[ocrates] goes on.
But it is impossibly [?][193] deep—Should be read again & again. This is only an outline.

15th July [19]08

---

[189] *Symposium*, 222c.
[190] Woolf's handwriting becomes increasingly illegible from this point until the end of her commentary on the *Symposium*. I have therefore rendered only the completely legible parts.
[191] This could also be "He carries you."
[192] This could also be "chopping," but I cannot be sure.
[193] This could also be "imperfectly."

GN59 Verso

There is also the beautiful story
of the old man, & his life in harmony with nature.[194]

GNN60

28th July [1908]

Virgil. 4th Georgic

Close account of way to keep bees. Their hive should be by a stream, with stones in it, where they can sun themselves in spring. Far from beasts & noises. The Kings fight, & you must choose their superior & kill the others. The different kinds have different markings. Some are spotted with gold scales. In this description, words, clearly, are used with such accuracy, but [yet?] twisted out of their ordinary relations that an unacademic [?] scholar must miss half.[195] There is something in the exquisite delicacy & brightness of the description of inanimate things; have wh.[ich] puts one/me in mind of Popes Rape of the Lock.[196] & the same kind of play upon meaning. The bees signify a state & its wars. Habits of bees. Loyalty to kings. How they kill themselves when worn out.
220. Bees [are] thought by some to have a divine spirit in them on account of their instincts. Some think there is a god in side[?] of beasts & a man, all that has in short; so that they never die, but are recalled to the stars & live there. This is something like the Buddhist view. The diseases of bees. How to tell when they are ill. Remedy—kill a calf, & bees will breed from its blood. Aristaeus taught this method. He was a son of Apollo turned shepherd on earth, & he lost his bees, & complained to his mother—she sat beneath the flood, singing among her maidens (this is like Sabrina, in Roman). Most exquisite myth of Aristaeus. He had is asked [?] sent [?] by his mother to [catch?] Proteus, to ask why his bees are dead.[197] Proteus has to

---

[194] This extract refers to Virgil's *Georgic IV*.
[195] Unfortunately, this sentence is not entirely clear.
[196] Alexander Pope's *The Rape of the Lock* (1712, 1714, 1717).
[197] According to Virgil, Aristaeus was the son of Apollo and Cyrene, a Nymph. Feeling ruined after having lost his bees, he complains that his mother has forsaken him. On hearing his cries, Cyrene, who had been sitting in a cave along with other Nymphs, invites him over and tells him that he should catch Proteus, the crafty sea-deity famous for his prophetic powers, and ask him why his bees are dead.

GN60 Verso

At cantu commotae Erebi de sedibus imis,
umbrae ibant tenues simulacraque luce carentum,
quam multa in foliis avium se milia condunt,
vesper ubi aut hibernus agit de montibus imber:
matres atque viri defunctaque corpora vita
magnanimum heroum, pueri innuptaeque puellae,
impositique rogis iuvenes ante ora parentum—[198]

GN61

be seized. He tells Aristaeus how Orpheus is his enemy because A. had frightened Eurydice, [2] & a snake seized her. Orpheus goes to seek her in the shades.[199] Souls like flocks of startled birds. He sang, & charmed them—but looked once on Eurydice & she sank back forever.[200] He mourns her all day long, as the sad nightingale among the poplars. The matrons tore him asunder for slighting them, & his dead head went down stream, crying Eurydice. A:[ristaeus] is told how to kill bulls, & bees breed from them.

    This is the song I, Virgil made, while Caesar was conquering & making laws.

Lovely![201]

---

[198] This is another indication of Woolf's fascination with the kingdom of Hades. In this passage, Proteus is describing to Aristaeus Orpheus trip to Hades: "From the crannies of Erebus they flocked about him like birds that hide in the leaves when dusk or breaking weather drives them from the hills—grown men and women, the strengthless forms of heroes drained of their brimming life, young boys and girls, young men set on the pyre while their parents watched" (*Georgic IV*, 471-477; *The Georgics*, trans. Robert Wells, Manchester: Carcanet, 1982, 93). See also Woolf's engagement with Book XI of the *Odyssey* in this manuscript.

[199] Meaning the underworld.

[200] According to the legend, Orpheus successfully negotiated Eurydice's return to the world of the living with Persephone, Pluto's wife. The condition was that under no circumstances should he turn around to look at Eurydice while she was walking behind him on their way back up to the land of the living. Unfortunately, just as Orpheus saw the first glimpses of daylight, he turned around to see whether Eurydice was still with him. In doing so, he violated Persephone's condition and Eurydice was sent back to Hades forever. Orpheus lamentations were cut short by a group of maenads who tore his body from limb to limb. His severed head echoed Eurydice's name until he eventually died.

[201] We cannot be certain as to whether Woolf is being sarcastic here. By writing "Lovely!" she may be referring to the myth of Orpheus and Eurydice; it could also be, however, that she is externalizing anti-war feelings, or expressing squeamishness at Orpheus' severed head bobbing down the river calling out Eurydice's name.

GN62

Ajax. Sophocles[202]
Dec 7th [1908]

Odysseus outside the tent of Ajax. Athena stands over him. He does not want to see Ajax in his madness. There is something far more gentle to him as a man in the sight than to Athena, a goddess. She insists—for to laugh at ones enemy is good."[203] Ajax comes out. She gibes—displays [?] him in all his insanity.[204] "see how great the gods are Odysseus."[205] "I pity him—I pity in him his fate as my own. Shadows we are."[206] This is profound; the meditation of a reflective man, like Hamlet. The individual makes him think [?] of all men.
The Chorus of Salaminian sailors.
They reflect that the great are easily subdued [?] by scandal:[207] no one believes ill of an insignificant man. Yet both great & small are necessary to each other. Ajax is great-minded. His enemies chatter like a flock of birds when he is absent; they fly & fall silent when he emerges. Let him [Ajax] come forth then & do away with the rumours.[208]
Tecmessa comes in & tells the story of the madness & slaughter. They hear Ajax shouting within. He had been wont to take sorrow silently. He [Ajax] is calling for his son Eurysakes] & Teu Teucer.[209] Are they never going to stop hunting? I am perturbed.[210] The irritability of a sick & unhappy person.

---

[202] After the death of Achilles, it was Ajax who fought bravely to protect the body of the dead hero. However, the Greek generals, Agamemnon and Menelaus, decided that his armor, made by Hephaestus himself, should go to Odysseus. Incensed at their decision, Ajax decided to avenge his honor, but was overwhelmed by divine madness sent by Athena. He ended up slaughtering the cattle thinking the animals to be Agamemnon, Menelaus and the Greek army. Having realized what he had done, he decided to take his life by falling on his own sword.
[203] Athena here insists that Odysseus should see Ajax.
[204] Athena is talking to Ajax.
[205] Maybe Woolf is quoting to demonstrate Athena's partiality.
[206] Odysseus' reply; perhaps we should pay some attention to Woolf's quotation here inasmuch as it denotes some degree of pessimism and subservience before the divine.
[207] This could also be "easily subject to scandal."
[208] The chorus does not believe that their leader is guilty of such ignominy.
[209] Teucer, Ajax's half-brother.
[210] This could also be "I am destroyed."

GN64[211]

He [Ajax] comes out, and asks the sailors to kill him—asks for one more sight of Odysseus.
Ajax laments his son [Eurysakes] & the [...]—questions how he is to meet his father. Shall he go to Troy & die there alone. [2] to the heights—seas that have known him & shall know him no longer. Tecmessa implores him to think of her. He took her country, her parents are dead; she [will] not stay but [with] him. Tecmessa dwells upon herself as a slave woman would, whose affection must always be partly selfish—like a servants.
Difficult for us to understand the story of Ajax. Seems such a trifling matter about a prize—but that his honour is aimed at; mixture of vanity & a sense [?] that he has made himself ridiculous. Enough ruling [?] of any vote [or role?] to be a tragic figure—partly because there is something impulsive in his glory over sheep & his bloody hand. Ajax [is] thinking of his life with its unspoken sadness, wonders what the use of living can be—each day advancing him to the limit of death & drawing him back again. Tecmessa has hidden Eurysakes, the son, during his fathers madness. He [Ajax] sends for him—& says that he wont be frightened of blood being, his fathers son. "O son, may you be happier than your father—in all else like him." The days of ignorance are best, until we [one?] learn [learns?] to joy or sorrow. When you come to them, prove yourself my son. He commends him to Teucer. Tells Tecmessa to go within & lock the doors. A woman is a pitiable thing. But a doctor has no charms when a wound calls for the knife.[212]

GN65

Ajax has a long speech. How we must obey those in power. Lovely conclusion: night gives way to day, the storms are hushed. "Must not men obey?"[213] Ends up with "I go where I must go—[...] shall hear that [...] of my unhappiness I have found peace."[214] I have found peace "seswsmenov" comes down on it assiduously [?]. They [the chorus of Salaminian sailors] interpret it innocently.[215] He goes off. They sing a song of joy to Pan. Tecmessa comes from Teucer. Calchas has proph-

---

[211] There is no page 63.
[212] Ajax implies that nothing can be gained from trying to heal a wound that can only be cured by "the knife"—that is, suicide.
[213] Line 675.
[214] Lines 685-692.
[215] The implication is that Ajax is trying to allay his comrades' suspicions that he is about to kill himself, and has succeeded.

esied that unless they keep Ajax indoors today he will die. He was guilty of hard words to Athena, saying that he did not want her help. Flouted the gods.

GN65 Verso[216]

[Sketch of the chorus of the Greek camp, the Salaminian sailors, or Ajax' tent and of the ships].[217]

Chorus of Salaminian Sailors
tent of Ajax
Odysseus & Athena
Ships & sea

GN67[218]

48. Athena—do you know how great the gods are?
125. Ορω γαρ, ημας ουδεν οντας αλλον πλην ειδωλ['], οσοιπερ ζωμεν, η κουφην σκιαν.[219]
190. Take this to heart & never rebel [?] against the Gods.
First chorus: The great are more easily attacked than the small. Both great & small do help [?] in alliance.[220]
Perhaps the Gods had been insulted, & therefore sent this madness.
290. Vigorous description Ajax [?] of madness.[221]
320. Ajax howled at these words of weakness.
330. T.[ecmessa] asks them [the chorus] to help her.
She complains that she has had a double woe—grudging cries heard.
343. The fretfulness of Ajax. T. fears that he called for her son. Ajax greets the sailor with emotion as his only friend.
365. Horror of hubris [?]—slaughter of sheep by such a man

---

[216] On the back of p. 65, there exists a sketch by Woolf of a potential setting of the first scene of the tragedy, depicting Ajax's tent, the Greek ships, and Odysseus with Athena.
[217] Woolf has drawn a sketch depicting the above.
[218] Woolf is here attempting a line-by-line translation.
[219] Rendering this in English verse, Jebb writes: "For I see that we are but phantoms, all we who live, or fleeting shadows" (Jebb, 31). An exact translation would perhaps be: "For I see that in life we are nothing but ghosts living in darkness."
[220] Lines 160-161.
[221] In fact, Tecmessa's account of Ajax's madness is given in lines 295-310.

380. Dread of being laughed at.[222]
391 Search [?] of T:[ecmessa] sustained. Wish to die with him.
Peevish & submissive—vaguely bewildered by the
greatness of her fate.
395. Darkness my sole light [...].
T.[ecmessa] remembers A.[jax]'s habits, always like an observant wife.
410. A.—addresses beautiful place that will see him no more.
430. A.'s lament for Telamon [?] lost: his father.

GN68

460. Questions [?] what he is [...]—conventional heroic figure—disgraced at home—therefore cant go back; to die at Troy wd please the Greeks.
470. Ultimate death is to die honourably,[223] wh.[ich] will do him credit in the eyes of his father.[224]
475. What joy is there is day following day, pushing us forward, now drawing us back, from the verge—of death (γε κατθανειν) - only death of the [4].
476. Empty hopes are undignified.
485. Prayer of Tecmessa—I too have suffered—have no mother, father or home. She has [?] the words [?] [2] mother & father, but returns to herself [?][225]
540. Ajax asks for his son—see not to be able to see impatience.
545. Address to his son—time—what is the meaning of "Life is sweeter when you know not feeling—until one learns to know joy or pain"?[226]
That wd mean simply knowledge is best when—then he supposes an intermediate stage between knowing & ignorance—worse than either—
590. Ajax no longer owes service to the Gods.

---

[222] Line 380 gives Ajax's impression of Odysseus as a "tool of evil" (κακων οργανον).
[223] I am not certain of this sentence, but it would definitely reflect Ajax's objectives.
[224] These comments are mostly illegible; in the original, Ajax is wondering how he could return to his father, Telamon, in honor; since he has been deprived of Achilles' armor, he cannot go back empty-handed; if, however, he were to kill as many Trojans as possible that would only please Agamemnon, Menelaus and Odysseus; and given what they did to him, he is not inclined to do so; therefore, the only option is to die honourably by taking his own life (430-480).
[225] Tecmessa here addresses Ajax and pleads with him to remember that she too was a free and wealthy man's daughter, a daughter he took on as a wife. If he were to perish she would be turned into a slave taunted by the rest of the Greeks, and so would his son (485-520).
[226] Addressing his son, Ajax says that life is sweeter when one has no sense (when one is a child), but when one is older one gets to know joy and suffering (554-556).

Tecmessa presents her entreaties.
A.[jax] is shut into his tent.
595. Chorus—they have a beauty
650. A fine speech. Ajax amazed at the way the ~~Gods~~ [...] do things.[227] He has [?] [...] truly—explains his change of mood & his anxiety to go to [?] T[ecmessa].

GN69

670. Is he [Ajax] speaking his own thoughts; revealed to him by calm reflection; is he deluding the chorus; or does Sophocles speak here?
αρχοντες εισιν, ωσθ" υπεικτεον.[228]
Here then comes one of the most beautiful passages in the play; it is romantic, rather than Greek (if that has meaning). All things give way [?]—slow & [...]: shall not we too be discreet?[229]
To most men the harbour of [...] is [...] that is.
σεσωσμενον:[230] comes down with a drop on that word.
790. Ajax had insulted the gods. & Athena [by saying that] he didn't need their help. Long speech of messenger—rather dull.
815. Ajax fixes the sword given him Hector in the hostile land of Troy—and falls on it?
His only ~~message to~~ request of Zeus is that a messenger shall come and ~~bury~~ bid Teucer bury him.
The ~~Furies~~ Erinyes to watch how he was killed by Greeks. No excuse. [Says] No word of abuse against the Gods, or asks for mercy. He says farewell to Salamis, his country, his father[,] mother & Athens. Says farewell to hoes [?] & rivers,[231] all [?] mentioned [...]
865. Jumps & falls on his sword.
925. Stubborn heart "fated to work ταλας[232] [?] evil doom."

---

[227] Here, Woolf has crossed out "Gods" and written something in tiny letters; unfortunately, the new word is illegible.
[228] Line 668; "they are leaders/rulers, so we must comply" (my translation).
[229] Line 677.
[230] The line (692) is "κειν νυν δυστυχω, σεσωσμενον" (even though I am now suffering, I will be saved)
[231] Woolf's handwriting is not clear at all here; Ajax invokes the sacred soil of Salamis, Athens, the springs and rivers of his land, and the plains of Troy, before falling on his sword (855-865).
[232] "ταλας": wretch; long-suffering person. The line is "εμελλες ,ταλας" (you were fated, poor man) (928).

940. You can speculate—I feel.[233]
960. Fine speech by T: I have greater pain than they [the Greeks] joy. & he [Ajax] has what he wanted—why shd they mock then?
1016. Telamon didnt laugh even when he was happy.[234]
1035. I wd believe that all things are planned by the Gods, [says] Teucer—seeing the coincidences in Hector's fate & Ajax's.

GN70

1075: Menelaus upon government. Fear & shame are necessary for the rule of a state.
We cant do as we like: & we may pay for it.
1200. Chorus—[…] of the man who first invented war. Kept them from love. Longing for Athens.

GN71

Ajax

The story of the Ajax is as follows: the flocks of the Greek army have been slaughtered. A spy has seen Ajax slinking into his tent along by [the] shore. Odysseus has tracked him [Ajax] to his tent. He is about to enter when Athena appears & tells him that Ajax has killed the cattle, thinking them the Greek fort. She [Athena] had made him mad. When his madness leaves him, & he sees what he has done, he is overwhelmed. His wife & the chorus attempt comfort. He pretends to listen; but indeed go (sic) out to a solitary place not to ask pardon but to kill himself.
He is discovered by Tecmessa; & Menelaus & Agamemnon refuse him burial. Teucer insists; but Odysseus persuades the generals to give way. Ajax had been insulted by the decision of the Atreidae to award the arms of Achilles to Odysseus.[235] ____

The impression left by the story is complex of course. I should say that the points which Sophocles had in view were to represent an heroic human being in conflict

---

[233] This is in fact line 942; Tecmessa is addressing the chorus.
[234] There is a fine piece of sarcasm here: in his speech, Teucer is wondering how Telamon (Ajax's father) will receive him now that the latter is dead; "Yes, Telamon will receive me with a smile, a man who wouldn't smile even when he was happy" (lines 1008-111).
[235] "Atreidae" refers to Agamemnon and Menelaus, the sons of Atreus.

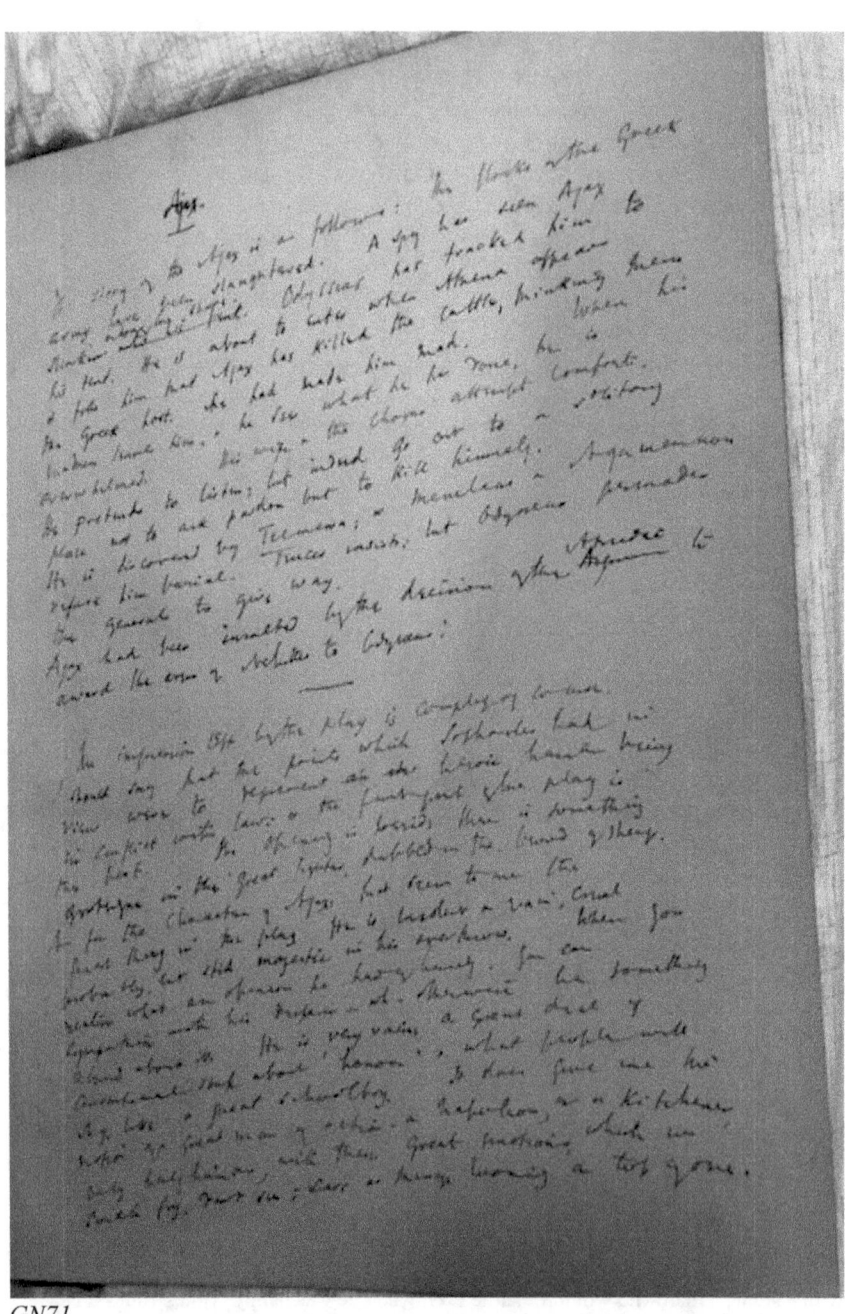

with law. & the first part of the play is the best. The opening is horrid. There is something grotesque in the great fighter dubbed in the blood of sheep. As for the character of Ajax: that seemed to me the finest thing in the play. He is insolent & vain, cruel probably; but still, majestic in his overflow. When you realise what an opinion he had of himself, you can sympathise with his despair—wh[ich] otherwise has something absurd about it. He is very vain; a great deal of conventional stuff about "honour," & what people will say, like a great schoolboy. It does give one this notion of a great man of action—a Napoleon or a Kitchener,[236] only half-human, with these great emotions, which is [in?] small fry dont see [?]; save as things looming on top of one.

GN72

He [Ajax] impresses Odysseus; moves him to a profound sigh. What shadows we are! All who see him are understandable [?] The character of Tecmessa is subtle also. She is a slave & selfish as a slave;[237] her 2nd thought for herself, wh.[ich] like a slave she has a servile dependence on A:[jax] which is pathetic. She is not large eno[ugh?] "to tell [?] the truth [?] about [...] worries him; & yet she is faithful as a dog: like an animal [...] too of inexplicable alarms.

It is difficult of course to pull the ~~whole~~ play sufficiently together to judge it as comprised of different parts leading to a crisis. Probably. If I could read quickly, I shd not find the end so scattered.

Besides the characters, there seems to be a concerted wish to bring out the strength of necessity. Menelaos talks of fear ~~& law~~ being necessary in a state: he wants to show that there is something which must be obeyed, although it is unpleasant. I think S.[ophocles] meant this himself.

This I suppose is what makes him, compared to the rest,[238] a contented poet; not a revolutionary. But then, the view seems to me fine, though sterile; & expressed by arid people, like M[enelaos] & Agamemnon.

Ajax fails because he has a stubborn heart, & must break himself against fate. Ajax never seems conscious of anything unseen. Even when he says farewell, it is

---

[236] Lord Kitchener (Horatio Herbert Kitchener, 1850-1916), of the Second Boer War (1899-1902).

[237] I cannot be sure whether Woolf's branding of Tecmessa as "selfish" here is the upshot of her Victorian/British-Imperial upbringing. To be sure, Tecmessa says nothing that, given the circumstances, an ordinary wife would not say, so I suggest that Woolf's treatment of Tecmessa here is rather unfair—especially if we consider her overall sympathy for Ajax (*GN* 71); he may be insolent and vain, but also "majestic."

[238] Given that Woolf had already read the *Ion* in this notebook, we may be justified in thinking that she refers to Euripides here.

to places, & never to his father or mother. Death he treats as an important person; one will have time eno[ugh] to talk to him.

An entirely material mind; but also he sees the finest side of [the] matter.

He has noble speeches, much hatred in them, & no submission, save when it is (presumably) feigned.

The choruses, sung by sailors, have a rough kind of beauty and pathos: they long for home & love, [but are] kept out there [in Troy] on the shore, wet with sea mists. In these choruses I can see now & then, the inimitable style, a music of words—transcending meaning—such as people claim for S.[ophocles].

GN73

Jebbs (sic) introduction [to *Ajax*]

He says that modern readers complain that the last part is dull, not understanding the unity of the play. The fact is that the play does not end with the suicide of Ajax; but that the climax is really the questions whether A[jax] shall be buried or not. His intention to kill the Greeks deserved punishment; that was made clear by the messengers account of Teucers reaction to before Ajax died; & the punishment is whether he [Ajax] shall be buried, & thus [be] counted a hero or not.

He is buried because, in his last speech to the chorus, he made it clear (to us) that he repented; thus Athena made Odysseus the instrument of herself, & he obtained the burial rites.

The difficult point is to decide how one takes reads Ajax' speech—the splendid one with the lines about winter & day & men learning discretion in it. Some think that he [Ajax] did not attempt to deceive the chorus; some that all his speeches were purely ironical. Jebb traces a change of mood, but not a change of purpose. He thinks that A[jax] had been softened by the appeal of his wife, & that he had returned to the ordinary human standard, & had seen his folly. At the same time he wished to deceive the chorus; there is also some irony in his speech. He says (what I think fine) that he could not have used such polemic imagery had he wished merely to veil his satire.

I think one may believe that he realised some for a superior to his own; & saw the folly of strife; at the same time, I think he never respected the Atreidae, looking upon them merely as a temporary & rather quite accidental ma part of the machine.

GN74

Jan: 11ᵗʰ: 09 Frogs. [of Aristophanes]

The first hundred of lines I found easy—they go with such speed & the jokes aren't hard. Then it became much more difficult than a Sophocles. For one thing there are allusions wh.[ich] I dont follow, & so go hopelessly astray; then the words are impossible—so that I made heavy going. What I perceive duly is an immense vitality—ideas springing up, on all sides—some lyric beauty in the choruses—& a rude boisterous kind of joking, mainly about parts of the body are cruelly[239] mentioned. This seems to be the groundwork of the play. I see more clearly the wit of the contest between Euripides and Sophocles[240]—the truth of the criticism. It has great vitality too, one imagines the enthusiasm of the audience at the [1], and the political jokes & advise (sic). A man of genius giving the likeness of his age—it must have been exciting.

I feel however that I have had read so roughly—deeply to further the sense—that I have missed an infinite number of meanings and beauties. I think however that it must be a vigorous play still because with all the hindrance I read with interest; one imagines that A:[ristophanes] has great range—must be have to tremendous pathos & true beauty.

---

[239] This could be "crudely."
[240] This must be a mistake. The dramatic contest in the *Frogs* is between Aeschylus, the dramatist of heroes, and Euripides, the sceptic. I am not sure why Woolf mentions Sophocles here.

GN75
Bickley Rogers on ~~Ar~~ Frogs[241]

The play was produced in 405! Two months after [the] death of Euripides—4 of the deaths [3] after the victory at Arginusae![242] ... The structure of the play is very queer; as though ~~tacked~~ incongruous pieces were tacked together. Dionysus goes to fetch Euripides; & suddenly, without reason its (sic) said that a contest is going forward between Euripides and Aeschylus for the right to the poetic throne. Then the contest follows, & at the end of it Pluto speaks for the first time & reminds D:[ionysus] of what he came for. D.[ionysus] then says (in contrast to his early meaning) that he will take the best counsellor (not poet) back to the world with him. ~~He~~ There are many things to be noted about the contest. When Euripides ~~quotes~~ says that A's [Aeschylus'] lines are always homeric, he quotes a Homeric line each to show the likeness. It is always in the same metre. Then, giving this up, he quotes lines at random, adding the sound of the lyre: they are faulty, & make no sense in themselves.
A:[eschylus], in criticising Euripides, adds ["]lost his oil jar["] to the end of the lines.[243] It is a

GN76

pure joke, for no one suggests that the break in the line is a bad thing. He also strings together different lines, & shows that they each have a defect, imperceptible to us. He invents a monody in the Euripidean manner satirising the way in which Eu-:[ripides] made servant girls talk in the traditional tragic strain about lost cocks.[244] We have a work about the antipathy between Euripides and Aristophanes. The old

---

[241] While Woolf is using the 1902 translation by Benjamin Bickley Rogers (*RN* 69), my notes below are taken from the second edition (1919).

[242] Naval battle at Arginusae (405 BCE) between the Spartans and the Athenians.

[243] Here, we have the famous ληκυθιον (phial, jar) test. Rogers explains that "Euripides was fond of commencing his plays ... with an historical narrative, which was occasionally prefaced by some philosophical apophthegms; and Aeschylus proposes to show that as a rule, within the first three lines, the words ληκυθιον απωλεσεν (s/he lost his/her [oil] jar) ... can be so tacked on as *to complete the metre and complete the sense*" (Rogers xxiv; emphasis maintained).

[244] According to Rogers, while Euripides criticizes Aeschylus for over-using the Homeric hexameter, the latter attacks the former on the grounds of trivialising the monody—a standard feature of Euripidean drama—by turning what in fact ought to be a vehicle for narrating heroic acts into stories about "spinning-girls" who lost their domestic cocks (Rogers xxxiv). While it is not clear, based on these few lines, that Woolf really understood the jokes either by Aeschylus or Euripides, she appears to be aware of the fact that they were indeed jokes.

comedy was akin to tragedy: [it] depended on the recognition of Dionysus & the mysteries wh.[ich] he represents. No [?] ~~the~~ tragedy seemed [?] to believe in this any longer, then the old Comedy[245] came to an end.

GN76 Verso[246]

86	16	18
26		14
—		—
60		32

4.10
___

52
56

---

[245] In the manuscript, the word "comedy" is written thus: "Comεδη;" also, the /o/ looks more like the Greek /σ/, and the /X/ like an /I/. Simon Goldhill insightfully suggested to me that the word was in fact a Greekified form of "comedy."
[246] Woolf has done a couple of sums here. It is not known to what these refer.

GN77

Notes [Plato's *Phaedrus*][247]

25th May

Lysias has been talking on Love. Phaedrus has the volume with him. S. [tells] a myth. Are they [myths] true or not?[248] What a labour to explain them all! Meanwhile, people knew better of the strange monster [...]. Let us know the nature of that heart first.

Lysias" argument that one ought to yield to non-lovers rather than to lovers. It is more enjoyable, more secure, jealousy of lovers. Love a physical passion that proves [?] Lovers have had judgment.

Argument begins by So.[crates] telling [a/the] story of a boy youth & lover. His lover tried to persuade him that he did not love him: & argued that that So:[crates] was right to [...] love, to find out if it were good or bad. There are 2 ruling principles—one of desire in pleasure, one of good. That wh.[ich] leads us to pleasure is called υβρις[249]—has many shapes. But the owner of this desire is called of [by?] the name of the predominant shape. ~~If the desire~~ The irrational desire wh.[ich] is led away by his engulfment [?] in beauty to vanquish all the rest of them [?] is called love.

They have a friend [...] & definitely [?] & low [?].

Taken wh[?] argument that as a lover is selfish & wd wish to keep his lover subservient, his influence must be worse than that of a non-lover.

---

[247] Brenda Silver suggests that Woolf might have been working from an edition that used to belong to her brother Thoby, by W. W. Thompson (*RN* 169). However, given that there is no such indication and, what is more, that the commentary is rather perfunctory, I would speculate that Woolf wrote this from memory.

[248] While it is clear in the manuscript that Woolf has written "nor," it does not make any sense. Perhaps she meant to write "not."

[249] Greek for "hubris."

No More Missed Connections: A Lesson in Transpersonal Feminism with Virginia Woolf, Audre Lorde, and Adrienne Rich
Erica Gene Delsandro

Beginning with A Conclusion

Virginia Woolf's 1937 novel, *The Years*, ends without Nicholas's anticipated peroration: "'Now for the peroration,' [Renny] said ... 'No,' said Nicholas, holding back the curtain. 'There you are mistaken. There is going to be no peroration—no peroration!'" (431). Nicholas's refusal to give his speech, on the one hand, denies the Pargiters at Delia's party any ceremonial conclusion to their evening, and, on the other hand, withholds from Woolf's readers any interpretive key to the novel's ending. The ending remains uninterpreted, like the unintelligible song the caretaker's children sing at the party, beautiful but enigmatic. Morning breaks on the Pargiter family party, leaving the characters and Woolf's readers on the cusp of a new day, suggesting that the novel's ending might usher in new beginnings. However, Nicholas's unspoken peroration shadows the conclusion, coloring the "beauty, simplicity and peace" of the dawn with uncertainty (435). John Whittier-Ferguson, writing about repetition and war in the novel, acknowledges the Janus-faced character of the ending: there is "a hopeful reading" that celebrates the "complexities of life" and "a darker, equally plausible reading that insists on fragmentation and meaninglessness (246).[1] Readers finish the novel, asking with Eleanor, "'And now?'... 'And now?'" (434-45). Not surprisingly then, the conclusion of *The Years* compels many scholars to evoke and explore Woolf's own assessment of the novel: as she explains to Stephen Spender in a letter, "Of course I completely failed" (*L6* 116). But, as this essay will argue, in her failure resides our feminist lesson.

What began as my interest in Nicholas's forever unspoken peroration has evolved into an obsession with the numerous unfinished, unspoken, and uninterpreted articulations in the novel, both public and private. It seems as though Nicholas is not the only character whose communications are thwarted or unrealized. As Maren Linett has highlighted, "the novel is laden with interruptions, with truncated conversations and thoughts," ultimately claiming that "the text emphasizes these intrusions" (342).[2] A feminist reading of the novel, however, perceives not only

---

[1] Whittier-Ferguson goes as far as to suggest that *The Years* can be seen as "an antinovel" (232).
[2] In her article, Linett "hope[s] to join current efforts toward more nuanced inquiry into Woolf's often conflicting and sometimes troubled political position," particularly her anti-Semitism (341). She does so by focusing on Sara's preoccupation with the "Jew having a bath" (*TY* 339), an oft-quoted exchange with North in the "Present Day" section of the novel.

the abundance of unrealized attempts at communication but also their gendered nature. It seems as though the women in *The Years* cannot communicate with each other, cannot effectively convey their thoughts nor bring their conversations with each other to fruitful conclusions. In fact, nearly every time a woman tries to connect with another woman, something interrupts the gesture, intervenes or distracts, incites insecurity, or invites critique. Whether it is age—the unassailable obstacle between Eleanor and Peggy—or class—the unspoken barrier between Kitty and Rose—productive affiliation among the novel's women is regularly denied. Often read as an example of modernist form in its late modernist evolution, *The Years* seems to *showcase* unrealized female affiliations, potentially representing Woolf's evolving gender politics as much as her evolving modernist aesthetic. If *The Years* is an example of both Woolf's gender politics *and* modernist style in the late 1930s, the incomplete and unsuccessful connections can help us think through some questions that this essay will entertain: How do we read *The Years* as not only modernists but also as feminists? What *connections can we make* across time and through texts as readers, scholars, and teachers?

Concurrent with my recent return to *The Years*, I was revising my Feminist Literary Theory syllabus. The undergraduate course focuses on theories of reading and revising, authorship and identity, that are simultaneously embodied in and theorized by literature written by women, straight and queer, cisgender and trans, western and colonial. Of course, Woolf figures prominently in the syllabus. But instead of positioning myself as a modernist and a Woolfian when I teach the course, I lean into my role as a Women's and Gender Studies teacher whose pedagogical emphasis is not theory but praxis, not icons but intersectionality, not the rise of the novel but the power of story. With this approach guiding me, I chose to incorporate some of the most significant voices in twentieth-century American feminism: Audre Lorde (1934-92) and Adrienne Rich (1929-2012). Their fierce appraisal of feminism, racial politics, and homophobia invigorated my course syllabus and, in the process, recontextualized my reading of *The Years*. Of course, the differences among Woolf, Lorde, and Rich are numerous. And yet, as I reread these authors in tandem, I realized unexpected affiliations among them, affiliations across time, text, race, and class that have enlivened their texts for me as a feminist reader. Nancy K. Miller's conception of the transpersonal zone offers a way to theorize the relations that grew out of my reading and teaching practices linking Woolf to Lorde and Rich—and linking me, a twenty-first-century feminist scholar, to them. For Miller, the transpersonal zone is constituted by "the many complex processes of identification and disidentification [that] take shape in the connective tissue that binds together language, custom, practice, cultural memory,and the archive" ("Getting Transpersonal" 168). In this transpersonal exploration, I hope to displace "the emphasis from the vertical axis" to the "horizontal axis of chosen relations" asking, with Miller, "what kind of story emerges?" ("A Feminist Friendship Archive" 69).[3]

This essay is divided into two main sections and a conclusion. In the first section I offer a corrective reading of Thomas Davis's recent examination of *The Years* as a historical novel by revealing the importance of gender politics in Woolf's family saga. Here I focus on the missed connections among women that abound in *The Years*, highlighting the difficulty women have making meaningful associations within patriarchal structures like family and nation.[4] The perspective gained in the first section of this essay is then elaborated on in the second. Lorde and Rich explore at great length the difficulty in feminist affiliations across race, class, age, and sexual orientation, examining in their writing and activism the struggle that remains unsurmountable for the female characters in *The Years*. Motivated by the missed connections that have plagued feminism, Lorde and Rich provide models for feminist affiliations that explicitly address the differences in race, class, age, ability, and sexual orientation that have, for so long, acted as obstacles in understanding and collaboration among women. In this section, I also turn to Jane Marcus's early feminist essays on Woolf in order to explore the productivity of reading transpersonally. Finally, in the conclusion, I entertain the consequences of this line of thinking for our current feminist modernist endeavors, encouraging contemporary feminist scholars to attend to what Carolyn Heilbrun calls "unmet friends" in order to cultivate a transpersonal zone of reciprocity and intellectual intimacy (137). And in this transpersonal zone I pose the question: How can revision help us to reimagine the dominant narratives of modernism and feminism that mold our reading, scholarship, and teaching?

Woolf and Gendered History, Or, Modernist Missed Connections

I have been trying to come to a conclusion about *The Years*' relationship to Woolf's gender politics in the 1930s. Thankfully, Woolf scholars have provided me with outstanding resources regarding the place *The Years* holds in Woolf's literary oeuvre and how it exemplifies her evolving feminism, and this paper is

---

[3] Miller's essays referenced here explore academic memoir, autobiography, and biography while theorizing an alternative to interpersonal relationships along a vertical axis, seeking, thus to investigate lateral or adjacent relationships that emerge through mutual influence, shared reading and writing practices, and friendship.

[4] That women have a difficult time collaborating and creating coalition is not surprising given a patriarchal hierarchy that has historically positioned women as objects for men to possess. In this structure, women must compete with each other for access to the resources distributed by men. This is not a new insight. See sources as varied as Simone de Beauvoir's *The Second Sex* (1949, 1952) and Naomi Wolf's *The Beauty Myth* (1991).

shaped by their work.[5] Early feminist scholars, perhaps most notably Jane Marcus, redirected scholarly attention to Woolf's late work (*The Years*, *Three Guineas*, *Between the Acts*), and, in their wake, contemporary scholars have found a rich repository of material in Woolf's 1930s writing—her letters, diaries, and drafts, as well as her fiction. Importantly, as outlined by Clara Jones in *Virginia Woolf: Ambivalent Activist* (2017), Marcus spearheaded the American challenge to the Woolf estate, represented by Quentin Bell and his biography of Woolf. At the least, the debate about how to characterize Woolf drew "attention to the need for close and detailed research into the nature of Woolf's political engagements" (Jones 11). And it is this revised Woolf—no longer a recluse in an ivory tower—that has been championed by contemporary scholars. Alice Wood is exemplary, as she evidences Woolf's "transition from high to late modernist aesthetics" by elaborating on Woolf's interest in "documenting the movement of her times throughout the 1930s and examining the socio-political contexts in her literary output" (11). Jones and Wood join scholars such as Anna Snaith, all of whom find Woolf's "real world" investments—to borrow a phrase given prominence by Alex Zwerdling—imperative to a comprehensive study of her late writing.

Additionally, modernist examinations of war and pacifism have also turned to Woolf with new eyes. Vincent Sherry, Sarah Cole, Paul K. Saint-Amour, and Charles Andrews, to name just a few, present keen readings of Woolf's work as deeply engaged in negotiating the culture of war and peace that is the context for the Great War as much as it is the context the 1930s.[6] Moreover, modernist scholars for whom Woolf figures as one of several representative writers of late modernism have also aided my study of Woolf in the 1930s. Jed Esty, Marina MacKay, and, most recently, Thomas Davis have all enriched the perception of the late modernist context in which high modernism evolved with and into a prewar and wartime Britain in the 1930s and 1940s. And yet, even with such a rich archive, I am still left with questions, frustrated especially with modernist scholars who approach Woolf's late fiction without adequate attention to the gender politics so imperative to Woolf in the last decade of her life. For example, how can Thomas Davis, in his book *The Extinct Scene: Late Modernism and Everyday Life* (2015), fully examine Woolf's work in the 1930s without taking into consideration her feminist ruminations—excavated by the feminist scholarship gestured to above—so prevalent in her diaries and letters and the motivation for so much of her literary output in the decade? Thus, like Renny at Delia's party, I continue to seek a peroration: a lesson about what *The Years* means not only to modernist studies but also to feminist studies.

---

[5] I am indebted to scholars of *The Years* such as Mitchell Leaska and Grace Radin for their archival and manuscript work, and benefit from more recent interest in the novel exemplified by scholars such as Elizabeth Evans, Christine Froula, Karen Levenback, Maren Linett, Merry Pawlowski, Anna Snaith, Judy Suh, and Alice Wood.

[6] Vincent Sherry's *The Great War and the Language of Modernism* (2003), Sarah Cole's *At the Violet Hour* (2012), Paul K. Saint-Amour's *Tense Future* (2015), and Charles Andrews's *Writing Against War* (2017) all situate Woolf prominently in their examinations of war, military culture, violence, and pacifism.

Davis attempts to give *The Years* the critical attention it deserves in late modernist studies through his thoughtful reading of it in *The Extinct Scene*, which takes up the scholarly turn towards objects and the ordinary. In his chapter on *The Years*, Davis reassesses the novel, joining "renewed attention to the tangled aesthetic and political problems of Woolf's novel" (*Extinct* 75). Building on the perception that "the everyday [is] the scene where the historical crises of the 1930s attain legibility," Davis troubles the division—aesthetic and historical, at times both—between modernism in the 1930s and the realist fiction that has long characterized 1930s literature in the academy. In doing so, he argues that the historical novel offers Woolf a vehicle for leveraging modernist aesthetic attentions in service of a political analysis that reveals an aprogressive philosophy of history (*Extinct* 69). In his examination of Woolf and Christopher Isherwood, Davis convincingly argues that both authors "recalculate the construction of character and plot"—the formal features prioritized in studies of the historical novel—"divesting themselves from the prevailing sense of history as a rational process," thus transgressing "the historical novel's generic parameters" (*Extinct* 69).[7]

Davis secured my interest through his commitment to troubling the divide separating modernism and realism and his perception that *The Years* critiques a progressive (read: patriarchal) philosophy of history. However, when I finished reading his chapter on *The Years*, I was left wanting. In his examination of *The Years*, Davis's "superb analysis" (to quote Allan Hepburn's review), fails to take into account the function of gender: not only Woolf's gendered position as an established modernist writing a historical novel, but also the gendered realities of the characters he examines in his close readings.[8] Let me summarize my critique with an example. Although Davis convincingly argues that it is through "Delia's and Rose's daydreams and fantasies" that the history they inherit is "most clearly reconfigured," and that their "daydreams express complex desires for greater autonomy" ("The Historical Novel" 12), he neglects to address their gendered identities and positionality vis-à-vis the patriarchal, imperial history which they are simultaneously inheritors of and disenfranchised from.[9]

In his reading of Rose, Davis attends to the oft-quoted scene during which Rose, a child in the "1880" section, steals off to Lamley's alone, imagining herself "Pargiter of Pargiter's horse…riding to the rescue" (*TY* 27). The humor of this scene

---

[7] Woolf and Isherwood prove an interesting pairing. See my "Modernism and Memorials: Virginia Woolf and Christopher Isherwood" in *Woolf Writing the World: Selected Papers from the 24th Annual Conference on Virginia Woolf*, eds. Pamela L. Caughie and Diana L. Swanson, Clemson UP, 2015, 30-36.
[8] He enacts a similar oversight in his reading of Christopher Isherwood's *The Berlin Stories* (1939); although a discussion of sexuality is not completely absent, it does not carry enough analytical weight in his analysis.
[9] The particular quotations used here are from the essay version of Davis's chapter, "The Historical Novel at History's End." Davis does not ignore their gendered identities; rather,

derives from gender dissonance. (And the horror: the scene concludes with Rose being confronted by a male exhibitionist, thus confirming the necessity of gender analysis and an accounting of heteronormativity.) Rose is a young girl, prohibited from leaving the house without her brother, Martin, as her male chaperone, and yet in her make-believe universe, she assumes the role of a military man: "Now the adventure has begun ... Now she must provide herself with ammunition and provisions…now she had her pistol and her shot" (*TY* 26). Later, in the "Present Day" section of the novel, also attended to by Davis, what was implicit in 1880 is made explicit when Martin declares his sister Rose the "very spit and image… of old Uncle Pargiter of Pargiter's horse," an assessment which motivates the following exchange:

> "Well, I'm proud of it!...proud of my family; proud of my country; proud of…"
> "Your sex?" [Martin] interrupted her.
> "I am," she asseverated. "And what about you?" (*TY* 416)

Here, Woolf alludes to the gender politics that surround Rose, whose childhood military imaginings evolve into militant suffrage before World War I and then patriotic involvement in the war effort. How Davis can analyze the way Rose's daydreams and fantasies trouble a progressive philosophy of history without a concerted examination of the gendered politics prioritized by Woolf seems, to me, a regrettable omission. If the modernist in me applauds Davis's analysis, the feminist in me remains disappointed.

Disappointed, especially, in hoping to further my consideration of the various incomplete, aborted, and unspoken connections among the characters of the novel. These "missed connections," to borrow from contemporary lingo, occur between women and men throughout the novel. However, the most sustained and lamented missed connections are those among the novel's female characters. Let me continue with Rose. In the "1910" section of the novel, Rose arrives for luncheon at Maggie's and Sara's shared flat (*TY* 162). Years of cohabitation have given Sara's enigmatic mode of communication a patina of familiarity to Maggie, but Rose's intrusion into their domestic space seems to highlight the impossibility of connection amongst the women. "'It's ages since we met,'" Rose begins, shaking hands with her cousins, wondering silently to herself why the desire to visit had overcome her when she met Maggie in the shop earlier and why she yielded to it (165). Shared memories about familiar furniture initiate conversation—"But there

---

he chooses not to consider them significant to his analysis. He recognizes that their daydreams are "coded in explicitly imperial terms" but does not examine how the imperial and patriarchal history they inherit is also the means of their national, social, and historical disenfranchisement. See pages 82-91 of *The Extinct Scene*.

was the crimson-and-gilt chair; she recognized it with relief. 'That used to stand in the hall, didn't it?' she said"—confirming the significance of Davis's attention to the ordinary and to objects (*TY* 165). Rose admits to living in the neighborhood in the past, a confession met with incredulity by Sara, who only associates Rose with Abercorn Terrace, the Pargiter family home: "'Can't one live in more places than one?' Rose asked, feeling vaguely annoyed, for she had lived in many places, felt many passions, done many things" (166). But Rose's many places and passions, the many things she had done, go unspoken: "Her past seemed to be rising above her present. And for some reason she wanted to talk about her past; tell them something about herself that she had never told anybody—something hidden…" (166). However, as the conversation continues Rose finds herself considering the futility of it all:

> They talked, she thought, as if Abercorn Terrace were a scene in a play. They talked as if they were speaking of people who were real but not real in the way in which she felt herself to be real…What was the use, she thought, of trying to tell people about one's past? What was one's past?… Why did I come, she thought, when they only laugh at me? (167)

Rose desires to share her past with her two female cousins: her childhood adventure to Lamley's, her suffragist politics, her romance with another woman all rise to the surface of Rose's consciousness and yet remain unspoken. Her effort to connect seems futile; the women's words reach each other over luncheon but their meaning, at least for Rose, seems impossible to convey and capture.

The above is one of many vignettes in *The Years* that illustrate the missed connections I am interested in, missed connections oriented around gendered positionality—a positionality Davis's otherwise astute analysis overlooks. Rose, a frequently studied character in the novel, is not only a make-believe military man as a child but also a militant suffragist and a patriotic supporter of World War I as an adult, thus reforming the patriarchal history she inherits.[10] And during luncheon with her cousins, Rose's hints at a same-gender attraction, an attraction erased from and silenced by the very patriarchal and heteronormative history in which the vote has finally given her a voice. Yet, in the vignette summarized above, Rose is confronted with political indifference and heteronormativity through Maggie (she seems detached and refuses to join Rose so she can finish mending the dress she will wear to the next evening's party) and political refusal and queer disability through

---

[10] Davis may perceive Woolf's historical novel as troubling the very concept of history as progressive but Rose, at least, is a champion of progressive politics and her character necessitates the assumption of historical progress. Perhaps a wrench in Davis's analytical gears? I would argue not. Rather, an opportunity for a more nuanced gender analysis.

Sara (she is associated with the radical politics of *Antigone* and is marginalized because of her decreased able-bodiedness and relationship with a homosexual man, Brown). And Rose finds herself unable to connect with her cousins across these social identity differences, differences put into relief next to their shared gender identity. Thus, although they inherit the same patriarchal and imperial history, their respective experiences of that history are distinct, their degree of disenfranchisement differs, and their desires, consequently, range from acquiesence (Maggie), to refusal (Sara), to reformation (Rose). These very significant differences remain obstacles in *The Years*, keeping Woolf's female characters from affiliating, connecting, communicating.

Whittier-Ferguson declares *The Years* "a novel that refuses all gestures toward closure and celebrates open-endedness," and I do not disagree (232). However, considering Woolf's engagement with gender politics in the decade—as Radin early explained, "the story of the writing of *The Years* begins with an idea conceived in a bathtub on a January morning in 1931, an idea for a feminist essay to be based on a talk Woolf was to give the next night" (1)—I can't help but wonder if some of the "open-endedness" is less celebratory and more critical or pedagogical. Again, prioritizing a feminist reading of the novel compels readers to account for the ways in which affiliations among women are left unrealized, and moreover, what lessons these missed connections teach us.

In addition to the example above, drawn from the "1910" section, readers can turn to the "Present Day" that concludes the novel. In this long section, the interactions between Eleanor, the eldest Pargiter sister, and Peggy, her niece and a member of the younger generation, offer additional missed connections that speak to the importance of gender politics for a reading of *The Years* as a historical novel. Let's begin with Eleanor's surprising curse—"'Damned—...bully!'"—uttered as she tears and then flings the evening paper with a photo of Mussolini onto the floor (330). Peggy is shocked at first, then amused, "[f]or when Eleanor, who used English so reticently, said 'damned' and then 'bully,' it meant much more than the words she and her friends used" (331). Their generational difference becomes only more pronounced here, as Eleanor's exclamation follows a brief exchange about the first time she ever saw an airplane:

> "I said to Miriam, 'Is that a bird? No, I don't think it can be a bird. It's too big. Yet it moves.' And suddenly it came to me, that's an aeroplane! And it was!...I remember reading it out in the paper, and someone—your father, I think—said: 'The world will never be the same again!'"
>
> "Oh, well—" Peggy laughed. She was about to say that aeroplanes hadn't made all the difference, for it was her line to disabuse her elders of their belief in science, partly because their credulity amused her, partly because

> she was daily impressed by the ignorance of doctors—when Eleanor sighed.
> "Oh dear," she murmured.
> She turned away from the window.
> Old age again, Peggy thought. Some gusts blew open a door: one of the many millions in Eleanor's seventy-odd years; out came a painful thought; which she at once concealed—she had gone to her writing-table and was fidgeting with papers—with the humbled generosity, the painful humility of the old.
> "What, Nell—?" Peggy began.
> "Nothing, nothing," said Eleanor. (329)

Generational difference has already taken center stage in this interaction between Eleanor and Peggy well before Eleanor's angry outburst upon seeing Mussolini's photograph in the evening paper. According to Peggy, airplanes hadn't irrevocably changed the world, whereas to Eleanor and her generation, they had. And Eleanor's memory—the first time she saw an airplane in the sky—and Peggy's laughing dismissal of its significance—earned, she seems to suggest, from her experience as a woman of science—alludes to the challenge of connecting across the divide between youth and age. And, in this instance, youth and age are marked by distinct experiences of the Great War. Eleanor, in her fifties at least during the war, hid in basements during air raids with her contemporaries—see the "1917" section of the novel—while Peggy, much younger at the time, lost her brother, Charles, in battle (336). Although both women experience the Great War from the vantage point of the home front, their generational positions influence their perspective on a war that, in the "Present Day" section, is still the Great War, not the First: Eleanor from the generation whose patriotism supported it, Peggy from the generation whose experience of war questioned the cost of patriotism.

And yet to stop there would be to disregard the role their gender plays in their respective experiences of wartime. As women, neither Eleanor nor Peggy could actively participate in the war; however, as women, both are significant others to men who fought: Eleanor is the aunt of North and Charles, and Peggy is their sister. Their distinct proximities to the loss of Charles and the survival of North—among other men unknown to readers—arguably shape their thoughts on the war. What those thoughts are, however, are left largely unspoken. Eleanor, confronted with a painful thought after remembering the first time she witnessed an airplane in the sky, offers no explanation to her niece. Was she remembering the air raid from the "1917" section? Was she remembering someone she lost in a war changed by aerial attacks? "'Nothing, nothing,'" she responds when Peggy presses her to continue (329).

Peggy, too, does not elaborate on her experience of the war. Rather, in the cab on their way to Delia's party, when passing a statue of a nurse holding out her hand in the theater district, Peggy declares that the statue "[a]lways reminds me of an advertisement of sanitary towels" (336). It is Eleanor's turn to be shocked at Peggy's remarks: "a knife seemed to slice her skin, leaving a ripple of unpleasant sensation" (336). But she quickly blames the bitterness in Peggy's voice on the loss of her brother, Charles, "a nice dull boy who had been killed" (336). Eleanor reads the words etched into the pedestal and reflects, "'The only fine thing that was said in the war,'" to which Peggy sharply replies, "'It didn't come to much'" (336).[11] What didn't come to much? The war? The sentiment inscribed on the statue's base? Peggy does not elaborate. Instead of using this moment to delve deeper into their experiences of the war, the losses they sustained as women on the home front, and their generational vantage points, the ensuing pause "seemed to hold them in the light of some thought that they both wished to put away" (336). "'Don't people wear pretty clothes nowadays?'" Eleanor inquires, breaking the silence and ultimately rejecting a moment of potential connection (336).

This scene, ripe for analysis under the historical, object-oriented rubric proffered by Davis, begs for a gendered lens. That both women are unmarried—Eleanor, arguably, challenging Victorian constraints, and Peggy, potentially, taking advantage of educational and professional opportunities for women emerging during and after the war—is significant as it determines their proximity to the men of the Lost Generation; they are aunts, sisters, friends, but not wives. Moreover, their ages create an obstacle that neither knows how—or wants—to overcome, as Eleanor belongs to a "wonderful generation," according to Peggy, of "[b]elievers" (331) and Peggy, according to Eleanor, lives a life "much more interesting than [mine] was" (333). What might these women gain from a deeper connection? How might they benefit from exploring their affiliations? Readers of *The Years* will never know. And, arguably, this is significant to Woolf's evolving gender politics in the 1930s.

Before I close this section, it is important to remember Woolf's own attempts at female affiliation in the 1930s. Perhaps the most salient for the purposes of this essay is her rich and complicated relationship with the composer Dame Ethel Smyth (1858-1944), a woman whose gender politics are mirrored in Rose and whose feminism both vexed and inspired Woolf. A letter to Smyth from Woolf in January 1931 (referenced by Radin [1]) is exemplary of Smyth's role in encouraging Woolf's thoughts on gender, as it links speeches the two women gave to London National Society for Women's Service (LNSWS) to "a sudden influx of

---

[11] The statue commemorates the British nurse Edith Cavell, who was executed in Belgium by the Germans in 1915. The words inscribed on the statue's base are Cavell's last words to an Anglican priest on the eve of her execution: "Patriotism is not enough, I must have no hatred or bitterness for anyone" (Hussey 53).

ideas" which eventually became, first *The Pargiters*, and then *The Years* and *Three Guineas* (*L4* 280).¹² In fact, Woolf begins her speech for the LNSWS, posthumously published as "Professions for Women" (1942), with a characterization of Smyth's achievements as a composer and feminist, portraying her as "one of the race of pioneers, of pathmakers [who] has gone before and felled trees and blasted rocks and built bridges and thus made a way for those who came after her" (Leaska xxvii-xxviii).¹³ Smyth, notorious for her role in the prewar militant campaign for women's suffrage, and equally notorious, some would argue, for "making scenes" as an advocate for her compositions, played an important role in the political and cultural emancipation of British women, and was beginning to play an integral part in Woolf's reflections on egotism, women's history, and gender politics (St. John 178).

As an admirer and close friend to Mrs. Emmeline Pankhurst, Smyth dedicated two years of her life (1910-1912) to women's suffrage generally and to Pankhurst's Women's Social and Political Union (WSPU) particularly. During these two years, Smyth put her career on hold—except to compose "The March of Women," the official anthem of the WSPU—in order to conduct at rallies, break windows, write pro-suffrage articles, and eventually serve a prison sentence with Pankhurst at Holloway. Her involvement with militant feminism encouraged Woolf initially to describe Smyth as "*one of the ice breakers, the gun runners, the window smashers*" (Leaska xxvii).¹⁴ Woolf's early draft of her LNSWS speech continues, revealing, I would suggest, Woolf's ambivalence regarding Smyth's role in the fight for women's rights: "*The armoured tanks, who climbed the rough ground, drew the enemies fire, and left behind her a pathway—not yet smooth and metalled road—but still a pathway for those who come after her*" (Leaska xxvii). Considering the pacifist holding the pen, the military rhetoric found in the original manuscript suggests Woolf may have had some misgivings regarding her new friend's feminist tactics. Ultimately, though, Woolf does borrow from her early description of Smyth for her characterization of Rose's tactics in *The Years*.

Moreover, Woolf's admiration of Smyth was tempered by her own strong desire for anonymity, a quality that Woolf associated with unconsciousness and

---

¹² Woolf's diary records a similar sentiment: "I have this moment, while having my bath, conceived an entire new book—a sequel to a Room of One's Own—about the sexual life of women: to be called Professions for Women perhaps—Lord how exciting! This sprang out of my paper to be read on Wednesday to Pippa's society" (*D4* 6). The book mentioned in both quotations begins as the novel-essay *The Pargiters*, but eventually is revised into two separate texts, *The Years* and *Three Guineas*. See Leaska for *The Pargiters* and Woolf's 1931 speech for the LNSWS.
¹³ As mentioned above, the speech is published in Leaska's *The Pargiters* and differs from the posthumously published "Professions for Women." All quotations below are from Leaska.
¹⁴ The italics indicate cancelled portions of the typescript, editorially restored for publication in order to illustrate the evolution of the manuscript.

that, for her, was necessary for the production of great art. In *A Room of One's Own*, it is Shakespeare's incandescent mind that represents the desired state of unconsciousness: "We are not held up by some 'revelation' which reminds us of the writer" (56). There is no "revelation" reminding the reader of the author's personality, suggesting, as Anna Snaith argues, that for Woolf, "egotism is restrictive" and "an impediment to the flexibility necessary for creativity" (48). Smyth's egotism stands in direct contrast to Woolf's description of Shakespeare's anonymity. Calling Smyth a "blazing egoist" in a letter to Vita Sackville-West (*L4* 272), Woolf was reacting to Smyth as many of her friends did, with a mixture of "pleasure, mockery, and wariness" (Lee 587). Woolf's diary illustrates her mixed reaction to Smyth. Sometimes Woolf is charmed by Smyth's unconventionality and sincerity: "Ethel stood at the piano…in her battered felt, in her jersey & short skirt conducting with a pencil…but everything she does with such forthrightness and directness that there is nothing ridiculous. She loses self-consciousness completely" (*D4* 9). Here Smyth is not portrayed with contempt; rather, she is concentrating on her art, oblivious to the world of convention and decorum. Other times, as Woolf becomes more attentive to, and more a victim of, Smyth's egotism, she is overwhelmed by disdain for Smyth's self-serving theatrics: "Sense of drum & blare: of Ethel's remorseless fangs: her irresistible vanity…how tawdry how paltry…& the sense of the futility of it all" (*D4* 12). Here, artistic unconsciousness is replaced by Smyth's insatiable desire for recognition and success in her male-dominated field.

Despite Woolf's aversion to Smyth's militant politics and gender-fueled egotism, Hermione Lee proposes that through their letters they became each other's "psychologists," Smyth's egotism giving Woolf permission to speak directly and reflectively about her own life (587). Lee credits "Ethel's self-absorption and enthusiasm" for inspiring "a new kind of autobiographical writing in Virginia's letters," connected, Lee offers, "to her lifelong argument about egotism, and to the political questions she was asking about the effects on women's lives and writing of anonymity, silence and repression" (587).[15] However, as Lee notes, it was "their argument over egotism" that was "the key reason why the friendship could not be kept up at its initial pitch" (594). Regardless, the confluence of egotism, politics, gender, and history became the crucible for Woolf's fictional experiments as the 1930s progressed, her correspondence with, and reflections on, Smyth providing an opportunity to further hone her thinking about gender, egotism, history, and their relationship to feminism. And since, as many scholars have noted, Smyth is the model for Rose in *The Years*, it seems careless to examine the novel without

---

[15] Jane Marcus, along with Hermione Lee and Herbert Marder, are scholars who give Woolf's relationship with Smyth the critical attention it deserves. Smyth's impact on Woolf's thinking during the 1930s is often trivialized, a view that Woolf's caricatures of Smyth only encourage, despite the predominance of letters and references to Smyth in the last two volumes of Woolf's collected letters.

close attention to the gender politics that buttress Rose's trajectory in the novel. That Woolf's once intense and intimate relationship with Smyth cooled over their differing approaches to gender and artistry suggests that aborted affiliations among women—missed connections—impacted Woolf's writing in the 1930s and thus were constituent of her evolving modernist aesthetic. Consequently, I argue that we cannot successfully read *The Years* as a historical novel as Davis does until we grapple with the gender politics so poignantly represented in *The Years* through missed connections, or rather, failures of gendered affiliation.

Sister Outsider: Thinking Back through Our Literary Mothers?

Jane Marcus was one of the first feminist scholars to explore the relationship between Woolf and Smyth. In "Thinking Back Through Our Mothers," Marcus reads Woolf's relationship with Smyth as an example of mutual influence that, when placed among other friendships and mentorships, created a network of women who could both seek out their metaphorical mothers and amass an artistic and intellectual inheritance for their metaphorical daughters. For, as Marcus explains, "finding our mothers is no easy task" (7). Moreover, in Marcus's reading of Woolf's female affiliations, she perceives the opposite of Harold Bloom's famous "anxiety of influence," suggesting that networks of women "afford the woman writer *relief from anxiety*, acting as a hideout in history where she can lick her wounds between attacks on the patriarchy" (8, emphasis mine). Although there is anxiety detectable at times in Woolf's commentary on Smyth, Marcus's point is important, and has been taken up more recently by Jean Mills in her book on the rich relationship between Woolf and the classicist Jane Ellen Harrison.[16] In *Virginia Woolf, Jane Ellen Harrison, and the Spirit of Classicism* (2014), Mills introduces the concept of the transpersonal to Woolf scholars as a way to imagine the mutuality of influence Marcus explores nearly twenty-five years earlier. Mills, leveraging the transpersonal, extends Marcus's reading, offering feminist scholars, I would argue, a way to see themselves as participating in transpersonal feminist affiliations. For Mills, borrowing from Nancy Miller, thinking transpersonally makes visible and values "'other categories of significant others, those to whom one is related by affinity (profession, passion, politics) but not (or not necessarily) by blood or marriage'" (qtd. in Mills 4). Valuing other categories of significant others—dare I suggest readers to authors, scholars to subjects?—shifts the primacy of the vertical axis, such as

---

[16] Marcus was a mentor of Mills and, as I was reading their work in tandem, I was witness to yet another transpersonal zone as Mills and Marcus continue to speak to each other through their work, illustrating the intellectual friendship both during Marcus's lifetime and its continuance after. A special thank you to Jean Mills for corresponding with me about her relationship with Marcus.

in traditional mentorship, and reveals relationships (and aspects of relationships) that are "lateral" or "interjacent in nature," emphasizing "interactive project[s] of shared ambitions and objectives" (Mills 4). And isn't this how Woolf scholars might characterize their relationship with Woolf and her work? The indie-folk band the Indigo Girls were on to something when they described reading Woolf as "a telephone line through time."[17] In this and the final short section, I will explore the transpersonal telephone line that links Woolf to second-wave feminists Audre Lorde and Adrienne Rich and, by extension, links them to us.

"A room of one's own may be a necessity for writing prose," writes Lorde, thinking back through her literary foremother, Woolf, "but so are reams of paper, a typewriter, and plenty of time … When we speak of a broadly based women's culture, we need to be aware of the effect of class and economic differences" ("Age, Race, Class, and Sex" 116). Class difference is but one aspect of identity Lorde attends to in her writing, as she was deeply committed to recognizing the various vectors constituting one's social location. Arguably one of the fiercest voices articulating intersectional feminism in the late twentieth century,[18] Lorde teaches us the lesson that remains unlearned in Woolf's *The Years*. The various missed connections in the novel derive from and are oriented by an inability to affiliate across and through difference. Although scholars such as Alison Light and Mary Wilson have shone a much-needed light on the role class plays in Woolf's writing and life, social and economic status is but one of many identity vectors that Woolf's female characters grapple with and are stymied by, especially in their desire and ability to affiliate with other women. For example: Kitty remains isolated from other women by her class position; Eleanor and Peggy, Sisyphus-like, attempt to connect across the social chasm created by generational difference; and Sara, rendered a female Peter Pan by her disability and assumed asexuality, exists in queer proximity, near but unknowable, to her sister and female cousins. Needless to say, Woolf scholars particularly and feminist modernist scholars more generally may benefit not only from thinking *back* through Woolf's literary mothers, but also *forward* through her metaphoric daughters. Turning to Lorde and Rich in the context

---

[17] The most relevant lines of the song "Virginia Woolf" on *Rites of Passage* (1992) are: "They published your diary / And that's how I got to know you / The key to the room of your own and a mind without end / And here's a young girl / On a kind of a telephone line through time / And the voice at the other end comes like a long lost friend / So I know I'm all right."

[18] R. Claire Snyder explains in her essay, "What is Third Wave Feminism? A New Directions Essay," how many self-identified third wave feminists inaccurately claim writers like Lorde as third wave feminists because of their commitment to intersectional analysis, one of the main tenets of contemporary feminist analysis. Although Lorde certainly shares with contemporary feminism an understanding of intersectionality, her role in American feminist discourse in the 1960s, 1970s, and early 1980s positions her firmly within the second wave of feminism. Kimberlé Crenshaw is credited with introducing the term intersectionality into feminist discourse in the late 1980s.

of the transpersonal allows me to enact, playing off of Davis, an aprogressively historical feminist reading.

In "The Master's Tools Will Never Dismantle the Master's House," Lorde articulates the patriarchal lesson that Woolf seems to have learned all too well, if the missed connections in *The Years* are any indication: "As women, we have been taught either to ignore our differences, or to view them as causes for separation and suspicion rather than as forces for change" (112). Lorde goes on to explain that "without community there is no liberation, only the most vulnerable and temporary armistice between an individual and her oppression. But community must not mean a shedding of our difference, not the pathetic pretense that these differences do not exist" (112). Although Woolf may have struggled with her own competing desires regarding a community of women—perhaps arriving at her ideal form in the Outsiders Society of *Three Guineas*—feminist modernist scholars have had to take Lorde's advice seriously in order to gain space and voice within male-dominated modernist studies. And yet, Lorde's experience as an outsider in the academy continues to teach us: as feminist scholars and teachers of modernist literature we continue to grapple with generational difference, heteronormative privilege, racial inequality, imperial inheritance, cisgender dominance, and ableism. Consequently, Lorde's words cut across the millennial divide: "The failure of academic feminists to recognize difference as a crucial strength is a failure to reach beyond the first patriarchal lesson. In our world, divide and conquer must become define and empower" (112).

And if we doubted Lorde's commitment to connecting across difference, the essays in *Sister Outsider* (1984) enact the practice that Lorde preaches. Particularly in "Letter to Mary Daly" and "An Interview: Audre Lorde and Adrienne Rich," Lorde invites, incites, and makes imperative not only the recognition of difference but also coalition building upon the very foundation of difference defined. In "Letter to Mary Daly," Lorde indicts the "old pattern of relating" between white women and women of color which is "sometimes protective and sometimes dysfunctional," adding that "we, as women shaping our future, are in the process of shattering and passing beyond, I hope" (67). Writing of Daly's *Gyn/Ecology* (1978), Lorde explains: "What you excluded...dismissed my heritage and the heritage of all other noneuropean [*sic*] women, and denied the real connections that exist between us" (68). Lorde elaborates:

> This dismissal stands as a real block to communication between us. This block makes it far easier to turn away from you completely than to attempt to understand the thinking behind your choices. Should the next step be war between us, or separation? Assimilation within a solely western european [*sic*] herstory is not acceptable. (69)

Lorde's compassionate but incisive critique of Daly's work identifies what Mariana Ortega, borrowing from Marilyn Frye, calls "loving, knowing ignorance": "an ignorance of the thought and experience of women of color that is accompanied by both an alleged love for and an alleged knowledge about them" (Ortega 57). In this context, Daly's loving perception of women of color does not erase her ignorance and dismissal of their history and experience. Although the vector of difference is race, Lorde's letter evokes an intersectional imperative. As the citations above illustrate, race is the difference elided in Daly's book, and yet, in so doing, Daly implicitly endorses a monolithic definition of woman, one that Lorde rightfully identifies as western European in derivation, and by extension, invested with imperial, racist, heteronormative, and cisgender privilege. The latter list of feminist keywords may be more commonplace in twenty-first-century feminist discourse than they were in 1979, but their significance and salience resonates throughout her public epistle, demonstrating the intersectional perspective necessary for feminist affiliations, according to Lorde.

Although there may not be an interpretative straight line connecting Lorde's essays in *Sister Outsider* and Woolf's *The Years*, I encourage us to constellate them, recognizing their differences and seeking affiliations concurrently, enacting a reading practice that mirrors the politics Lorde requests of her feminist colleagues. In other words, I encourage us to realize the transpersonal zone which Woolf, Lorde, Rich, and contemporary feminist scholars activate and inhabit. As a white, well-positioned, British woman, Woolf is implicated in the western European herstory Lorde reproaches Daly for assimilating her into, and yet the missed connections outlined from *The Years* suggest that Woolf recognized the danger of perceiving difference as an obstacle—rather than a foundation—in cultivating connections among women. As suggested above, it is when Rose encounters Sara's narrative of her life—Sara's incredulity that Rose could have lived anywhere but Abercorn Terrace—that she balks in frustration. Rose's desire to connect with her cousins remains, and perhaps is encouraged by her urge to correct Sara, but her frustration arises from the knowledge that Sara has assimilated, to use Lorde's term, her life into a narrative of Sara's own making, a too-narrow history dominated by family ties and dismissive of her suffragist politics (of which the Pargiter rumor mill must have made Sara aware). In fact, Sara's initial description of Rose (before she even enters the room) reverberates with echoes of Rose's childhood adventure, militant politics, and patriotic labor during the war, and anticipates Martin's refrain characterizing her as the "spit and image … of Old Uncle Pargiter of Pargiter's Horse" (416) in the "Present Day" section: Sara chants, "'Rose of the flaming heart; Rose of the burning breast; Rose of the weary world—red, red Rose!'" (164). Sara seems to demonstrate toward Rose the kind of loving, knowing ignorance that Ortega describes. Her evocative description suggests to the careful reader that she knows

Rose—perhaps even admires her—and yet her inability to imagine that Rose lived anywhere but Abercorn Terrace reveals the ignorance accompanying her loving perception. Rose attempts to reach across the distance reinforced by Sara's loving, knowing ignorance by inviting her and Maggie to her meeting: "She wanted to conceal the thing that interested her the most; she felt extraordinarily shy. And yet she wanted them to come" (*TY* 171). Reaching out and making herself vulnerable, Rose reiterates her desire for affiliation over assimilation. Whether or not such connection is achieved the novel does not reveal as the narrative, jumping ahead to Rose's meeting, shifts to another pair of missed connections, Eleanor and Kitty, leaving the reader uncertain as to whether Rose was able to rekindle the connection sparked when she ran into Maggie at the shop: "And it was odd, considering how little she knew of them ... how strongly, sitting there at the counter before Maggie saw her, simply from the sound of her voice, she had felt—she supposed it was affection?—some feeling bred of blood in common" (162).

Before continuing, I must state the obvious: the political stakes for Woolf and Lorde are not the same. Despite being politically and economically disenfranchised as a woman in the late nineteenth and early twentieth centuries, a positionality Woolf explored in-depth in *A Room of One's Own* and *Three Guineas*, Woolf's race and national identity bestowed upon her significant privilege, especially in comparison to working-class, non-white, and colonial women.[19] Similarly, although Woolf's intimate relationships suggest that she was not exclusively heterosexual, she was married to Leonard Woolf, thus allowing her to benefit from heterosexism.[20] In contrast, Lorde was less able to avoid social prejudice and her life was irrevocably impacted by racism, sexism, and homophobia. She characterizes her positionality as follows: "As a forty-nine-year-old Black lesbian feminist socialist mother of two, including one boy, and a member of an interracial couple, I usually find myself a part of some group defined as other, deviant, inferior, or just plain wrong" ("Age, Race, Class, and Sex" 114). And it is her particular intersectionality that provides her the epistemic authority to articulate what is, arguably, a critique applicable to Woolf: "As white women ignore their built-in privilege of whiteness and define *woman* in terms of their own experience alone, then women of Color become 'other,' the outsider whose experience and tradition are too 'alien' to comprehend" (117).

---

[19] Although Woolf famously declares in *Three Guineas* that "[a]s a woman I have no country. As a woman I want no country. As a woman my country is the whole world" (129), it would be naïve to take her words as a renunciation of citizenship, real or rhetorical. Rather, Woolf's oft-quoted declaration acts as an indictment of the misogyny and sexism embedded in the nationalist, imperialist project, a project that, for centuries, disenfranchised women, marginalizing their experiences and silencing their voices. Throughout her life, Woolf benefitted from her Englishness even as she honed a critical approach to nationalism and imperialism.
[20] Woolf's marriage to Leonard did situate her firmly within heterosexual privilege but Leonard's Jewishness meant that Woolf, as his wife, experienced the anti-Semitism with which Leonard was already familiar. See Rosenfeld (200).

Different historical and cultural circumstances notwithstanding, Lorde's insight helps us more responsibly perceive the vectors of power distinguishing her second wave, American feminism from Woolf's British, interwar gender politics while simultaneously revealing the ways in which the two are in constellation together. Although Woolf provocatively claims the label of outsider in *Three Guineas*, she is an outsider in gender alone, thanks to her race, class, and national identity. Consequently, what Woolf feared most upon the publication of *Three Guineas* were unfavorable reviews and falling out of favor with friends. Lorde's fears differ greatly. "Some problems we share as women," she admits, but "some we do not. You fear your children will grow up to join the patriarchy and testify against you, we fear our children will be dragged from a car and shot down in the street, and you will turn your backs upon the reasons they are dying" (119). Just as Woolf's interwar writings still resonate with our twenty-first-century culture, so, too, do Lorde's words find chilling corollaries in politics today.

Ultimately, to read Lorde and Woolf in tandem, I am confronted with the challenge of "define and empower" when I inherited "divide and conquer" ("Master's Tools" 112). In her interview with Adrienne Rich, Lorde provides examples of the kinds of missed connections she experienced throughout her life, like those in *The Years* that obstruct potentially productive affiliations among women. She explains to Rich how she spent her coming of age trying out "other ways of getting and giving information"—patriarchal ways, masculinist ways, heteronormative ways ("An Interview" 81). "People were talking all around me all the time—and not either getting or giving much that was useful to them or to me," Lorde explains, marking this recognition—of difference, of not listening, of not knowing—as integral in her turn toward poetry and its relationship to her evolving her feminist politics (81-82). Interestingly, Lorde's characterization could easily be employed to describe the frustration of various women in *The Years*, such as Rose or Peggy, as they seek to cultivate relationships with other women. Woolf's women in *The Years*, as far as readers know, never achieve the recognition of difference and its revelations that are so vital to Lorde's poetry and politics.

However, perhaps this is how Woolf and Lorde speak across time and through texts, through *our ability to connect the two*, recognizing their differences as strength for our feminist work. *The Years* ends in the "Present Day": for modernist scholars, Woolf's final chapter indicates the 1937 of the novel's publication, but for feminist readers interested in exploring what Davis identifies as Woolf's aprogressive philosophy of history, the final chapter's "Present Day" can be a temporal tesseract into the moment of reading, Lorde's late twentieth century or our early twenty-first century. Reading Woolf through the lens of Lorde offers a political richness and feminist dimensionality missing from readings of Woolf through a strictly modernist framework. Reading both forward and backward through feminist history and women's texts opens up the space while simultaneously cultivating feminist imagination.

A Feminist Modernist Peroration

"As women, we have been taught either to ignore our differences, or to view them as causes for separation and suspicion rather than forces for change" ("The Master's Tools" 112). I would like to conclude by encouraging feminist modernist scholars to take Lorde's words from "The Master's Tools" to heart—empathetically and politically, but also academically and intellectually. In our research, our teaching, and our interactions with each other, feminist modernist scholars should move beyond the missed connections that emerge from the ignorance and suspicion of difference (as well as the equally problematic loving, knowing ignorance). In our scholarship, this means looking for possibilities as well as critiques, seeking out what might have been as much as what was. In our reading, it means, as Mills explains of Woolf's reading of Harrison, "discern[ing] new plots, new models, which [we] then [can] translate, revise, or recreate" for our twenty-first-century purposes and passions (Mills 6). As Rich reminds us, "One of the dangers of a privileged education for women is that we may lose the eye of the outsider" ("What Does a Woman Need to Know?" 3).[21]

Taking the missed connections of *The Years* as our cue, Woolf's novel offers us a lesson to learn as much as a text to analyze and interpret. And in taking ourselves seriously as students of Woolf's gender politics, we will see the ways in which Woolf's writing responds to and reverberates in other feminist texts, both from Woolf's past and her future. To do so would be to read Woolf's fiction not only as literary scholars read novels but also as makers read models: if, as Davis argues, Woolf provides us with an aprogressive philosophy of history, let us not be hindered by the confines of the teleological narratives so treasured by male modernists and their subsequent scholars. Instead of employing inherited patriarchal models of tradition, individual talent, and anxiety of influence, let us lean into a feminist historicity in which networks trump icons, in which history flows backward

---

[21] The concept of the outsider was resonant for Woolf, Lorde, and Rich, each theorizing their outsider status differently and yet each attentive to the political importance of the epistemological vantage point provided when viewing the establishment from the margins. A passage from Rich's "What Does a Woman Need to Know?" is particularly illustrative here: "Gradually, those flashes of insight, which at times could seem like brushes with madness, began to demand that I struggle to connect them to each other, to insist that I take them seriously. It was only when I could finally affirm the outsider's eye as the source of legitimate and coherent vision, that I began to be able to do the work I truly wanted to do, live the kind of life I truly wanted to live, instead of carry out the assignments I had been given as a privileged woman and a token" (3-4).

as well as forward, and in which we think through our daughters as much as we do our mothers. Let us, in the words of Carolyn Heilbrun, "transform that literary exercise [reading] into friendship" (138).[22] Let us create, enact, and prioritize a transpersonal feminist reading practice.

What kinds of stories would emerge, to paraphrase Miller, if we enacted a transpersonal feminist reading practice? I had an opportunity to find out in my Feminist Literary Theory course, mentioned earlier, in which I eschewed the vertical axis of historicity for a more aprogressive orientation that privileged affiliations and thematic reverberations. The telephone lines through time cut forward and backward, across and through. My students, accustomed to progressing linearly and teleologically, were at first disoriented by a more associative organizational structure. Before too long, though, I found them intellectually liberated, making connections among authors and texts usually kept separate by period, generic, or identity categories. Consequently, all the authors we studied and the texts that we read came to life in new ways through these transpersonal associations. Moreover, the students were encouraged to foster relationships with authors and texts they might otherwise have dismissed because of their seemingly assailable position in a particular period, as a certain genre, or within a specific identity category. The work of feminist theorizing came to life in the space and time of the classroom, as typical academic boundaries were trespassed and common intellectual conventions disregarded. Literary theory was the ostensible subject of the course, but transpersonal feminist reading was the practice, and, as a result, together my students and I cultivated a revisionary ethos that motivated us to reimagine our relationships with feminist writers and their relationships with each other.

Here, I turn to one of Lorde's contemporaries, Adrienne Rich. Rich fostered and maintained a robust relationship with Lorde, seeming to respond to Lorde's challenge that as feminists we must recognize, empower, and build upon difference. Similar to Lorde, Rich is committed to "the challenge flung by feminists at the accepted literary canon, at the methods of teaching it, and the 'astigmatic' view of male literary scholarship" ("When We Dead Awaken" 189). For Rich, a white woman, to continue this feminist work requires the recognition and integration of black as well as lesbian feminism, political movements raising their voices in the 1970s both in the academy and on the street. The optimal strategy for such integration, according to Rich, is revision. Not just textual revision. For Rich, revision is a political rallying cry and a feminist modality. Literary revision. Scholarly revision. Feminist revision. In "When We Dead Awaken," written for the Modern Language Association Conference in 1971, Rich urgently reminds us that "[r]e-vision—the

---

[22] Heilbrun's elaboration on the concept of "unmet friends" is worth quoting here: "Women catch courage from the women whose lives and writing they read, and women call the bearer of that courage friend" (138).

act of looking back, of seeing with fresh eyes, of entering an old text from a new critical direction—is for women more than a chapter in cultural history: it is an act of survival" (190). To imagine the potentiality in Rich's statement is to circle back to Woolf. Revision, the act of rewriting, was a practical strategy for Woolf as evidenced by the numerous drafts of her speeches, essays, stories, and novels, many bleeding into each other.[23] As a metaphor for exploring her feminist position, revision acts as a political strategy, as illustrated in *Three Guineas* in which Woolf "turn[s] and turn[s] about," to use Melba Cuddy-Keane's phrase, in her replies to the three anonymous letter writers seeking her opinion.[24]

And revision is what I attempted in my Feminist Literary Theory course, and what I hope to offer in this essay: to revise Davis's reading of Woolf's *The Years* and to reimagine Woolf's work as a literary conduit, connecting the literary past she both inherited and was disenfranchised from with feminist literary future, hers and ours. As Rich explains in her essay "Toward a More Feminist Criticism," "[t]he survival of the women's movement, as of any revolutionary movement, depends directly on that of our communication networks" (85). Thus, Woolf's own missed connections, as illustrated in her life as well as in *The Years*, can become our feminist lesson, highlighting the importance—and the urgency—of affiliating across and through difference, be it race, sexual orientation, class, age, or ability. Moreover, taking a cue from Davis's reading of *The Years* as offering an aprogressive philosophy of history, Woolf's novel provides a model of thinking not only back through our mothers but also forward through our daughters—not only revising the past but also simultaneously reimagining the future, all in the space of ours, and Woolf's, "Present Day," to return to the last chapter of *The Years*. And perhaps it is in the imperative of the present that the peroration of *The Years* resides: "Then she turned round into the room. 'And now?' [Eleanor] said, looking at Morris ... 'And now?' she asked, holding out her hands to him" (434-35). The penultimate paragraph of the novel compels us to remain anchored in our present moment, imagining a new feminist day in which our literary mothers and daughters *speak to each other through us*.

And thus I arrive at our peroration: listen and write across time and texts. Revise and reimagine.

---

[23] In fact, *The Years* and *Three Guineas* are, in Woolf's mind, one book, as many scholars have noted. On Friday, June 3, Woolf writes in her diary: "Anyhow, that's the end of six years of floundering, striving, much agony, some ecstasy: lumping the Years & 3 Gs together as one book—as indeed they are" (*D5* 148).

[24] Although Cuddy-Keane does not directly address *Three Guineas* in her discussion of the "turn and turn about" method, her analysis of Woolf's strategy has greatly influenced my reading of Woolf's epistolary polemic.

Works Cited

Andrews, Charles. *Writing Against War: Literature, Activism, and the British Peace Movement*. Northwestern UP, 2017.

Cole, Sarah. *At the Violet Hour: Modernism and Violence in England and Ireland*. Oxford UP, 2012.

Collis, Louise. *Impetuous Heart: The Story of Ethel Smyth*. William Kimber, 1984.

Cuddy-Keane, Melba. *Virginia Woolf, the Intellectual, and the Public Sphere*. Cambridge UP, 2003.

Davis, Thomas. *The Extinct Scene*. Columbia UP, 2015.

———. "The Historical Novel and History's End: Virginia Woolf's *The Years*." *Twentieth-Century Literature*, vol. 60, no.1, Spring 2014, pp. 1-26.

Esty, Jed. *A Shrinking Island: Modernism and National Culture in England*. Princeton UP, 2004.

Heilbrun, Carolyn. *The Last Gift of Time: Life Beyond Sixty*. Dial Press, 1997.

Hepburn, Allan. Review of *The Extinct Scene: Modernism and Everyday Life*, by Thomas Davis. *Modernism/Modernity*, vol. 23, no. 2, April 2016, pp. 469-471.

Hussey, Mark. *Virginia Woolf A-Z: The Essential Reference to Her Life and Writings*. Oxford UP, 1995.

Jones, Clara. *Virginia Woolf: Ambivalent Activist*. Edinburgh UP, 2017.

Leaska, Mitchell A., editor, *The Pargiters by Virginia Woolf. The Novel-Essay Portion of* The Years. Harcourt Brace Jovanovich, 1978.

Lee, Hermione. *Virginia Woolf*. Vintage, 1999.

Light, Alison. *Mrs. Woolf and the Servants*. Penguin, 2007.

Linett, Maren. "The Jew in the Bath: Imperiled Imagination in Woolf's *The Years*." *Modern Fiction Studies*, vol. 48, no. 2, Summer 2002, pp. 341-361.

Lorde, Audre. "Age, Race, Class, and Sex: Women Redefining Difference." *Sister Outsider*. Crossing Press, 2007.

———. "An Interview: Audre Lorde and Adrienne Rich." *Sister Outsider*. Crossing Press, 2007.

———. "The Master's Tools Will Never Dismantle the Master's House." *Sister Outsider*. Crossing Press, 2007.

———. "An Open Letter to Mary Daly." *Sister Outsider*. Crossing Press, 2007.

MacKay, Marina. *Modernism and World War II*. Cambridge UP, 2007.

Marcus, Jane. "Thinking Back Through Our Mothers." *New Feminist Essays on Virginia Woolf*, edited by Jane Marcus. U of Nebraska P, 1981.

Marder, Herbert. *The Measure of Life: Virginia Woolf's Last Years*. Cornell UP, 2000.

Miller, Nancy K. "A Feminist Friendship Archive." *Professions 2011*. Modern Language Association of America, 2011, pp. 68-76.

Mills, Jean. *Virginia Woolf, Jane Ellen Harrison, and the Spirit of Classicism*. The Ohio State UP, 2014.

———. "Getting Transpersonal: The Cost of an Academic Life." *Prose Studies*, vol. 31, no. 3, December 2009, pp.166-80.

Ortega, Mariana. "Being Lovingly, Knowingly Ignorant: White Feminism and Women of Color." *Hypatia*, vol. 21, no. 3, 2006, pp. 56-74.

Radin, Grace. *Virginia Woolf's* The Years*: the Evolution of a Novel*. U of Tennessee P, 1981.

Rich, Adrienne. "What Does A Woman Need To Know?" *Blood, Bread, and Poetry*. W. W. Norton & Company, 1986.

———. "Towards a More Feminist Criticism." *Blood, Bread, and Poetry*. W. W. Norton, 1986.

Rosenfeld, Natania. *Outsiders Together: Virginia and Leonard Woolf*. Princeton UP, 2000.

Saint-Amour, Paul K. *Tense Future: Modernism, Total War, Encyclopedic Form*. Oxford UP, 2015.

Sherry, Vincent. *The Great War and the Language of Modernism*. Oxford UP, 2004.

Snaith, Anna. *Virginia Woolf: Public and Private Negotiations*. Palgrave, 2000.

Snyder, R. Claire. "What is Third Wave Feminism?: A New Directions Essay." *Signs: Journal of Women in Culture and Society,* vol. 34, no. 1, 2008, pp. 175-96.

St. John, Christopher. *Ethel Smyth: A Biography*. Longman, 1959.

Whittier-Ferguson, John. "Repetition, Remembering, Repetition: Virginia Woolf's Late Fiction and the Return of War." *Modern Fiction Studies* vol. 57, no. 2, Summer 2011, pp 230-253.

Wilson, Mary. *The Labors of Modernism: Domesticity, Servants, and Authorship in Modern Fiction*. Routledge, 2016.

Wood, Alice. *Virginia Woolf's Late Cultural Criticism*. Bloomsbury, 2015.

Woolf, Virginia. *The Diary of Virginia Woolf, Volume IV, 1931-1935*. Edited by Anne Olivier Bell and Andrew McNeillie. Harcourt Brace, 1982.

———. *The Diary of Virginia Woolf, Volume V, 1936-1941*. Edited by Anne Olivier Bell and Andrew McNeillie. Harcourt Brace, 1984.

———. *The Letters of Virginia Woolf, Volume IV, 1929-1931*. Edited by Nigel Nicolson and Joanne Trautmann. Harcourt Brace Jovanovich, 1978.

———. *The Letters of Virginia Woolf, Volume V, 1932-1935*. Edited by Nigel Nicolson and Joanne Trautmann. Harcourt Brace Jovanovich, 1979.

———. *The Letters of Virginia Woolf, Volume VI, 1936-1941*. Edited by Nigel Nicolson and Joanne Trautmann. Harcourt Brace Jovanovich, 1980.
———. *A Room of One's Own*. Harcourt, 2005.
———. *Three Guineas*. 1938. Harcourt, 2006.
———. *The Years*. 1937. Harcourt, 1965.
Zwerdling, Alex. *Virginia Woolf and the Real World*. U of California P, 1986.

Maps of Her Own: Virginia Woolf In and Beyond the Archives

Diane F. Gillespie

In 1971, boxes of Leonard and Virginia Woolf's personal books began to arrive at Washington State University (WSU) Libraries in Pullman, Washington. Some of the books contained maps, once important to the Woolfs as students, travelers, and observers of a changing world. A flat cardboard box filled with forty-nine individual maps came with them. What might we learn from cartographical materials that survived decades of traveling, house moving, and even two world wars? We can think about these reminders of Virginia Woolf's life and writing in several interrelated contexts:

1. Archival studies. Librarians, cultural historians, theorists, and researchers are interested in the functions and value of archival collections, how they are housed and preserved, and what users' experiences are like. Looking at the Woolfs' books and maps is different from examining unpublished letters or diaries, manuscripts, typescripts, or proof copies in other kinds of literary collections. In Manuscripts, Archives and Special Collections (MASC) at WSU, the individual maps are now in separate files.[1] Julia King and Laila Miletic-Vejzovic's *Short-title Catalogue* includes an "Introduction" to the Woolfs' books (Gillespie vii-xx) plus details of publication and information about the existence of book plates, inscriptions, and annotations. Even so, whether the Woolfs inherited, purchased, or received individual items as gifts or for review is not always clear. Neither is it clear, unless titles contain a word like "atlas," which books contain maps.[2] Nor can we be sure who used an item and when. References in outside sources—biographies, chronologies, letters, and diaries—sometimes help. Still, although archived materials provide a valuable beginning, it helps to think beyond the books and outside the box.

2. The surviving maps, and others Virginia Woolf mentions, have auto/biographical contexts. As her diaries make clear, maps were important in Virginia Stephen's family background and self-education. In a lifetime of urban and rural walking, she knew and used ordnance and topographical maps as practical aids to exploration, discovery, and protection against getting lost. Guide books richly illustrated with maps accompanied her on foreign travels. Atlases provided two-dimensional overviews of continents and the world. Throughout Virginia Woolf's life, maps offered ways to visualize not only her own country's history and culture but also those of other places impacted by internal and external changes.

---

[1] Cage 665 is designated as "Maps from the Library of Leonard and Virginia Woolf." Manuscripts, Archives and Special Collections, Washington State University Libraries, Pullman, WA. The list of maps is available online.
[2] The *Short-title Catalogue* is available online. Searches for individual items in the Washington State University Libraries' online catalogue include "maps" among descriptive details.

3. In historical and theoretical contexts, the Woolfs' cartographical materials fit an increasing emphasis on geography and spatial theory in literary and cultural studies, including feminist and related post-colonial responses. Accordingly, maps are not just nouns but verbs, not just artifacts but actions taken by geographers and mathematicians who map local and global territories and thus reify the values and power structures of specific time periods. Prior to, and even during Woolf's lifetime, hierarchical values affected cartography as well as verbal record-keeping done by those with appropriate education and power. As Virginia Woolf realized, the results reflected a nation not only with mapped geographical boundaries but also with social and cultural spheres that limited the education, economic power, and autonomy of women. On a larger scale, cartographers mapped boundaries around international territories within which hierarchies similar to those at home metaphorically mapped and limited the autonomy of subject peoples.

4. Reflecting these boundaries and/or reacting against them, writers of fiction mapped metaphorically the physical and psychological itineraries of their characters. Virginia Woolf's fiction is thus the fourth context where map as well as globe metaphors serve purposes of thematic and character development. In the biographical section of this essay, I will mention a few instances in which Woolf's fiction reflects her own experiences with maps. In the theoretical section, *A Room of One's Own* and *Three Guineas* are especially relevant to a discussion of Woolf and maps. The final section, however, emphasizes the cartographical trope. It includes not only additional references to maps, books, and globes but especially Woolf's use of map imagery in characterization and social criticism. Instead of a study of one or two novels, this section supports and augments ongoing scholarly discussion with a cartographical medley of Woolf's fiction.

When we discover maps to which Virginia Woolf had access, maps that accompanied her life of walking and traveling, and maps mentioned or used metaphorically in a number of her writings, we see that cartography helped her to contemplate relationships among places and between present and past as people traversed and marked the natural world. Maps provided orientations to cities, countries, or continents, and revealed what places and names cultures prioritized. With measured boundaries, lines, names, and symbols, maps both defined and confined human experience. Their abstract, austere impersonality could never provide what Virginia Woolf considered most important. Metaphorically, she tried to map how it felt to be alive and to move about in these charted spaces. She challenged the apparent "granite-like solidity" of geographical measuring and naming with the "rainbow-like intangibility" of actual, biographical, and fictional lives (*E4* 473).

I

What was in the Woolfs' box of maps and what books added to their cartographical milieu? Leonard Woolf's 1815 map of Kandy Town in Ceylon (Sri Lanka) is the earliest of the individual maps.[3] London is well represented with maps and pamphlets, more up-to-date ones no doubt having replaced earlier ones.

---

[3] Two later maps of Ceylon are dated 1953 and 1956.

Dates range from a "List of Principal Streets in London" (1917) to bus and underground railway maps (1937). Still surviving are London Transport's bus schedules backing a large, colored map of routes for London's "Central Areas" (1937). The "Underground Railway Map" (1937) includes three brightly-colored maps: a large one of city underground lines, a mid-sized one of lines that access art galleries, museums, public buildings, and churches, and a small one of lines in theatre and cinema locations. Also notable is Bartholomew's large, fold-out, colored "Town Plan of London Central Area" (undated) indexing principal streets. Two of three black-and-white maps in an undated "London Street Guide" ("The City" and "Underground Railways") are badly faded, but "Theatreland" is readable.

Following the purchase of their first automobile in 1927, the Woolfs needed road maps.[4] Most of the surviving European ones, including twenty Michelin Guides, however, date from the 1940s and 1950s, after Virginia Woolf's death. Only the "Bretagne Carte Regionale" Shell map (1936) survives from before 1941. In England, however, the Woolfs may have used the "principal motoring routes" marked on a colorful map of "London's Countryside: A Map-Guide for the Antiquarian Tourist and Sportsman" (c. 1924). Oversized and torn in the middle, it includes Guildford, Sevenoaks, Maidenhead, and St. Albans along with golf courses, woods, and viewpoints [Figure 1]. Several Ordnance Survey maps are dated in the mid-1930s, during Virginia Woolf's last decade. They include a large "Layered Map of England and Wales" (1935), plus ones of "The Forth, Clyde and Tay" (1934), "Glasgow and the Middle West" (1934), "Eastern Highlands" (1934), and "Skye and the Outer Hebrides" (1934). These maps may be results of Woolf's remark to Ethel Smyth in 1933 that she does not

Figure 1. Cover, "London's Countryside: A Map-Guide for the Antiquarian Tourist and Sportsman." Philips' Series of Map Guides No. 2. George Philip & Son (c. 1924). MASC.

---

[4] Robin Adair and Ann Martin detail the roles of motor cars in modern consumerism and in the lives and relationships of Virginia Woolf, family, and friends.

"at once visualize Hebrides, Skye, and the rest" of the British Isles (*L5* 218). Finally, the Woolfs' box contained two much used topographical maps (1931) of Rodmell and environs covered by Virginia and annotated by Leonard.

Although I could not search for maps in every volume the Woolfs owned,[5] I found (and keep finding) more than enough to indicate their importance. It is clear, for example, that both Stephens and Woolfs often relied on texts and maps in travel guidebooks to orient themselves to unfamiliar places. Fifteen volumes of *Handbooks for Travelers* remain and range from 1899 to 1930 (King 11-12). They are by Karl Baedeker (1801-1859), prolific developer of well-known guides for the growing nineteenth-century tourist market.[6] Obviously used, probably by more than one traveler at different times, one or two of the books in MASC include pressed leaves or, in the case of the Greek guidebook, museum ticket stubs.[7]

Although Virginia Stephen had neither a formal university education nor the opportunity to travel abroad confidently on her own, she had her own early travel experiences with family and friends. Her initials and dates remain in several travel-related books. Inside Baedeker's *Northern France* (1899), for example, she penciled "V S. 1905. April" on the title page. Another example is Edmund G. Gardner's *The Story of Florence* (1903) with its black-and-white, fold-out map of Florence and its clarifications of historical and political changes, foreign place names, and boundaries. Inked inside the front cover is "A.V.S. Venice. April. 1904"[8] [Figure 2]. The same inscription and date appear in another book useful for travel, Augustus J. C. Hare's *Venice* (1904).[9] A bookplate with "AVS 1908" is in Horatio Brown's *Venice: An Historical Sketch of the Republic* (1895).

Virginia Woolf packed, then referred to such map-filled guides and histories in diary accounts of early trips (e.g., *PA* 257, 315, 319, 331-332). Often she provided reactions the authors omitted. "Baedecker [*sic*] will count the statues; . . . but the final work must be done by each fresh mind that sees them," she writes in Greece in 1906 (*PA* 319). To her, the stadium at Olympia looks rather like "a very

---

[5] One reason is that, after Leonard Woolf's death, a number of the books, especially signed first editions, went to individual bidders or other libraries (Gillespie, "Introduction" xv).

[6] Karl Baedeker hired a cartography specialist to do folding maps for inside the front covers and city maps to inset in the texts. Baedeker also included "references…to appease the literary minded traveler" thus fostering a spate of literary guidebooks and maps (Bulson 3-10) as well as maps as frontis- and end-pieces in classic novels (Hegglund, "Introduction" 9).

[7] Amanda Golden (101) reproduces four tickets and a schedule from Greek sites found in Baedeker's *Greece* (1909) in MASC. She thinks this edition "could have provided a reference when Woolf was composing *Jacob's Room*" (100).

[8] This book is not listed in the *Short-title Catalogue*. MASC continues to purchase books known to have been owned by the Woolfs (Gillespie, "Introduction" xvi).

[9] Other identifications in travel books include "Sidney Woolf Middle Temple" in *Handbooks for Travellers in France*, Parts 1 & 2 (1882) (King 97) and "A. L. Stephen. Venice April 9th 1904" in Augustus Hare's *Florence* (1900) (King 98). Leonard Woolf signed Baedeker's *Norway, Sweden, and Denmark with Excursions to Iceland and Spitsbergen* (1909), and his drawings and annotations appear in *Southern France Including Corsica* (1907) (King 11-12). MASC.

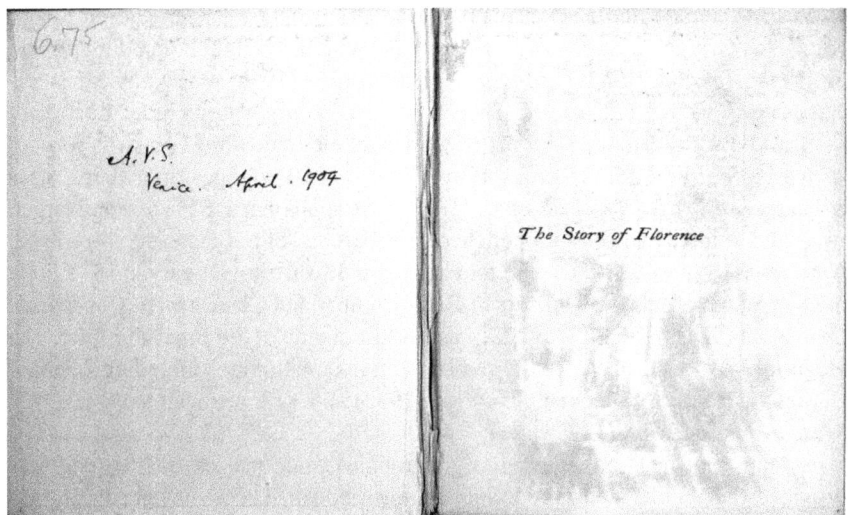

Figure 2. Inscription in ink by Virginia Stephen in Edmund G. Gardner's The Story of Florence *(1903). MASC.*

disorderly pagan graveyard," and her "vagrant mind dwells" instead on "thyme growing by the pillars, & fine grass" (*PA* 319). In a 1905 review called "Journeys in Spain," Virginia Stephen had already noted how a traveler relies on Baedeker for necessary and abundant information but not for reading "pleasure" (*E*1 44).[10] She prefers an account that is "as much a guide-book to the mind of the man that wrote it as it is to any definite region of the earth's surface" (*E*1 44). In later essays like "To Spain" (1923), Virginia Woolf advises a traveler on the "precipice" of "departure" not only to fix in her mind the "homely things" she is leaving behind, but also to welcome entry into a "new society" where people live, dress, and worship differently (*E*3 361). On a train through France, she wishes she could create, like painters, the "visual beauty" outside (*E*3 363). In Spain itself she finds the Sierra Nevada "indescribable, unthinkable. The mind's contents break into short sentences. It is hot: the old man; the frying pan; it is hot; the image of the Virgin; the bottle of wine; it is time for lunch;…it is hot" (*E*3 363). Guide books with their facts and maps cannot recreate the physical sensations of being alive in a foreign place.[11]

When they married in 1912, Leonard and Virginia Woolf contributed their Baedekers to their shared library, then added more along with L.V. Bertarelli's

---

[10] No handbook by Baedeker on Spain remains among the Woolfs' books in MASC.

[11] Virginia Stephen found E. M. Forster's *A Room with a View* (1908) "very amusing" (*L*1 372) and must have enjoyed his second chapter, "In Santa Croce with No Baedeker." Miss Lavish absconds with the guidebook she thinks will prevent Lucy Honeychurch from seeing and feeling the real Italy. Even without an initial source of information about the Basilica, Lucy begins to enjoy her experience there. *A Room with a View* is no longer among the eleven books by E. M. Forster in MASC (King 78).

Northern Italy and *Southern Italy* (1924 and 1925). The Woolfs acquired Arthur Kingsland Griggs' *Paris for Everyman* (1924) with forty-eight colored maps, and even *The Handbook of Palestine and Trans-Jordan* (1934), edited by Sir Harry Luke and Edward Keith-Roach. Their combined library also included historical/ political books illustrated with maps. One example is Edward Hertslet's *Map of Africa by Treaty: With Numerous Maps* (1894).[12] Two volumes of Wilbur Cortez Abbott's *The Expansion of Europe...*(1919) have small maps in the text and larger, two-page, colored maps of Europe. There is also a copy of E. Lipson's *Europe in the Nineteenth Century...* (1916) with fold-out maps of Austria-Hungary in 1878, Italy in 1815, and the Balkan Peninsula in 1912. Cumberland Clark's history of *Britain Overseas* (1924) from 1497 to 1921 has a fold-out map of the British Empire. The Hogarth Press itself occasionally published books with maps including Leonard Barnes's account of *The New Boer War* (1932) and Y. Z.'s travel account, *From Moscow to Samarkand* (1934).[13]

Maps and facts collected into geographical dictionaries and large atlases provided the Woolfs with important reference books. These oversized volumes document the cultural characteristics, imperial influences, and commercial connections of a vast and changing world. Titles alone indicate ambitious goals and coverage. The earliest, published in 1773, contains a two-page world map (two hemispheres and a circle above for high latitude countries and the north pole) and sixteen page-sized maps. By Frederic Watson, et al., this book is entitled *New and Complete Geographical Dictionary: Containing a Full and Accurate Description of the Several Parts of the Known World, as Divided into Continents, Islands, Oceans, Seas, Rivers, Lakes, Etc.*[14] Watson and his collaborators provide a dictionary of place names, visual renderings of inhabitants, and vistas of various places. Descriptions include information on climate, language, trade and manufacture, topography, important sites and curiosities, religion, customs, longevity, morals, rituals, political and church government.

More current for the Woolfs than Watson's geographical dictionary was J. G. Bartholomew's large *Citizen's Atlas of the World: Containing 156 Pages of Maps and Plans, with an Index, a Gazetteer, and Geographical Statistics* (1912) [Figure 3].[15] This once red-covered atlas (now recovered and rebound by MASC)

---

[12] These two volumes have the armorial bookplates of "John Dawson Mayne" (1828-1917) who was a prominent British lawyer, acting Advocate-General of the Madras Presidency, member of the UK privy Council, and author of the authoritative *Mayne's Hindu Law*. How these volumes came into the Woolfs' combined library is unknown.

[13] This book is listed in the *Short-title Catalogue* under its title (King 81).

[14] Watson's book is signed, not quite legibly, inside the front cover, "Charles Harrison or Jamison [?] Sutton Place" with an even more illegible signature on the next page: "M. Woolf [?]," possibly Marie de Jongh Woolf, Leonard Woolf's mother.

[15] Five generations of Bartholomews, including J. G. Bartholomew (1860-1920), produced maps and atlases until the company merged with Harper Collins in 1989. Its subsidiary, Collins Bartholomew, continues to publish maps.

has another two-page, world map with a circle for each hemisphere and four circles above representing water, land, northern, and southern hemispheres. In addition to maps covering each continent and country, the atlas contains both a black-and-white map showing the growth of the British Empire and a colored one showing the 1911 British Empire defined by the traditional red. Also included are maps that color-code German, French, Russian, and Dutch possessions and even a map showing degrees of successful mapping of territories throughout the world. Specialized maps chart world vegetation, climates, religions, races, commerce, and population densities.

Sandor Radó's *Atlas of To-day and To-morrow* (1938) is the most recent book of maps in the Woolfs' collection. Reflecting a

Figure 3. Title Page, J. G. Bartholomew's The Citizen's Atlas of the World: Containing 156 Pages of Maps and Plans, with an Index, a Gazetteer, and Geographical Statistics *(1912). J. Bartholomew, 1912. MASC.*

period torn by world conflicts, his title is less confident as is his intent "to provide…a snapshot photograph of our rapidly changing world" through "a cartographic record of all that bewildering mass of contemporary political and economic problems" (ix). Radó's emphasis is on continual changes that do not come easily. The defining word is "struggle." One section, "The Struggle for the Division of the World," maps who has colonized what territories as well movements of capital, resources, armaments, and manpower from 1876 to 1913, 1914 to 1930, and since 1931. Included is a map of League of Nations membership. Subsequent parts of the atlas provide well over two hundred small maps documenting "Great Powers and Colonial Empires," "The Struggle for World Markets," "The Struggle for Control of Communications," "State, Nationality, Religion, and Race," and finally "State and Society." The latter charts industrialization, national income, political freedom, forms of government, the "struggle" of ideologies, and for suffrage. Change also is reflected in a small pamphlet the Woolfs owned called *The Atlas of the War: 15 Maps* [Great Britain is number 14] *with Explanatory Text* (1939) including a note by J. N. L. Baker. This atlas charts resources, imports and exports, manufacturing, and, where appropriate, changing boundaries.

Because her participation in Leonard Woolf's writings on international government and imperialism and their professional collaboration have been established,[16] we can conclude that the Woolfs' interest in world affairs and the maps documenting them was mutual if not similarly pursued and expressed.[17] Although we cannot always be certain Virginia Woolf studied all the cartographical materials she and Leonard Woolf owned or that she herself never mixed up Armenians and Albanians (*MD* 182), it is clear that her growing geographical knowledge was wide-ranging. One attempt to survey the central and "mentioned or visited" locations in her novels finds not just sites in London (mostly west end), but also references to Oxford and Cambridge, the Isle of Skye or Hebrides, Manchester, Scarborough, and Windsor/Eton, as well as Paris, Rome, Venice, Constantinople (Istanbul), Athens, Berlin, Madrid, and New York ("Londonist" 2). Included too is every continent except Antarctica and "even the North Pole gets two mentions" ("Londonist" 3).

II

Maps were practical givens in Virginia Woolf's everyday life. Although the earliest ones have not survived, young Virginia Stephen's accounts make clear that she often walked or bicycled with maps at hand. At Netherhampton House in 1903 explorations with her siblings enabled all of them "to find out our position in the world" (*PA* 188). She also loved "solitary walks" (*PA* 197, 285). At Blo' Norton in 1906 her "usual walk" had "the interest of a *discovery*, because," she wrote, "I go, *armed with maps* into a strange land" (*PA* 312; my emphases). Virginia Stephen thus alludes to the origins of maps in exploration and military campaigns. "I tramp the country with a map, leap ditches, scale walls and desecrate churches," she wrote to Violet Dickinson, "making out beautiful stories every step of the way" (*L1* 234).[18] Initially she takes their accuracy for granted. As historians of cartography observe,

---

[16] See, for example, Michèle Barrett, Wayne K. Chapman, Wayne K. Chapman and Janet M. Manson, and, on the Woolfs' "shared ideology" (125), Patricia Laurence.

[17] Leonard Woolf's use of maps and occasional reviews of books with maps would be a separate essay.

[18] Among these early writings done at Blo' Norton Hall was "The Journal of Mistress Joan Martyn" (*CSF* 33-62, 295).

however, map makers are selective, even biased or inaccurate, about what they include and exclude (Monmonier 121-2). Bicycling to Kenninghall, Virginia and her siblings, for instance, could not find a famous Saxon burial ground placed there by their Ordnance map.[19] They searched the graveyard thoroughly. No one they asked could help. So much for "the authority of the map," Virginia Stephen declared but, because it was so hard not to take "the map's word for it," they "consecrate[d] a mound in some gentleman's Park" (*PA* 313-14). Relating what is on the map to what one sees sometimes involved doing the opposite, "steering by windmills & towers" to find one's position on the map (*PA* 311), an ongoing conversation between visual experience and cartographical abstraction.

Although, as Holly Henry argues, the narrative "scoping strategies" Virginia Woolf learned from telescopes are at the center of a late story, "The Searchlight" (137), Mrs. Ivimey's ancestor "taught himself all he knew" by reading "old books ...with maps hanging out from the pages" (*CSF* 270). So Virginia Stephen's early self-education came in part from reading "the literature of...exploration and conquest" (Marcus, "Registering" 183). Among such books were editions of Richard Hakluyt's voyages which made her "dream of...obscure adventurers" (*D3* 271).[20] Virginia Stephen also owned twelve volumes of a new edition of Edward Gibbon's *Decline and Fall of the Roman Empire* (1820) containing maps and her bookplate. Gibbon's history, with its now-loose covers, was inscribed to her by her brother Adrian Stephen [Figure 4].[21] These accounts established a foundation for reading, alluding to, and writing essays about other accounts of empire, exploration, and adventure in distant places. The Woolfs' books by Joseph Conrad, for example, include *Heart of Darkness* where Charles Marlow refers to maps showing the "'many blank spaces on the earth'" as his introduction to the "'glories of

---

[19] The Ordnance Survey of Great Britain (OSGB) goes back to the late eighteenth century. Different projections and scales were used until after World War II when one "unified National Grid referencing system" and "a single Transverse Mercator projection" were introduced for all maps (Perry 134-5).

[20] MASC has one five-volume edition of *Hakluyt's Collection of Early Voyages, Travels, and Discoveries of the English Nation* (1809-12). Since it has Virginia Woolf's bookplate, however, it probably was purchased after her marriage. *The Principal Navigations, Voyages, Traffiques and Discoveries* . . . is in eight volumes, but the Woolfs' library contains only volumes two and three. Probably the edition Virginia Stephen knew in her early years was *Voyages of Hawkins, Frobisher, and Drake: Select Narratives from the Principal Navigations of Hakluyt* (1907) which contains notes and maps (King 95). MASC. Andrew Thacker notes geographical links in Woolf's thinking between Hakluyt, Sir Walter Raleigh, and Shakespeare (417, cf. *E2* 91). The three books by Raleigh remaining among the Woolfs' books include *Shakespeare* (1907) but not any of his travel writings (King 183).

[21] By the time Woolf wrote "The Historian and 'The Gibbon'" in 1937 (*E6* 81-91), she had the twelve volumes at hand plus other autobiographical and biographical resources (King 85-86). MASC.

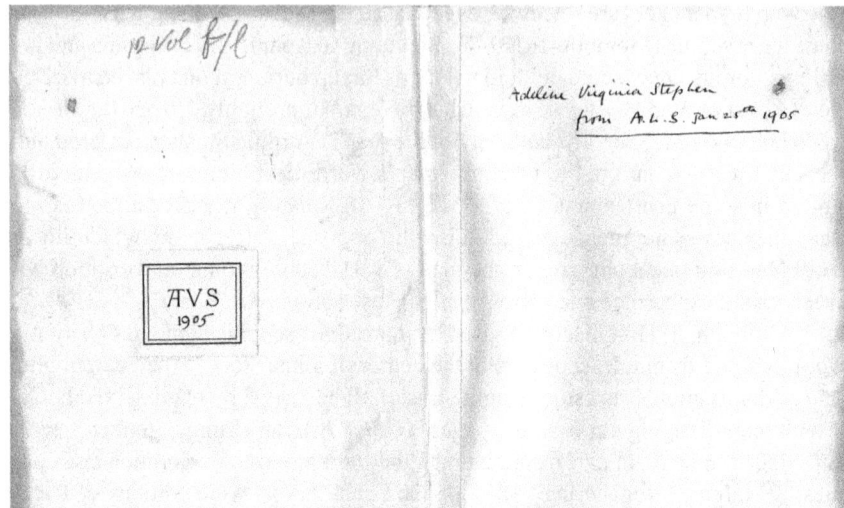

Figure 4. Inscription by Adrian Stephen to Adeline Virginia Stephen by Adrian Stephen, Jan. 25th 1905 in vol. 1 of Edward Gibbon. *The History of the Decline and Fall of the Roman Empire. New ed. 12 vols. T. Cadell and W. Davies, 1820.* MASC.

exploration'" (52).[22] *The Travels of Marco Polo The Venetian* with a map inside the front cover and facing page joined the Woolfs' books in 1926.

Virginia Stephen grew up in a society in which men traditionally went, maps in hand, for long hikes, walking tours, or climbs. In the countryside, she continued an activity, although arguably not always an attitude, important to men in her own family. To generations of Stephens, outdoor exercise connoted masculinity, moral self-discipline, therapy,[23] and even compensation or penance for self-indulgence (Annan 97 n3, 33). Maps were important. Leslie Stephen traced some of his ascents in the Swiss Alps on existing maps, participated in the Alpine Club's desire to improve their accuracy with revisions and annotations, and pondered philosophically

---

[22] Among the Woolfs' books are six volumes of Joseph Conrad that predate *The Voyage Out* (three of them signed by Leonard). The ten entries remaining include the first Uniform Edition of *The Works of Joseph Conrad*. Eight of the twenty-two volumes have Woolf's small bookplates in them, with the handwritten date "1923" (King 50-51). In addition to allusions to Conrad in her fiction and references in her essays, Woolf wrote a number of essays on him (e.g. *E*2 140-143, 158-60, 226-228), as well as "Joseph Conrad," a longer tribute when he died in 1925 (*E*4 227-233).

[23] Virginia Stephen's early journals, begun in 1897 while she gradually recovered from the breakdown following her mother's death, indicate that the Stephens' family doctor, David Elphinstone Seton, prescribed four hours out of doors every day (*PA* xvi).

"questions of perspective" (Hollis 30, 36). Not surprisingly, Virginia Woolf, women, walking, and writing, in various combinations, have been topics of considerable scholarly interest and some disagreement, mostly in the context, not of maps, but of modernism defined as urban.[24] In rural settings, women's ability to find their way about and observe freely is also controversial.

"While one certainly finds...equations of topographic overview and masculine power," David Matless nevertheless thinks that "the open air is also...a space of equal access for women and men where restrictive definitions of feminine conduct could be overcome" (200). Prior to and during the interwar period in England, books advocating exercise in the open air included "pictures of girls with maps" (Matless 205-06). Although primarily the production of educated men and their priorities, a map was still in some ways a "travel text available to women" since "unlike fictional or historical discourse, the words on maps are subjectless, verbless suggestions" of sentences women potentially could complete and spaces they might actually occupy (Frederick and Hyde xxvii-xxviii).

In actual rural landscapes, however, women as subjects of walking narratives could encounter problems maps were unlikely to anticipate. Without them, walkers could become lost and, even with them, potentially vulnerable. Virginia and Vanessa Stephen, for instance, staying at Bognor in 1897, took off on their bicycles with "no map, no watch, and no knowledge of the country." When mist increased and footpaths ran out, they "had to plough on as best we might in 6 inches of sticky clay" (*PA* 33). Mud-covered, they encountered nothing more threatening, however, than mocking schoolboys. In 1903 Virginia Stephen records in detail another such mapless experience, again treating discomfort and disorientation with mock-heroic humor. Pursuing a "tortuous & difficult path" and getting lost, she and Vanessa "were brought to a stop by hearing male rustic voices, alarming to pedestrians of the womanly sex" (*PA* 190-91). These men were hay makers who, instead of providing clear directions, teased the sisters about encountering dangerous cows.

Variations on bovine and masculine encounters emerge in Woolf's later fiction. In *Night and Day* (1919) baby Katharine Hilbery in her perambulator was threatened by a bull, possibly only a cow, in a field (154). Although in *To the Lighthouse* (1927), Mrs. Ramsay walks sedately accompanied by Charles Tansley and Lily Briscoe strolls with William Bankes, "rash and impulsive" Minta Doyle is the one likely to "flounder across" a stream if necessary and to fear "nothing—except bulls" (*TTL* 74). Woolf's self-mockery about alarming male voices and potential bovine dangers reappears in *Orlando* (1928). To the young male Orlando who climbs a hill and confidently observes "his own great house" as "a spot compact

---

[24] In Woolf's writing, Rachel Bowlby posits a transgressive *flâneuse*, a counterpart to the *flâneur*, the "man about town with ample leisure and money to roam the city and look about him" (194). Anna Snaith, however, detects more ambivalence about female urban freedom where the city offers women "a combination of danger and freedom, of conspicuousness and anonymity" (37).

and mapped out," solitary walking presents no threats (20). To the female Orlando, however, walking alone even on her own charted estate makes her wonder if she will meet "poachers or game keepers or…errand-boys" or some other "male form … hiding behind a furze bush" or even "some savage cow…lowering its horns to toss her" (*O* 247). By the 1930s, Virginia Woolf's use of the phrase, "'taking the bull by the udders'" was a mocking feminist riposte to Wyndham Lewis's taking "'the cow by the horns'" (Marcus, "Taking" 137-38). It was also a culmination of decades of threats, humorous at least in retrospect, that female walkers would not find on printed maps.

Limited or not, maps linger in people's memories. In *To the Lighthouse*, Mrs. Ramsay thinks how she, along with the "map of the Hebrides," would be "wound in…[the] hearts" and preserved in the memories of those like Paul Rayley and Minta Doyle who had visited there (170). In 1905, when Virginia Stephen took a commemorative trip to the real setting for *To the Lighthouse*, she noted that while the Cornish landscape had not "changed in eleven years, or in eleven hundred," her own "point of view" was altered (*PA* 283). When she walked by herself over "a great distance of the surrounding country," sometimes "in the teeth of heavy rain storms," she noted, "the map of the land … [had become] solid in my brain" (*PA* 283, 285). She was the one, however, who added to a mental map her emotional response to people's fond memories of Julia Stephen. She was the one who responded with exhilaration to what she calls "all moods of the air & the earth" (*PA* 285-86).

When Virginia and Leonard Woolf bought Monk's House, Rodmell, in 1919, Leonard recalls how Virginia spent "an hour, two hours, or even more" walking over the downs, through the water-meadows, or along the river bank (*Downhill* 149-50, 155; *Journey* 70-71). To any earlier maps of the area that have not survived and to maps they had begun to accumulate for enthusiastic motor trips, they added two topographical maps of the rural Rodmell countryside. These 1931 editions[25] now in MASC help us recreate the paths Virginia Woolf occasionally bicycled but mostly walked alone during the last decade of her life.[26] Diaries and letters provide a complementary calendar as well as her heightened sensory and emotional responses not only to the beauty of the downs but to changes, like the "irresponsible building" in the countryside around Rodmell (Jones 85).[27] The Woolfs' topographical maps do not include identifiable little squares for what Virginia Woolf considers tawdry "Villa Jones[es]" (Jones 75). If, as J. B. Harley notes, a map's visual narrative reflects values like "ethnicity, politics, religion, or social class" (5), then the Woolfs'

---

[25] The 1931 editions are based on Ordnance Surveys taken in 1872 and revised in 1929.
[26] Another early, small book of maps, volume one of the *British Road Book* (1897) published by the Cyclists' Touring Club and covering the Southern Counties (Kent to Cornwall), includes Lewes to Newhaven and Seaford.
[27] Speculators were spoiling nature with housing developments for people who had no thought of rural preservation or community. Having sought a rural refuge herself, Woolf was both complicit with, and angry about "a threateningly mobile middle class [increasingly] bent on invading the countryside" (Jones 76).

topographical maps indicate traditional priorities. Named not only are downs and hills, established farms and orchards, roads and railroad lines, reservoirs and mills, but also schools, village churches, vicarages, and rectories.

Leonard and Virginia Woolf did not accept the territory precisely as defined by these two maps. Most footpaths are marked with double dotted lines, but the couple exercised their own power and possession by covering and labeling each map as well as by marking and annotating routes that looped out from, and back to Rodmell, their geographical and psychological center. Clearly wanting to preserve them, Virginia Woolf covered one map with black paper and affixed a light-blue, hand-printed "Rodmell and Brooks" label. The other she covered in blue paper and added a terra cotta label, lettered "Rodmell & Telscomb" [Figures 5 and 6]. Precisely when after 1931 she did this is difficult to tell. The maps—each 26 x 20 inches with a scale of six inches to a mile—are contiguous. Together, they show the area from Lewes (upper left) to Piddinghoe (lower right). The writing, difficult to reproduce, is in Leonard's trembling hand. Sometimes now-blurred red ink augments smudged pencil marks to indicate distance or to add details helpful to the Woolfs, like "Faint Track," "Double Wire," "Gate," "Grass," or "Plough"—along

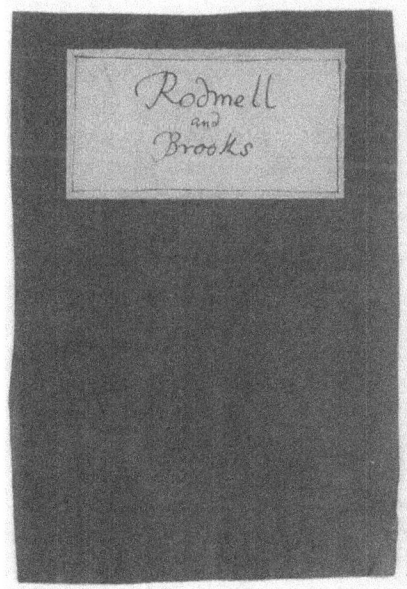

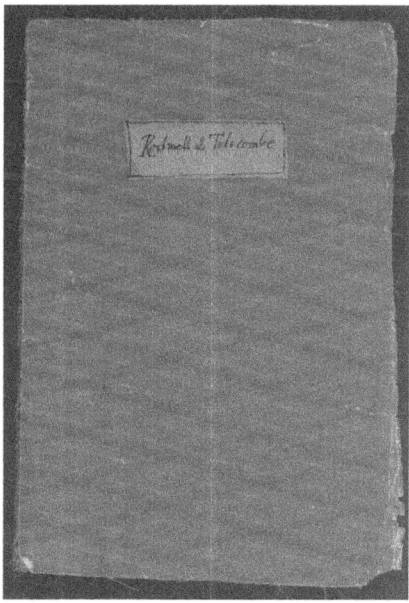

Figure 5. "Rodmell and Brooks." Cover by Virginia Woolf for topographical map (1931). MASC.

Figure 6. "Rodmell and Telscombe." Cover by Virginia Woolf for topographical map (1931). MASC.

with abbreviations for perhaps "Fence Gate," "High Gate," and "Foot Bridge."[28]

In letters and diaries, Virginia Woolf briefly notes walking in some of the directions marked and on her usual routes towards the river. Often she records only the direction and that she has been "making up" her writing while she walked. She records a Sunday "Walk to Southease" (*D5* 325), for example, as "walking this mildish day, up to Telscombe" while inventing what became "The Leaning Tower" (*D5* 266). Again, she is "making up" on another Telscomb walk that, on the return, looped by "Mount Misery" (*D5* 291). In 1938, she had recorded an account of an old woman who had lived on that site, who had "turned queer" and "drowned herself." Woolf notes that the body was found near Piddinghoe. The woman had chosen a time, Woolf speculates, "when the tide was high in the afternoon" (*D5* 161). Although Leonard knew of Virginia's preoccupation with the site and the story, he did not mark any rise or building "MM" on the map. The marked routes provided variety, but Virginia Woolf continued to include her "usual walk"—the one south along the river (*D5* 161). Not surprisingly, both Leonard and Vita Sackville-West linked the site with Virginia Woolf's own suicide. Vita quotes Leonard as having said, after Virginia's death: "'When we couldn't find her anywhere, I went up to a derelict house which she was fond of in the Downs, called Mad Misery [she called it "Mount Misery"], but she wasn't there'" (Stape 81).

Since the Woolfs, especially Virginia, had been walking the countryside around Rodmell for over a decade, it is possible that the marked maps had other uses. That all this work was done exclusively for other people and not themselves seems unlikely, but as artifacts the maps are silent. Did they help to anchor the Woolfs in the local and familiar when, during the London Blitz, Monk's House became their primary residence? Did these covered and personalized maps represent an assertion of Englishness in the face of Hitler's broadcasted rants, military planes growling overhead, and worries about imminent invasion? Although the Woolfs had many people, especially from London, visiting during the 1930s, did guests go walking with these maps? The diaries record conversing and playing bowls instead. When visitors finally left her in peace, Virginia reports that she "walked miles," rather than "talked miles" (*D5* 238). Might these annotated maps have been potentially useful instead to people unfamiliar with the area and temporarily housed near Rodmell? Among them were troops, English and foreign (L. Woolf, *Journey* 66-8, cf. *D5* 322), wounded soldiers on leave (*D5* 289, 318), refugees, land girls (*D5* 291), or relocated urban mothers and children. Always essential to military strategy, including both defensive and offensive movements of troops and supplies, maps like the Woolfs' that indicated land and water areas, transportation routes, potential obstacles, and other landmarks could be extremely valuable during an invasion (Monmonier 125; Hegglund, "*Ulysses*" 169). "'Hide your maps,'" warned the newspapers, or anything else that could help invaders (Snaith 131).

---

[28] The "Characteristic Sheet" that explains the visual symbols and abbreviations published on these maps has not survived.

III

As we continue to move from maps read literally to maps used metaphorically, historical and theoretical relationships between mapping and writing become other relevant contexts. Cartographers traditionally used "a mosaic of points, symbols, lines, shadings, and coloring" to transmit visually their knowledge of environmental spaces (Wilford x, 13). Writers used words to transform "personal ... to transmittable knowledge," often using "map" and "mapping" as metaphors for "clarification, coherence, [and] plotting of information" (Wilford 3). Virginia Woolf scholars have been metaphorically mapping her life and works for decades, organizing and clarifying information into coherent biographies or editions of letters, diaries, and essays. Scholars have delineated historical, cultural, or geographical contexts and interests by tracing themes, images, and allusions in her fiction. They have clarified the overall structures of her texts and charted her characters' actual and psychological itineraries. Ever since E. M. Forster in "The Novels of Virginia Woolf" (1926) called the London of Woolf's *Night and Day* a "'topographical metropolis'" that "reveals [her characters'] psychology" (qtd. Squier 78), Woolf's city novels especially have invited place-centered scrutiny.[29] Detailing the travels of her work through different countries and languages, as Susan Friedman writes in *Mappings*, reveals Woolf herself as a "geopolitical" and a "transnational phenomenon" (115).

Ongoing interest in metaphorical mapping in modernist literary and cultural theory augments this scholarly work and reflects an altered and expanded relationship between cartography and writing. Although it may be that "every culture has engaged in some sort of mapping" (Turchi 1), the invention of the printing press in the fifteenth century facilitated both map and book production. Wars and conquest as well as increasing education, wealth, travel, and migration created consumer demands for both methods of communication, sometimes in the same publications. As Denis Cosgrove notes, however, our increasingly "politically, economically, technically and culturally globalizing world" has caused "a startling explosion of academic, artistic and cultural interest in 'cartography'" (3-4). Thus, in studies of literature and culture, as Robert T. Tally Jr. puts it, "*spatiality*" has emerged as "a key concept" (*Spatiality* 33, 3), one that encompasses mapping metaphors. Although readers have been orienting themselves to "fictional spaces... [as] real ones" as long as they have been reading novels, Eric Bulson writes, the disorienting effects of the modern world, "empire, mass culture, technology, and urbanization" (1-2) have changed the reading experience and fostered a shift

---

[29] Most recently, Lisbeth Larsson has generated detailed readings of the role of London in individual novels. The small, black-and-white, difficult-to-read London maps she uses to mark and number the walking routes and sites visited by Woolf's characters are from the Internet or Google Maps (see Elisa Kay Sparks's review in this volume).

from time as the defining descriptor of modernist and post-modernist literature to space and place. The map metaphor has evolved into "literary cartography," the ways "writers function as mapmakers," maps tell stories, and writing and space interact "to generate new places and new narratives" (Tally, *Spatiality* 45-46). To a literary scholar, then, "a narrative is simultaneously something that maps and something to be mapped" (Tally, "Introduction" 3). This is not to say that Virginia Woolf abandoned temporality for spatiality in her fiction. Instead, with the sensations and memories of "an ordinary mind on an ordinary day" as a primary concern (*E4* 160), she blended time, space, and place and did so in part by using cartographical images and metaphors.

Challenges to spatiality and its geographical base came in the 1990s from both feminist geographers and feminist literary scholars who objected to male domination of their disciplines and discussions of spatiality within them.[30] Gillian Rose proposes in 1993, for example, that geography is not universal or exhaustive as masculinist geographers have assumed; studies of space are "destabilized" when "the geographical desire to know" meets "the resistance of the marginalized victims of that desire" (159-60). Another example is Doreen Massey whose focus in 1994 is the anti-essentialist and dynamic ways in which "geography . . . influences the cultural formation of particular genders and gender relations" (177). In turn, class and gender play important parts in "geographical constructions of space and place" (Massey 180, 182). So far as "identity-formation" goes, Massey suggests, "the need for the security of boundaries" that counterposes "one identity against another" and rejects more fluid, unbounded definitions "is culturally masculine" (7), as are dualities between "the local and the global," private and public, women and men (9).[31]

Literary discussions had shifted in the 1980s for writers like Alex Zwerdling from Virginia Woolf's experimental techniques to her "social vision," her treatment of "historical forces and societal institutions" (3). In the 1990s as well, literary and cultural studies reveal and interrogate ways in which literary texts reflect cultural hierarchies including the "symbolic gendering of certain types of physical and social space as masculine or feminine," the representation and treatment of women's bodies and their mobility outside of predetermined boundaries and definitions, and the parallels between women's economic displacement and that of "colonized or dependent economies" (Higonnet 5, 12). Scholars interested in feminist and post-colonial theory thus joined "social vision" with considerations of space and place. Jane Marcus, writing of "Spatial Modernism" ("Registering" 181), gener-

---

[30] Robert T. Tally does include a short section on "Engendering Spaces" (132-135) in *Spatiality*.
[31] Jane Marcus discusses the difficulties of "feminist mappings of women's culture" and the need for critics to read "women's maps" of outsider status "not just metaphorically, but historically, contextually" ("Registering" 185-90).

ated discussion of "maps" in *The Waves* that revealed "boundaries between self and other, . . . classes and sexes, . . . the colonizers and the colonized" ("Britannia" 241). Kathy Phillips charted Woolf's multiple "connections among imperialism, war, and gender relations" (ix). Discussion of "Spatial Aesthetics" (Pearson 427), "'geographical imagination'" (Thacker 411), and "Literary Geography" (Larsson 7) in Woolf's work continues.

The Woolf's library certainly evokes a long masculinist and colonialist history of geography and map making. Reflecting traditions of education in science and mathematics, political power, and exploration, all the Woolfs' books with maps at WSU are by men.[32] In this context, it is time to say more about their early *New and Complete Geographical Dictionary...* by Frederic Watson, "M.A. Vicar of SUTTON, and Several other GENTLEMEN" (1773). The unattributed, black-and-white frontispiece [Figure 7] is captioned, "A professor of Geography shewing his Pupils the Situation of the different Nations of the World." Ensconced comfortably in a classical architectural setting, he directs three young men's gazes to a large globe. Two female allegorical figures, breasts partially bared, inspire him. One is History, who holds a book entitled *Voyages perform'd by British Seamen* and points towards a ship at sea in the background. The other is Urania who holds a Celestial Hemisphere, "to prove that Astronomy is essential to Geography." Below, a child points to a map of a fortified city, emphasizing the importance of geographical knowledge to military operations.

As *A Room of One's Own* (1929) and *Three Guineas* (1938) have established, Virginia Woolf was well aware of such gender-defined spaces and boundaries. She set out to reveal the psychological and emotional effects not only on women and the history of their lives and accomplishments, but also on men, on the resulting lopsided, hierarchical values that foster imperialism and war. *Three Guineas* especially makes clear that, throughout her career, Woolf has been interested in metaphorically mapping "two worlds," a potentially vibrant "world of women" often obscured within a hierarchical "world of men" (*TG* 53). Her narrator explicitly offers a bird's-eye view of the nation and states that, whatever "dangerous and uncertain theories" exist about psychological and biological differences between men and women, the facts prove that it is men, not women, who possess the "capital," "land," "valuables," and "patronage" (*TG* 17-18). She makes this cartographic project clear in an end note. We can begin to understand the effects of these inequities on gender differences, she says, by "chalking on a large-scale map of England [,] property owned by men, red; by women, blue" (*TG* 149n15).

---

[32] This dominance of cartography by men complements the perceived dominance of the humanities by male authors. In her father Leslie Stephen's library, as Beth Rigel Daugherty writes, "Woolf would claim there was no women's tradition; it existed," however suppressed, "but not...on Leslie's shelves" (14).

Figure 7. Frontispiece for Watson, Frederic, et al. A New &; Complete Geographical Dictionary: Containing a Full and Accurate Description of the Severall Parts of the Known World, as Divided into Continents, Islands, Oceans, Seas, Rivers, Lakes, Etc. London: G. Kearsly, 1773. The caption reads, "A Professor of Geography shewing his Pupils the situation of the different Nations of the World. History pointing to a Ship at Sea, signifying that by Navigation a knowledge of Geography is chiefly to be obtained. Urania descends, holding a Celestial Hemisphere, to prove that Astronomy is essential to Geography." MASC.

In this map of a British Empire in miniature, red would almost eclipse blue.

Woolf's endnote parodies maps and fact collecting that enforce power by ignoring and suppressing whole populations. It alludes to a tradition of colonial exploration, conquest, and map making that colors boundaries and spaces within them to define and assert control over subject peoples. In *Three Guineas*, however, Woolf's chalked map suggests neither the colonizers' pride of possession, nor even the resigned submission of those colonized. It solicits the collective anger of her readers. She has put red and blue colored chalks in her narrator's hand to assist in exposing such mapping and fact-gathering for what it is. Red is the main color not only of the British Empire, but of patriarchal authority and pageantry, even of war. For soldiers, says the narrator, "the red and the gold...are discarded upon active service," so "their expensive...splendor is invented partly in order to impress" and "to induce young men to become soldiers" (*TG* 21). Fury at such displays reappears when her "Outsiders' Society" members refuse to "merge...[their] identity" with men's in exclusionary groups (*TG* 105-06). Her narrator imagines "a monstrous male" who, like a cartographer mapping empires, is "childishly intent upon *scoring the floor of the earth with chalk marks*, within whose mystic boundaries human beings are penned,...; where, daubed red and gold,...[,] he goes through mystic rites and enjoys the dubious pleasures of power and dominion" (my emphasis). Meanwhile those penned, "'his' women, are locked in the private house," banned from "the many societies of which his society is composed" (*TG* 105-06).

To this startling exposé of immature cartographical gratification Woolf adds the "methodical," "dispassionate," "cold facts" of Joseph Whitaker's *Almanac for the Year of Our Lord*...(*TG* 45, 87). The two issues (1936 and 1938) that remain among the Woolfs' books chart a nation dominated by masculine professional hierarchies and boundaries. To these Woolf contrasts alternative spaces of intellectual liberty and true culture revealed by women's writing, just as she contrasts a successful, money-centered, hierarchical, masculine professional life to one that includes sensory pleasures, conversation, good health, and human relations (*TG* 72). Given women's lives in an England divided unequally into red and blue, Woolf's "outsider" has to conclude that "As a woman, I have no country. As a woman I want no country. As a woman my country is the whole world" (*TG* 109).

As Susan Friedman reminds us, however, the "daughters of educated men" are "both of and not of the educated classes, just as they are both of and not of the nation-state" ("Wartime" 31). Not only is Woolf product and part of her imagined map but also of the "whole world," much of which is divided among imperial powers into colored possessions. The ability to imagine and criticize the hierarchical map she experiences in her country and, by extension, abroad, the ability to reveal its effects not only on past and present women with whom she can identify, but also on the lives of men, suggests Woolf's goals. Consistent with her desire to see "men and women working together for the same cause" in *Three Guineas* (102) and like her goal for great minds and for literature in *A Room of One's Own* to be "androgynous" (102), so her implied goal for cartography is for nation and world to be more equally red and blue, even red-blue and blue-red. Blended on maps, red and blue would form shades of violet, like the typewriter ribbon and ink Woolf at times wittily and affectionately preferred for communications with Violet Dickinson (Hawkes 272) and Vita Sackville-West (*L6* 461), and like the purple ink she used to write *A Room of One's Own,* a manuscript now in the Fitzwilliam Museum, Cambridge.[33] Such an imaginary spin of the color wheel helps us as readers to understand Woolf's continued efforts to think "against the current, not with it" (*E6* 243), to sight "some real thing behind appearances" (*MOB* 72).

The stated claim of Watson's *Geographical Dictionary* is "to render the Science of GEOGRAPHY easy and intelligible to every CAPACITY." Although, judging from the Frontispiece, the potential students are young men, Virginia Woolf had both admirable "capacity" and access to an abundance of geographical materials, including many more recent than Watson's. Her awareness of them is apparent in her writing, but she did not use these resources as systematically and self-consciously as did male novelists like Melville, Joyce, and Pynchon. For them printed maps and guidebooks may have been "formative in the way space was represented" in their fiction (Bulson 15). Still, as Tally points out, "sometimes the very act of telling a story is also a process of producing a map" (*Spatiality* 46). Even if Woolf often relied on her mental maps of London, for example, to describe characters' movements in relation to their social identities and developing lives, she did not always go entirely "mapless" (Bulson 117). When she drafted "Mrs. Dalloway in Bond Street" (1923) then turned that story into *Mrs. Dalloway* (1925)*,* she must have consulted one of her London maps in order to sketch in a reading notebook a map focusing on "'Green Park,' 'Stratton St,' and 'Bond Street'" (Silver 240, B.2q, 19).[34] In the novel, therefore, she can keep her readers oriented with accurate and sufficient "narrative signposting" (Bulson 117) even when her characters seem more randomly conscious of their locations and more easily distracted by sights, sounds, thoughts, feelings, and memories. The geographical details she includes may make readers feel "at home in the world when they are not," an experience Eric Bulson calls "oriented disorientation" (2).

Maps provided Virginia Woolf with an awareness not only of local urban and rural spaces but also increasingly of national, international, even cosmic ones. We

---

[33] Leonard Woolf gave Virginia Woolf's autographed manuscript to the Fitzwilliam Museum in 1942. S. P. Rosenbaum published an edition of it in 1992. Both Ted Bishop and Gill Lowe discuss real and metaphorical types of inks and pens in Woolf's life and writing.

[34] In the 1930s Woolf sketched another map, this one a plan for "a study and bath at the top of Monk's House" (Rosner 186). In both urban and rural places, outdoor and indoor spaces complemented each other.

see her understanding of the maps' abilities to use boundaries, colors, and lines to reify empires both political and commercial. For Woolf, two-dimensional maps with their birds'-eye views or, as some would have it, "God's-eye or Godlike view[s]" (Edney 72), were intriguing and functional. Nevertheless, as Andrew Thacker puts it, Woolf uses "external geographical locations" and the maps that reflect and accept them, "to interrogate the inner psychology of her characters, as well as to explore wider political issues of gender and empire" (413). Cartographical imagery helped Woolf to create, character by character and novel by novel, maps of her own.

IV

The cartological trope in Virginia Woolf's fiction reveals multi-layered uses of geographical and cartographical perspectives, orientations, and boundaries. However impersonal, maps still could suggest actual and metaphorical itineraries, whether current, remembered, or anticipated, whether physical or psychological. Woolf certainly would have agreed with Beryl Markham (1902-1986) who, in 1936, was the first woman to make a grueling trans-Atlantic flight, solo and non-stop, *against* prevailing winds, from England to North America.[35] Unfortunately, Markham's memoir *Westward with the Night* (1942) appeared too late for Woolf to read. Still, Markham's mixed responses to maps are relevant to this discussion. She writes, "Were all the maps in this world destroyed…, each man would be blind again, each city be made a stranger to the next, each landmark become a meaningless signpost pointing to nothing" (245). On the one hand, she calls "a map…a cold thing,…humourless and dull, born of calipers and a draughtsman's board." A map's coastline reveals "neither sand nor sea nor rock" nor "mariner, blundering full sail in wakeless seas." We want stories of exploration and adventure, she writes, but "this brown blot that marks a mountain" shows no climbers risking their lives. We see no explorers courageously tracing new paths "with bleeding feet" through what on the map is "a valley," "a swamp," "a desert," or "a river" (Markham 245-46). On the other hand, Markham says, even if the "modest" map is "only paper and ink," it can make one contemplate "histories of hope or sagas of conquest" (246). Woolf was aware that scientific developments in cartography had eliminated figures of "dolphins and narwhals who," Katharine Hilbery recalls in Woolf's *Night and Day* (1919), "disport themselves upon the edges of old maps" (197) and figures of "ships, animals, monsters" that early mapmakers used to suggest past and future

---

[35] Beryl Markham (née Clutterbuck) was born in England but grew up in Kenya where she became the first woman licensed as a race horse trainer. With a commercial pilot's license, she worked as a bush pilot and flyer of game hunters, doctors, and mail. She determined in 1936 to become the first woman to fly from England across the Atlantic. Although she landed in Nova Scotia rather than New York, the flight was hailed a success. *West with the Night* was reissued in 1982 to much acclaim.

journeys (Hegglund, "*Ulysses*" 176). Still, to Markham, maps as well as written accounts in *Westward with the Night*, evoked memories of her own risky travels, sometimes over uncharted territory. She claims never to have "lost or thrown away" any map she has "flown by": "I have a trunk containing continents" (Markham 246).

Woolf made no direct reference to Markham or her record-breaking 1936 flight. She did know, however, about achievements, explorations, and even map-making done by other women in the 1930s. Amelia Earhart (1897-1937) had accomplished the same feat as Markham four years earlier, but in the opposite direction *with* prevailing winds. Woolf knew Earhart's *The Last Flight* (1937). In *Three Guineas* she quotes Earhart's encouragement of women "'to do for themselves what men have already done—and occasionally…have not done—thereby establishing themselves as persons, and perhaps encouraging other women towards greater independence of thought and action'" (186 n.46). Just as Charles Marlow in Joseph Conrad's *Heart of Darkness* describes his childhood "passion for maps" (52), so Earhart in *The Last Flight* remembers "'map-traveling,'" and using "maps in childhood games of make-believe, 'imaginary journeys full of fabulous perils'" (qtd. Frederick xxviii). Woolf also knew of at least one instance of women's map-making. In 1935, Anne Morrow Lindbergh (1906-2001) published *North to the Orient* (1935), a book about husband and wife's joint "attempt to map a new and uncharted air route from America to Asia in 1931" (Simpson 1-2, *D4* 335 and n6).[36]

Like Beryl Markham, Amelia Earhart, and Anne Morrow Lindbergh, Virginia Woolf knew and used maps, but she never went up in an airplane. Still, to Woolf flight "typifies the present day" (Beer 135). Maps provided substitute aerial views in both life and art and views from above were, in turn, like maps. In *The Years* (1937), for example, as Woolf metaphorically maps the Pargiter family's evolving London-centered lives from 1880 into the 1930s, Eleanor and Peggy look down from a window at a scene "like a map of London; a section laid beneath them." Then, looking upward from the same vantage point, Eleanor remembers seeing her "first aeroplane" (*TY* 328). Woolf's "Flying Over London," drafted in 1928 (*E6* 445-50) with imaginary views from above, is an example not only of her "airmindedness" in an era of "airplanes, airmen, and aerial views" (Delsandro 117) but of her familiarity with a map's similar limitations. Just as maps do not chart human thoughts and feelings, neither do "air values." What are merely abstract "blocks" seen from above turn out to be, according to "land values," "Rolls Royces in a row with city magnates waiting furious" (*E6* 449). Berta Ruck, popular novelist and fan of both flying and Woolf's *Orlando* (1928), wrote in a letter that "The Great Frost" and "The Great Damp" were like a "vivid, brilliant glimpse down onto English history" from an aeroplane. An amused Woolf replied that "it was something of

---

[36] Earhart's and Lindbergh's books are no longer among those in MASC.

that very effect I tried to give" (Gillespie, "Virginia" 120). That "brilliant glimpse down," however, is incomplete without Orlando's long-lived experiences of changes not only in sex but also in geography, history, and culture. In *Between the Acts*, a novel with no direct map references, old Mr. Oliver says he's heard that "'from an aeroplane...you could still see, plainly marked, the scars made by the Britons; by the Romans; by the Elizabethan manor house....'" (4). Ordnance maps, like those Virginia Stephen, then Woolf used, also may include everything from ancient burial mounds to contemporary roads, but again she wants to imagine into those local spaces people's lives. In this case audience members respond to Miss LaTrobe's village pageant and to each other as they play out their intimacies, insecurities, prejudices, and antagonisms in the intervals. Like *Orlando* itself, the pageant is a parody of English cultural evolution, but one now enacted on the brink of another, civilization-threatening world war.

Ultimately "a writer's country" is not a place you can visit, Woolf says in her early essay "Literary Geography" (1905), but rather "a territory within his own brain" (*E*1 35). Thus it is from his "own writings that one must draw one's impressions of the Dickens country," or Thackeray's, or Melville's (*E*1 35), or Virginia Woolf's own. When we look at literary cartography in Woolf's fiction, then, we often move back and forth in the same novel from actual places cartographers have mapped, places Woolf sometimes knew, to cartographical metaphors for characters' lives or for social structures and values that affect them. Sometimes maps are just maps. Sometimes they "acquire symbolic and thematic resonance, no longer functioning as mere guides for the location of story events" as they might do in more traditional novels (Hegglund, "Introduction" 10). Virginia Woolf's experiences with maps and with metaphorically mapping the lives of her characters represent simultaneous movements in perspective back and forth not only between present and past, but also between aerial and ground, outer and inner, and local and global. Twentieth century modernism, Jon Hegglund argues, is "metageographical" ("Introduction" 4). Traditional "classical narrative realism" is increasingly in tension with a movement "away from the local, human-centered scale of character-driven actions and plots toward a more detached overview of a wider global space" (Hegglund, "Introduction" 11).

Metaphorically mapping the consciousnesses of characters remains central in Woolf's fiction. Still, although we often can follow their physical movements and psychological developments among places and spaces that two-dimensional maps represent, Woolf expands her experiments with cartographical metaphors to include three-dimensional globes. Already in her early fiction, globes join maps as both objects and metaphors for the itineraries and shapes of characters' lives. Although I have found no evidence that the Woolfs owned an actual globe, they certainly encountered them.[37] In Woolf's fiction globes are sometimes outdated objects that create domestic atmospheres of earlier times. In *Night and Day*, "sallow globes" and artifacts like "cracked oil-paintings, and stuffed owls" suggest the early nineteenth century in the Otways' Stogdon House (197). In *The Years* Eleanor Pargiter visits her brother Morris at his mother-in-law, Mrs. Chinnery's home where an "old yellow globe…stood under the pleasant eighteenth-century picture of all the little Chinnerys in long drawers and nankeen trousers" (197).

Woolf's characters usually experience intimations of cartographical worlds or globes, however, not in domestic parlors but in the natural world. Already in *The Voyage Out*, we have the "infinite distances" (131), the "vast expanse of land" of South America that strikes Rachel Vinrace and Terrence Hewet as "uncomfortably impersonal and hostile" (210).[38] These views from crests of hills or mountain tops are so unlike the comfortable ones in England where, as on the Woolfs' maps, "the villages and the hills" are named and horizons are defined (*VO* 210). In South America Rachel and Terence imagine the "infinite sun-dried earth" in all its shapes and forms "widening and spreading" and being, as they would on the map of a continent or a world map in an atlas, "partitioned into different lands, where famous cities were founded, and," as an imperial perspective suggests to them, "the races of men changed from dark savages to white civilized men, and back to dark savages again" (*VO* 210).

Woolf's first three novels are richest in cartographical references and metaphors. Her first is thus already an interrogation of global imperialism. One of Virginia Woolf's books that is appropriately prominent is Gibbon's *Decline and Fall of the Roman Empire*. Appreciation of it is St. John Hirst's masculinist "test" for whether or not Rachel Vinrace has "got a mind" or is "like the rest of…[her] sex" (*VO* 154). When St. John gives her the first volume, Rachel carries it with a kind of fearful determination to measure up, "much as a soldier prepared for battle" (*VO* 176). Later, when "the style of Gibbon" is the subject of debate, Rachel cannot admire it. Failing St. John's test, she feels "that her value as a human being was lessened" (*VO* 201).

The Empire of interest in *The Voyage Out*, however, is British. In this first novel, Woolf's character relationships are metaphors for the ethical fragilities of nations as they create colored maps showing colonial and commercial empires. Frederic Watson's *Geographical Dictionary* (1773) includes an early map of South America, but J. G. Bartholomew's "Commercial Chart of South America" in 1912 shows in color which European countries dominated what portions.[39] "All

---

[37] Jane Garrity provides a helpful illustrated history of globe manufacturing and usage in England (129-131).

[38] Jed Esty looks at "Rachel's mind and the South American landscape" in *The Voyage Out* as "figures for each other, each prone to a certain formlessness" (133).

[39] Both Patricia Novillo-Corvalán and Lindsey Cordery suggest that Woolf knew more about South America than scholars previously have thought.

seemed to favour the expansion of the British Empire," muses Mr. Pepper on the voyage to that continent, "and had there been men like Richard Dalloway in the time of Charles the First," he thinks, "the map would undoubtedly be red where it is now an odious green" (*VO* 89).[40] Rachel Vinrace, who initially admires Richard Dalloway, has the illusion that even fashionable Clarissa Dalloway deals "with the world as she chose; the enormous solid globe spun round this way and that beneath her fingers" (*VO* 47). Woolf ironically replaces the professor and his globe in the frontispiece to Watson's *Geographical Dictionary* [Figure 7] with a woman, but one who mirrors for her husband his self-image as a morally superior "martyr... in the service of mankind," of what he calls "'dominion'" and "'progress'" (*VO* 64-65). Richard Dalloway's sudden sexual advance makes clear Rachel's naiveté. He thinks of the history of British "conservative policy... as though it were a lasso that opened and caught things, enormous chunks of the habitable globe" (*VO* 51). He asserts this characteristic masculine dominance not just over geographical territory but over women's bodies and brains, thus over their autonomy. Dalloway's advances and his criticisms, like St. John Hirst's of women's capabilities, confuse Rachel and prompt not only nightmares of pursuit but also an awareness of her "hedged-in" life (*VO* 82). Even the sea on which her group travels is not entirely an unmapped space for a woman's development and renewal but "merely another man-shaped vista" (Vlasopolos 80).[41]

As metaphors for Rachel Vinrace's psychological itinerary in *The Voyage Out*, globes turn from comforting to confining. At one point she feels herself within a "warm mysterious globe," not so much a three-dimensional printed orb as a bounded space "full of changes and miracles," a world from which the critical St. John Hirst seems excluded (*VO* 295). Terence Hewet, however, defends Hirst and dismisses Rachel as "'essentially feminine'" with "'no respect for facts'" and thus unable to understand his friend (*VO* 295). Rachel's "warm mysterious globe" of belonging is an illusion as she begins to discover and understand how she is defined by others and what the metaphorical marriage map looks like for women.

Night and Day also has both literal and metaphorical maps and globes. Maps and the specialty stores that carry them evidence public awareness of London's position in England and the British Isles, and on both continent and globe. Although Katharine Hilbery has in her head "an imaginary map of London, to follow the twists and turns of unnamed streets," she needs to buy "a large scale map of Norfolk in the map shop in Queen Street" (*ND* 445, 438). Katharine also confronts metaphorical

---

[40] Joseph Conrad's Marlow, not yet initiated into the ravages of traders and imperialists, is pleased by the "'vast amount of red'" on a trading company's "'large shining map'" because "'some real work is done there'" (55).

[41] Jed Esty notes that Rachel, "like Conrad's cloistered women in *Heart of Darkness*, represents the gendering of the imperial unconscious, the split between civilizing and chivalric ideals on the one hand and the grubby deeds of empire men on the other" (138).

maps of life charted for her by others. She struggles to locate her own, as well as Ralph Denham's "exact position," not just among places and spaces named and bounded on printed maps, but "upon the turbulent map of the emotions" (*ND* 332). There she tries to chart her true feelings about complex relationships and atypical feminine goals. A map of life made by her, not for her, involves holding "in her hands for one brief moment the globe which we spend our lives trying to shape, round, whole, and entire from the confusion of chaos" (*ND* 503). To go ahead with their mutual attraction, she also needs Ralph Denham to clarify his relationship with Mary Datchet, to "do what appeared to be necessary if he, too, were to hold his globe for a moment round, whole, and entire" (*ND* 503). If Woolf's characters, both female and male, are able to grasp and read them, globes offer metaphors for attempts to define individual needs and relationships and to grasp and control the itineraries of their own lives.

For Mary Datchet, globes and maps become positive tropes for the heady feeling that her work for women's suffrage is important. Her typewriter and telephone represent, like maps of international communication lines in the Woolfs' atlases, the "exact spot on the surface of the globe that all the subterranean wires of thought and progress came together" (*ND* 265-66). Mary's office is the center of her practical organizational abilities where she also envisions a "large scale map of England" augmented with colored pins to mark suffrage organizations in each county (*ND* 256). This confidence of being on the map herself and being able to assist in mapping national and global progress for women helps Mary to bear her unrequited love for Ralph Denham and thus to avoid the worst of Katharine Hilbery's "turbulent map of the emotions" (*ND* 332). What Katharine says about Mary, "'She's happy too…She has her work'" (*ND* 505), is roughly what Lily Briscoe later concludes about herself in *To the Lighthouse* as she struggles to map her unmarried life, conflicted relationships, and dedication to painting.

In *Jacob's Room*, Woolf's third novel, literal globes and maps indicate broad news coverage and travel possibilities.[42] The *Globe* is a newspaper (*JR* 98), the "*Globe Trotter* is an international magazine" (*JR* 138), and an insect carries in its head a "globe of the world" (*JR* 163). On a domestic level, lamps have globes (*JR* 12, 127, 136) and wine glasses are pleasingly globe-shaped (*JR* 75). So far as world maps go, a Miss Barrett visits "Bacon, the map seller, in the Strand" whose "large yellow globe" in the window is a symbol of his trade.[43] There the customer even can find and buy "maps of the Syrian desert" (*JR* 170-71). Map stores with their globes and maps both reflect and enlarge a Londoner's view of the world and

---

[42] Although they do not include her other writings, concordances by James M. Haule and Philip H. Smith are useful for tracing cartographical images in Woolf's novels.

[43] G. W. Bacon & Company went bankrupt in 1867 but reopened in 1870 at 127 The Strand.

facilitate travel, real or imaginary.

Used metaphorically, the globe image also suggests social boundaries, in this case for both sexes. Triggered by a letter from Jacob's mother are several paragraphs with the anonymous narrator contemplating the ways in which "life would split asunder without" letters; they "lace our days together and make of life a perfect globe" (*JR* 93). This routine round of letters representing teas, dinners, conversations, concerts, and appointments, however, make us worry, "Is this all?...Am I doomed all my days to write letters, send voices, which fall upon the tea-table, fade upon the passage, making appointments, while life dwindles, to come and dine?" Are even poets' letters capable of "reading, touching, penetrating the individual heart"? (*JR* 93). Routine letters and invitations, like printed maps or globes, have practical functions, but as metaphors for social and personal expectations they leave something essential undefined or omitted.

As Rose Shaw says, "The streets of London have their map; but our passions are uncharted" (*JR* 95). The "our" refers not just to Jacob and his male friends, but also to his mother, Betty Flanders, to women with whom Jacob has affairs, to Sandra Wentworth Williams, the married woman with whom he falls in love, and to a multitude of people adrift in unexamined routine and socially defined boundaries. Does Jacob Flanders define his own "perfect globe" (*JR* 93) before he becomes a casualty of World War I? Jacob's physical itineraries with his maps and guide books are metaphors for traditional masculine privilege in both education and mobility, advantages that groom a young man for confidence and success.[44] At Cambridge, while Jacob smokes by a window, his friend Timmy Durrant casually consults "the map" and makes plans for their trip to the Scilly Isles (*JR* 39). After Jacob's exploration of London on foot, from lower-class districts to ones representing affluence and power, he sets off for Paris, Rome, and Athens. Longing to spend a day walking in Greece, he instructs himself to "'look at the map'" (*JR* 141). In Olympia, he finds and observes statues with "his Baedeker" in hand (*JR* 145, 149). Jacob, as Amanda Golden points out (102), is "accurate and diligent" in his use of the guide book, but he is also "profoundly morose" (*JR* 149). The next day finds him reading an unnamed book (Gibbon perhaps?) that inspires an annotation "upon the importance of history" (*JR* 149-50). Even with his masculine privileges, Jacob remains in search of the metaphorical globe that can help him shape and define a satisfying life.

Mrs. Dalloway, much discussed, is an example of Virginia Woolf's literary mapping, not because she mentions actual or metaphorical maps or globes in the

---

The company was well known for its printed globes.

[44] Leslie Kathleen Hankins's experimental change of "Jacob" to "Judith" and male to female pronouns raises issues about what it might have been like if a woman of that time and place had been educated and free to move across boundaries as confidently as Jacob and other men of his class.

text but because her characters' itineraries take them through identifiable parts of London. The Woolfs' map collection reveals this much-charted city with sites associated with monarchy, government, culture, religion, education, recreation, and transportation clearly marked.[45] Recent readers like Lisbeth Larsson rightly emphasize how Woolf tracks characters through urban areas that are metaphors for the "fixed conditions…by which they have been shaped and through which they shape themselves" (10, 2).

The one direct map reference in *Mrs. Dalloway* is fraught with despair. Septimus Smith, distraught psychological victim of World War I, finds no solace in, or itinerary through a "map of the world" and other drawings he has made; "'Burn them!'" he cries before he plunges to his death (*MD* 224). The boundaries on Septimus's hand-drawn map, even if roughly accurate, cannot chart the effects on people's lives of international competition for geographical territories, abuses of subject peoples, or physical and psychological casualties of wars fought to attain, keep, or expand imperial power. Even maps like the one showing property and privilege in England that Virginia Woolf imagines chalking in *Three Guineas*—"men, red; …women, blue" (149 n15)—do not reflect the force used to maintain masculine hierarchies and privileges at home and abroad. When Martin and Sara have lunch in the 1914 portion of *The Years,* they recall that Rose has been imprisoned and is probably being force-fed for throwing a brick during a suffragette demonstration. Sara pounds the table and quotes with bitter irony, "'Roll up the map of Europe,' said the man to the flunkey, 'I don't believe in force!'" (*TY* 232). As Woolf indicates in *Three Guineas*, the European continent does not have a monopoly on tyrants.

In *The Waves* world maps are introduced in a seemingly benign fashion as important pedagogical tools aimed at the ideal of a "cartographically literate citizen" (Matless 202). Girls are schooled *en masse*, Rhoda says, "herded together under maps of the entire world" (*TW* 33). These "maps, green-baize boards, and rows of shoes on a shelf" remain equated in their memories with authority, with "monumental ladies" who taught "French, geography and arithmetic" (*TW* 125). Woolf's emphasis here is on the formal pedagogical exposure to, and acceptance of large, defined geographical spaces, anticipating the many countries the sun illuminates at noon in the fifth Interlude of the novel.

Motivations for empire building include acquisition of natural resources and establishment of trade routes and commercial markets. The Woolfs' 1912 *Citizen's Atlas* therefore includes maps that document global communication and commercial empires and their control of vast spaces, oceans as well as the continents they surround [Figure 8]. Shipping for travel and commerce is a theme throughout Woolf's work beginning in *The Voyage Out* with characters traveling from England to South America on one of Willoughby Vinrace's trading ships. In *Night and*

---

[45] See Elisa Kay Sparks's use of the Woolfs' London maps remaining in MASC.

Day, the Bond Street neighborhood prompts the "young" and the "ignorant," we are told, "to think the world one great bazaar, with...divans heaped with spoils from every quarter of the globe" (364). In "The Docks of London" (1932), Woolf refers to goods shipped from all over the world to be "transformed" for sale in the "garishness and gaudiness" of the "Oxford Street Tide" (*E5* 283). It is no surprise that the "large yellow globe" Fanny Elmer in *Jacob's Room* sees in "the window of Bacon, the map seller, in the Strand," is a modern one "marked with steamship lines" (170-71).

Louis in *The Waves,* self-conscious about an Australian accent that identifies him with a distant British colony, is the culmination of this theme. He has played a part in his company's efforts to "send ships to the remotest parts of the globe" (169). Thus, as the Woolfs' atlas shows, he has helped "to score those lines on the map...by which the different parts of the world are laced together." Metaphorically he has "roll[ed] the dark before...[him], spreading commerce where there

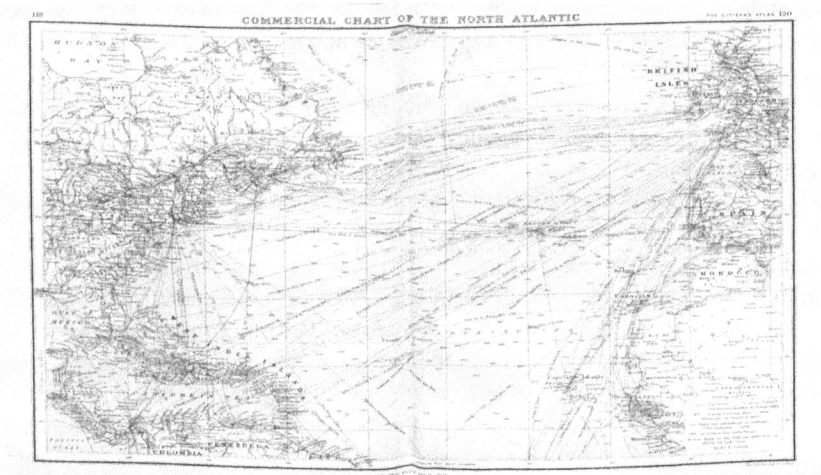

Figure 8. "Commercial Chart of the North Atlantic" from J. G. Bartholomew's The Citizen's Atlas of the World: Containing 156 Pages of Maps and Plans, with an Index, a Gazetteer, and Geographical Statistics *(1912). J. Bartholomew, 1912. MASC.*

was chaos" (*TW* 168). Whether Louis is complicit in economic empire building, trapped by it, or conflicted by both,[46] Woolf makes clear that his satisfaction with professional authority and respectability in a well mapped commercial empire has brought, as he maps his private life, "little natural happiness" (*TW* 201).

Similarly, in "Scenes from the Life of a British Naval Officer," a short story probably written late in the year *The Waves* appeared (*CSF* 306), Virginia Woolf introduces "Captain Brace…in his cabin with a map spread on the…table in front of him." Whether political or commercial, his imperial mission in the Red Sea is assumed (*CSF* 232). Like Louis's, the Captain's personal happiness—suggested here by a "photograph of a lady's head"—is elusive. This time, however, technology joins maps as a trope for impersonal, even mechanical human relationships. The Captain lives among "white faced instruments" that "divided[,] measured, weighed and counted in seven or eight different ways simultaneously" (*CSF* 232). The Captain considers those around him mere hands, saluting or serving him, "white hands" seen, "not white" ones "dismissed" (*CSF* 233). The precision, order, exactitude of his fifty years at sea have transformed him into an unfeeling machine or brute, his "telescope…[becoming]…an extension of his eyes as if it were a horn casing" (*CSF* 234).

Another ship's captain in Woolf's fiction comes to mind, Marmaduke Bonthrop Shelmerdine in *Orlando*. He also relies on his "map and compasses" (257), in this case to meet the "most desperate and splendid of adventures—which is to voyage round Cape Horn in the teeth of a gale" (252). Whether Shelmerdine's role, never directly mentioned, is empire expansion or governance, he maintains a lively long-distance, personal relationship with Orlando. She is an adventure in herself, a ship in "'full sail,'" her "roughly 300-year span of…life" simultaneous "with the establishment and consolidation of the oceanic British Empire" (Graber 165). When Orlando finds herself at last in the twentieth century, though, she scoffs at some kind of "pyramid, hecatomb, or trophy" in London that sums up this history. She mocks the "conglomeration…of the most heterogeneous and ill-assorted objects" that include "higgledy-piggledy" symbols of everything from domestic history to the reach of British imperialism. Orlando had never seen "anything at once so indecent, so hideous, and so monumental," and among her long list of "excrescences" are "extinct monsters, globes, maps, elephants and mathematical instruments" (*O* 232).

Maps like ones in the Woolfs' atlases that chart both political and commercial empires, however, can "distort reality" by generalizing, symbolizing, prioritizing,

---

[46] Jane Marcus reads Louis as "mostly complicit with Empire," says Tracy Savoie, who reads him as more conflicted (18). Louis's "imitation of Englishness … mocks colonial authority …and exposes the instability of colonial discourse and of the empire itself" (Savoie 16).

and politicizing the world (Monmonier xi-xii).[47] Virginia Woolf's "family on both sides, Stephens, Prinseps, and Pattles, had a long history of colonial work in India" (Marcus, "Registering" 183). Her great uncle, Henry Thoby Prinsep (1792-1878), chief secretary of the Calcutta Council, for example, was especially involved with controversies over mapping British holdings. The British, as Matthew H. Edney points out, "did not map the 'real' India" (26) or by extension the other territories they dominated. They thought they could scientifically "create order from social chaos" by imposing administrative power and knowledge that objectified cultures and territories (Edney 53). In *The Waves,* Bernard imagines Percival in India solving an "Oriental problem" at hand "by applying the standards of the West, by using the violent language that is natural to him" (136). Percival's death, thrown from his horse in India, positions him as both part of this imperialist tradition and casualty of it, one that anticipates the dissolution of Empire, a prospect welcomed as well as lamented, both quite possibly by Virginia Woolf herself.[48]

The Waves itself is Virginia Woolf's attempt to create a metaphorical globe that encompasses not only her characters' self-definitions as they mature but also imperialism as Percival leaves for India and dies there. Bernard tries to "'pretend that life is a solid substance, shaped like a globe'" and "'that we can make out a plain and logical story'" on it (*TW* 251).[49] As Jane Garrity suggests, the globe as a metaphor for "the characters' desire for wholeness" is inseparable from Percival and from the imperialist desire to conquer and hold territories by means of "violence and aggression" (124, 133). As Bernard struggles to seize "'this globe, full of figures,'" he realizes that the "'globe of life as one calls it'" with its "'walls of thinnest air'" is fragile and easily broken (*TW* 238, 256). By implication, so is the imperialist globe. Bernard's memory of Percival's death in India threatens the globe as a metaphor for his own struggles as a writer to grasp and control, as well as a metaphor for unified individual and collective lives. Bernard's identity contracts, expands, and disintegrates until what is left, as he imagines it was for an idealized and lost Percival, is a defiance of "Death...the enemy" (*TW* 297).

World atlases, globes, and technology may have helped Virginia Woolf to expand her perspectives beyond the possible "'ruin of civilization'" to "the repo-

---

[47] Government maps especially often practice "a censorship of secrecy to serve military defense and a censorship of silence to enforce or reinforce social and political values" (Thrower 122).

[48] Is Woolf's attitude towards Percival more ambivalent than anti-colonist, as Nels Pearson asks (433), because she finds herself, as James F. Wurtz suspects, both "critical" and "complicit" (98)?

[49] While she worked on *The Waves,* Woolf wrote an essay on John Donne (*E5* 349-66). She reflects Donne's "search for something whole, something lasting" as her characters "evoke the Donne-like figures of perceptually expanding and contracting, dividing and uniting globes or worlds" (Gillespie, "Through" 234).

sitioning of humans within the universe" (Henry 153). If we can contemplate the world and then the universe, however, then natural forces and vast spaces can in reverse destroy, ignore, or miniaturize us out of existence. Already in "Thunder at Wembley" (1924) Woolf had imagined the natural world overwhelming a carefully charted British Empire Exhibition, an Empire in miniature that still required "maps and guides and transportation" to visit (Marcus, "Registering" 183).[50] Metaphorically, "the Empire is perishing," Woolf writes, "the bands are playing; the Exhibition is in ruins. For that is what comes of letting in the sky" (*E3* 413). The power of the natural world reminds us that maps and globes, empires, other human constructions, and people themselves, are vulnerable and transitory. As atlases with different publication dates indicate, lines, colors, and names reflect the results of such historical changes, often occurring by gradual dissolution, too often by violence.

Such expansions include the "Time Passes" section in *To the Lighthouse* and especially the interludes in *The Waves* where the importance of individual struggles and achievements may be commemorated, but also diminished by cycles of nature and obliterated by vast geographical spaces. A glimpse of even further disintegration occurs appropriately in Woolf's last novel. In *Between the Acts,* Mrs. Swithin, whose "favourite reading" is "an Outline of History" (8), expands her vision beyond time.[51] She imagines the earth viewed from a cosmic space far beyond the clouds "that was blue, pure blue, black blue; blue that had never filtered down; that had escaped registration. It never fell as sun, shadow, or rain upon the world, but disregarded the little coloured ball of earth entirely" (*BTA* 23).

Looking back at her own life and career in "A Sketch of the Past," Virginia Woolf attempts a "philosophy" that returns from images and metaphors of maps and globes to a renewed contemplation of the word "world" (*MOB* 72). In *Three Guineas*, the narrator, one of the "daughters of educated men" (*TG* 4), had declared "the whole world" her country rather than one that has limited or denied her prosperity, education, and opportunity (*TG* 109). Now Woolf verbally remaps "the whole world," not as England where red dominates blue or even as a globe divided into multicolored empires, but as "a work of art." Instead of actual and psychological itineraries of individual characters or actual people, she envisions "all human beings" connected in a unifying "pattern," one "hiding behind the cotton wool of daily life" (*MOB* 72). On this metaphorical map of the creative imagination, the hierarchical, quantitative, essentially masculine "power-knowledge" (Harley 11) of traditional cartography cannot exclude lived-knowledge, the varied patterns experienced by all those existing outside the power grids—women,

---

[50] Jane Marcus reprints the map of The British Empire Exhibition, 1924 ("Registering" 184).
[51] H. G. Wells's *The Outline of History* (published as a single volume in 1920) is not among the Woolfs' books in MASC, but his less detailed preliminary, *A Short History of the World* (1924) is there (King 241).

socio-economic and racial minorities, the colonized. Virginia Woolf, with access to individual maps and to ones that illustrated or filled books, more importantly had a mind that contained not only countries, continents, and globes. She also could imagine a creative life of writing as ongoing journeys, as a series of challenging attempts to chart in words a final map of her own, the "whole world" as a unifying and unified "work of art" (*MOB* 72).

I wish to thank Trevor James Bond, Associate Dean of Digital Initiatives and Special Collections at Washington State University, Cheryl Gunselman, Manuscripts Librarian, and Julia King, Rare Books Cataloguer, for help with research and reproduction of images. I would also like to thank two anonymous readers who offered helpful suggestions. I presented preliminary versions of three parts of this essay at the Thirteenth Annual Conference on Virginia Woolf, Smith College, June 2003; at the Twenty-seventh Annual International Conference on Virginia Woolf, University of Reading, June 2017 (read for me by Eleanor McNees); and at the Twenty-Eighth Annual International Conference on Virginia Woolf, University of Kent, June 2018. A special thanks to the community of Woolf scholars for years of support and inspiration.

Works Cited

Abbott, Wilbur Cortez. *The Expansion of Europe*: *A History of the Foundations of the Modern World*. 2 vols. G. Bell, 1919. MASC.

Adair, Robin and Ann Martin. "A Driving Bloomsbury: Virginia Woolf, Vanessa Bell, and the Meaning of the Motor-Car." *Woolf Studies Annual,* vol. 24, 2018, pp. 75-99.

An Atlas of War: 15 Maps with Explanatory Text. "Note" by J. N. L. Baker. Oxford UP, 1939. MASC.

Annan, Noel. *Leslie Stephen: The Godless Victorian*. Random House, 1984.

Baedeker, Karl. *Northern France, from Belgium and the English Channel to the Loire, Excluding Paris and its Environs: Handbook for Travellers*. 3rd edition. K. Baedeker, C. Scribner's, 1899. MASC.

Barnes, Leonard. *The New Boer War*. Hogarth, 1932. MASC.

Barrett, Michèle. "Virginia Woolf's Research for *Empire and Commerce in Africa* (Leonard Woolf, 1920)." *Woolf Studies Annual,* vol. 19, 2013, pp. 83-122.

Bartholomew, J. G. *The Citizen's Atlas of the World*: *Containing 156 pages of Maps and Plans, with an Index, a Gazetteer, and Geographical Statistics*. John Bartholomew, 1912. MASC.

Beer, Gillian. "The Island and the Aeroplane: The Case of Virginia Woolf." *Virginia Woolf,* edited by Rachel Bowlby, Longman, 1992, pp. 132-61.

Bertarelli, L. V. *Northern Italy, from the Alps to Rome (Rome Excepted)*, edited by Findlay Muirhead, Blue Guides, Macmillan, 1924. MASC.

———. *Southern Italy, Including Rome, Sicily, and Sardinia*, edited by Findlay Muirhead. Blue Guides. Macmillan, 1925.

Bishop, Ted. "Getting a Hold on Haddock: Virginia Woolf's Inks." *Virginia Woolf and the World of Books: The Centenary of the Hogarth Press: Selected Papers from the Twenty -Seventh Annual International Conference on Virginia Woolf*, edited by Nicola Wilson and Claire Battershill, Clemson UP, 2018, pp. 2-18.

Bowlby, Rachel. "Walking, Women and Writing." *Feminist Destinations and Further Essays on Virginia Woolf*. Edinburgh UP, 1997, pp. 191-219.

Brown, Horatio. *Venice: An Historical Sketch of the Republic*. 2nd ed., rev., Rivington, Percival, 1895. MASC.

Bulson, Eric. *Novels, Maps, Modernity: The Spatial Imagination, 1850-2000*. Routledge, 2010.

Chapman, Wayne K. "Collaborative Reviewing by Leonard and Virginia Woolf." *Women in the Milieu of Leonard and Virginia Woolf: Peace, Politics, and Education*, edited by Wayne K. Chapman and Janet M. Manson, Pace UP, 1998, pp. 243-247.

———. and Marilyn M. Manson. "Carte and Tierce: Leonard, Virginia Woolf, and War for Peace." *Virginia Woolf and War: Fiction, Reality, and Myth*, edited by Mark Hussey, Syracuse UP, 1991, pp. 58-78.

Clark, Cumberland. *Britain Overseas: The Story of the Foundation and Development of the British Empire from 1497-1921*. K. Paul, Trench, Trubner, 1924. MASC.

Conrad, Joseph. *Heart of Darkness* (1899). *The Works of Joseph Conrad*. Uniform Edition vol. 22. J. M. Dent, 1923, pp. 45-162. MASC.

Cordery, Lindsey. "Virginia Woolf and South America: Border-Reading." *Virginia Woolf and the World of Books: The Centenary of the Hogarth Press: Selected Papers from the Twenty-seventh Annual International Conference on Virginia Woolf*, edited by Nicola Wilson and Claire Battershill. Clemson UP 2018, pp. 226-232.

Cosgrove, Denis. "Introduction: Mapping Meaning." *Mappings*, edited by Denis Cosgrove, Reaktion Books, 1999, pp. 1-23.

Daugherty, Beth Rigel. "Learning Virginia Woolf: Of Leslie, Libraries, and Letters." *Virginia Woolf and Communities: Selected Papers from the Eighth Annual Conference on Virginia Woolf*, edited by Jeanette McVicker and Laura Davis, Pace UP, 1999, pp. 10-17.

Delsandro, Erica. "Flights of Imagination: Aerial Views, Narrative Perspectives, and Global Perceptions." *Virginia Woolf: Art, Education, and Internationalism: Selected Papers from the Seventeenth Annual Conference* on *Virginia Woolf,* edited by Diana Royer and Madelyn Detloff, Clemson U Digital P, 2008, pp. 117-124.

Edney, Matthew H. *Mapping an Empire: The Geographical Construction of British India, 1765-1843.* U of Chicago P, 1997.

Esty, Jed. *Unseasonable Youth: Modernism, Colonialism, and the Fiction of Development.* Oxford UP, 2012.

Frederick, Bonnie and Virginia Hyde. "Introduction." *Women and the Journey: The Female Travel Experience,* edited by Bonnie Frederick and Susan H. McLeod, Washington State UP, 1993, pp. xvii-xxxiii.

Friedman, Susan Stanford. *Mappings: Feminism and the Cultural Geographies of Encounter.* Princeton UP, 1998.

———. "Wartime Cosmopolitanism: Cosmofeminisms in Virginia Woolf's *Three Guineas* and Marjane Satrapi's *Persepolis.*" *Tulsa Studies in Women's Literature,* vol. 32, no. 1, 2013, pp. 23-32.

Gardner, Edmund G. *The Story of Florence.* J. M. Dent, 1903. MASC.

Garrity, Jane. "Global Objects in *The Waves.*" *A Companion to Virginia Woolf,* edited by Jessica Berman, John Wiley & Sons, 2016, pp. 121-136.

Gibbon, Edward. *The History of the Decline and Fall of the Roman Empire.* New ed., T. Cadell and W. Davies, 1820. 12 vols. MASC.

Gillespie, Diane F. "Introduction." *The Library of Leonard and Virginia Woolf: A Short-title Catalogue,* edited by Julia King and Laila Miletic-Vejzovic, Washington State UP, 2003, pp. vii-xx.

———. "Through Woolf's 'I's: Donne and *The Waves.*" *Woolf: Reading the Renaissance,* edited by Sally Greene, Ohio UP, 1999, pp. 211-244.

———. "Virginia Woolf and the Curious Case of Berta Ruck." *Woolf Studies Annual,* vol. 10, 2004, pp. 109-138.

Golden, Amanda. "Textbook Greek: Thoby Stephen in *Jacob's Room.*" *Woolf Studies Annual,* vol. 23, 2017, pp. 83-108.

Graber, Darin. "*H. M. S. Orlando*: The Metamorphosing, Imperial Vessel." *Woolf Studies Annual,* vol. 24, 2018, pp. 165-183.

Griggs, Arthur Kingsland. *Paris for Everyman: Her Present, her Past, and her Environs.* Dent, 1924. MASC.

Hakluyt, Richard. *Voyages of Hawkins, Frobisher, and Drake: Select Narratives from the Principal Navigations of Hakluyt,* edited by Edward John Payne. Notes, maps, etc. edited by C. Raymond Beazley. Clarendon, 1907. MASC.

A Handbook for Travellers in France. 16th ed. 2 vols. Murray, 1882-84. MASC.

Hankins, Leslie Kathleen, editor. *Judith's Room: a posthumous collaboration with (and homage to) Virginia Woolf.* Making Waves Press, 2017.

Hare, Augustus J. C. and St. Clair Baddeley. *Venice.* 6th ed. G. Allen, 1904. MASC.

Harley, J. B. "Deconstructing the Map." *Cartographica,* vol. 26, no. 2, Spring 1989, pp. 1- 20.

Haule, James M. and Philip H. Smith. *Concordances to the Novels of Virginia Woolf.* Oxford Microform Publications 1981- .

Hawkes, Ellen, ed. *Friendships Gallery* by Virginia Woolf. *Twentieth Century Literature,* vol. 25, no. 3/4, 1979, pp. 270-302.

Hegglund, Jon. "Introduction: The Modernist Novel as Metageography." *World Views: Metageographies of Modernist Fiction.* Oxford UP, 2012, pp. 1-30.

———. "*Ulysses* and the Rhetoric of Cartography." *Twentieth-Century Literature* vol. 49, no. 2, 2003, pp. 164-192.

Henry, Holly. "From Edwin Hubble's Telescope to Virginia Woolf's 'Searchlight.'" *Virginia Woolf in the Age of Mechanical Reproduction,* edited by Pamela L. Caughie. Garland, 2000, pp. 135-58.

Hertslet, Edward. *The Map of Africa by Treaty: With Numerous Maps.* 2 vols. HMSO, 1894. MASC.

Higonnet, Margaret R. "New Cartographies, an Introduction." *Reconfigured Spheres: Feminist Explorations of Literary Space,* edited by Margaret R. Higonnet and Joan Templeton, U of Massachusetts P, 1994, pp. 1-19.

Hollis, Catherine W. *Leslie Stephen as Mountaineer: "Where does Mont Blanc end, and where do I begin?"* Cecil Woolf, 2010.

Jones, Clara. "Virginia Woolf and 'The Villa Jones.'" *Woolf Studies Annual* vol. 22, 2016, pp. 75-89.

King, Julia and Laila Miletic-Vejzovic, editors. *The Library of Leonard and Virginia Woolf: A Short-title Catalog.* Washington State UP, 2003.

Larsson, Lisbeth. *Walking Virginia Woolf's London: An Investigation in Literary Geography.* Palgrave Macmillan, 2017.

Laurence, Patricia. "A Writing Couple: Shared Ideology in Virginia Woolf's *Three Guineas* and Leonard Woolf's *Quack, Quack!*" *Women in the Milieu of Leonard and Virginia Woolf: Peace, Politics, and Education,* edited by Wayne K. Chapman and Janet M. Manson, Pace UP, 1998, pp. 125-43.

Lipson, E. *Europe in the Nineteenth Century: An Outline History Containing Eight Portraits and Four Maps.* Black, 1916. MASC

"Londonist." By M@. londonist.com/london/books-and-poetry/mapped-all-virginia-woolf-s-novels. 1-10. Accessed 22 June 2017..

Lowe, Gill. "'Penning and Pinning': Vita, Virginia, and *Orlando.*" *Virginia Woolf and the World of Books: The Centenary of the Hogarth Press: Selected Papers from the Twenty-Seventh Annual International Conference on Virginia Woolf,* edited by Nicola Wilson and Claire Battershill. Clemson UP, 2018, pp. 289-295.

Luke, Sir Harry and Edward Keith-Roach, editors. *The Handbook of Palestine and Trans-Jordan.* 3rd ed. Macmillan, 1934. MASC.

Marcus, Jane. "Britannia Rules *The Waves.*" *Virginia Woolf: A Collection of*

Critical Essays, edited by Margaret Homans, Prentice Hall, 1993, pp. 227-48.

———. "Registering Objections: Grounding Feminist Alibis." In Higonnet, pp. 171-93.

———. "Taking the Bull by the Udders: Sexual Difference in Virginia Woolf—A Conspiracy Theory."*Virginia Woolf and the Languages of Patriarchy,* Indiana UP, 1987, pp. 136-62.

Markham, Beryl. *West with the Night.* 1942. North Point, 1983.

Massey, Doreen. *Space, Place, and Gender.* U of Minnesota P, 1994.

Matless, David. "The Uses of Cartographic Literacy: Mapping, Survey and Citizenship in Twentieth-Century Britain." In Cosgrove, pp. 193-212.

Monmonier, Mark. *How to Lie with Maps.* U of Chicago P, 1991.

Novillo-Corvalán, Patricia. "Empire and Commerce in Latin America: Historicizing Woolf's *The Voyage Out.*" *Woolf Studies Annual,* vol. 23, 2017, pp. 33-62.

Pearson, Nels. "Woolf's Spatial Aesthetics and Postcolonial Critique." *A Companion to Virginia Woolf,* edited by Jessica Berman. John Wiley & Sons, 2016, pp. 427-440.

Perry, R. B. and C. R. Perkins. *World Mapping Today.* Butterworths, 1987.

Phillips, Kathy J. *Virginia Woolf Against Empire.* U of Tennessee P, 1994.

Polo, Marco. *The Travels of Marco Polo the Venetian.* Introduction by John Masefield. J. M. Dent, 1926.

Radó, Sandor. *The Atlas of To-Day and To-Morrow.* Victor Gollancz, 1938. MASC.

Rose, Gillian. *Feminism and Geography: The Limits of Geographical Kno*wledge. U of Minnesota P, 1993.

Rosenbaum, S. P., editor and transcriber. *Virginia Woolf; Women & Fiction; the manuscript version of* A Room of One's Own. Shakespeare Head P, 1992.

Rosner, Victoria. "Virginia Woolf and Monk's House." *The Edinburgh Companion to Virginia Woolf and the Arts,* edited by Maggie Humm, Edinburgh UP, 2010, pp. 181-194.

Ryan, Derek and Stella Bolaki, editors. *Contradictory Woolf: Selected Papers from the Twenty-First Annual International Conference on Virginia Woolf.* Clemson UP Digital Press, 2012.

Savoie, Tracy. "Caged Tiger: Louis as Colonial Subject in Virginia Woolf's *The Waves.*" *Virginia Woolf: Art, Education, and Internationalism: Selected Papers from the Seventeenth Annual Conference on Virginia Woolf,* edited by Diana Royer and Madelyn Detloff, Clemson U Digital P, 2008, pp. 16-20.

Silver, Brenda R. *Virginia Woolf's Reading Notebooks.* Princeton UP, 1983.

Simpson, Kathryn. "To 'Write About Mrs Lindbergh': Woolf, Flight, and Anne Morrow Lindbergh's *North to the Orient.*" *Virginia Woolf and The World of Books: The Centenary of the Hogarth Press: Selected Papers from the Twenty-Seventh Annual International Conference on Virginia Woolf,* edited by Nicola Wilson and Claire Battershill, Clemson UP, 2018, pp. 268-274.

Snaith, Anna. *Virginia Woolf: Public and Private Negotiations*. St. Martin's P, 2000.

Sparks, Elisa Kay. "Leonard and Virginia's London Library: Mapping London's Tides, Streams and Statues." *Virginia Woolf's Bloomsbury: Volume 1 Aesthetic Theory and Literary Practice*, edited by Gina Potts and Lisa Shahriari, Palgrave Macmillan, 2010, pp. 64-74.

Squier, Susan M. *Virginia Woolf and London: The Sexual Politics of the City*. U of North Carolina P, 1985.

Stape, John ed. *Virginia Woolf: Interviews and Recollections*. U of Iowa P, 1995.

Tally, Robert T. Jr., editor. "Introduction: Mapping Narratives." *Literary Cartographies: Spatiality, Representation, and Narrative*. Palgrave Macmillan, pp. 1-12.

———. *Spatiality*. Routledge, 2013.

Thacker, Andrew. "Woolf and Geography." *A Companion to Virginia Woolf*, edited by Jessica Berman, John Wiley & Sons, 2016, pp. 411-425.

Thrower, Norman J. W. *Maps and Man: An Examination of Cartography in Relation to Culture and Civilization*. Prentice-Hall, 1972.

Turchi, Peter. *Maps of the Imagination: The Writer as Cartographer*. Trinity UP, 2004.

Vlasopolos, Anca. "Staking Claims for No Territory: The Sea as Woman's Space." In Higonnet, pp. 72-88.

Watson, Frederic, et al. *A New & Complete Geographical Dictionary: Containing a Full and Accurate Description of the Several Parts of the Known World, as Divided into Continents, Islands, Oceans, Seas, Rivers, Lakes, Etc.* G. Kearsly, 1773. MASC.

Wells, H. G. *A Short History of the World*. Labour Publishing, 1924. MASC.

Whitaker, Joseph. *An Almanack for the Year of Our Lord . . .* by Joseph Whitaker. L. Whitaker, 1869- . 1936, 1938. MASC.

Wilford, John Noble. *The Mapmakers*. Alfred A. Knopf, 2000.

Woolf, Leonard. *Downhill all the Way: An Autobiography of the Years 1919 to 1939*. Harcourt Brace Jovanovich, 1967.

———. *The Journey Not the Arrival Matters: An Autobiography of the Years 1939 to 1969*. Harcourt Brace Jovanovich, 1969.

Woolf, Virginia. *Between the Acts*. 1941. Harcourt Brace Jovanovich, 1969.

———. *The Complete Shorter Fiction of Virginia Woolf*. New Edition. Edited by Susan Dick. Harcourt Brace Jovanovich, 1989.

———. *The Diary of Virginia Woolf*, Edited by Anne Olivier Bell, Harcourt Brace Jovanovich, 1977-1984. 5 vols.

———-. *The Essays of Virginia Woolf.* vol. 6. Edited by Stuart N. Clarke, Hogarth, 2011.
———. *Jacob's Room.* 1922. Harcourt Brace Jovanovich, 1950.
———. *The Letters of Virginia Woolf.* Edited by Nigel Nicolson and Joanne Trautmann. Harcourt Brace Jovanovich, 1975-1980.
———. *Moments of Being,* 2d edition, Edited by Jeanne Schulkind, Harcourt Brace Jovanovich, 1985. 6 vols.
———. *Mrs. Dalloway.* 1925. Harcourt Brace Jovanovich, 1953.
———. *Night and Day.* 1919. Harcourt Brace Jovanovich, 1948.
———. *Orlando: A Biography.* 1928. Harcourt Brace Jovanovich, 1956.
———. *A Passionate Apprentice: The Early Journals 1897-1909 of Virginia Woolf.* Edited by Mitchell A. Leaska, Harcourt Brace Jovanovich, 1990.
———. *Three Guineas.* 1938. Harcourt, Brace & World, 1966.
———. *To the Lighthouse.* 1927. Harcourt, Brace & World, 1981.
———. *The Voyage Out.* 1915. Harcourt, Brace & World, 1948.
———. *The Waves.* 1931. Harcourt Brace Jovanovich, 1959.
———. *The Years.* 1937. Harcourt Brace & World, 1965.
Wurtz, James F. "'I have had my vision': Empire and the Aesthetic in Woolf's *To The Lighthouse.*" *Woolf Studies Annual*, vol. 16, 2010, pp. 95-110.
Z., Y. *From Moscow to Samarkand.* Hogarth, 1934. MASC.

Guide to Library Special Collections

This list reflects updates or changes received by the end of 2018. Readers are advised to check an institution's website for the most current information. Suggestions for additions to this list are welcome.

Name of Collection: The Beinecke Rare Book and Manuscript Library

Contact: Timothy Young, Curator of Modern Books and Manuscripts
Nancy Kuhl, Curator of American Literature

Address: Yale University Library
P.O. Box 208240
New Haven, CT 06520-8240

URL: http://beinecke.library.yale.edu/

Access Requirements: Registration required at first visit.

Holdings Relevant To Woolf: General Collection includes autograph manuscript of "Notes on Oliver Goldsmith." Comments on Edward Gibbon, William Beckford Collection. Letters from Virginia Woolf in the Bryher Papers, the Louise Morgan and Otto Theis Papers, the Rebecca West Papers, the James Lees-Milne Papers, and the Mary Smyth Hunter correspondence. Related material: 41 letters from Vita Sackville-West to Violet Trefusis; files relating to Robert Manson Myers's *From Beowulf to Virginia Woolf* in the Edmond Pauker Papers.

Yale Collection of American Literature includes typewritten manuscripts of "The Art of Walter Sickert," "Augustine Birrell," "Aurora Leigh," "How Should One Read a Book?" "Letter to a Young Poet," "The Novels of Turgenev," "Street Haunting." Dial/Scofield Thayer Papers: manuscripts of "The Lives of the Obscure," "Miss Ormerod," and "Mrs. Dalloway in Bond Street." Letters from Virginia Woolf in the William Rose Benet Papers, the Benet Family Correspondence, Henry Seidel Canby Papers, the Seward Collins Papers, the Dial/Scofield Thayer Papers, and the *Yale Review* archive. Material relating to translations of Woolf in the Thornton Wilder papers. Related material: Clive Bell, "Virginia Woolf" (Dial/Scofield Thayer Papers); 43 letters from Leonard Woolf to Helen McAfee (*Yale Review*); 11 letters from Leonard Woolf to Gertrude Stein.

Name of Collection: The Henry W. and Albert A. Berg Collection of English and American Literature

Contact: Carolyn Vega, Curator

Address: The New York Public Library
Stephen A. Schwarzman Building
476 Fifth Avenue, Room 320
New York, NY 10018

Telephone: 212-930-0815
Email: carolynvega@nypl.org; berg@nypl.org
URL: https://www.nypl.org/locations/divisions/berg-collection-english-and-american-literature

Hours: Tue.-Sat. 10 am-5:45 pm
Closed Sun., Mon. and legal holidays

Access Requirements: A New York Public Library card and current government-issued photo identification are required to complete registration. If possible, please contact the division in advance to schedule your research visit.

Holdings Relevant to Woolf: The Virginia Woolf collection of papers (Berg Coll MSS Woolf) includes the manuscripts and/or typescripts of all of Woolf's novels except *Orlando*, including: *Between the Acts, Flush, Jacob's Room, Mrs. Dalloway* (notes and fragments), *Night and Day, To the Lighthouse, The Voyage Out, The Waves, The Years*; 12 notebooks of articles, essays, fiction and reviews, 1924–1940; 36 volumes of diaries; 26 volumes of reading notes; and correspondence with Vanessa Bell, Violet Dickinson, Shuhua Ling, Ethel Smyth, Vita Sackville-West and others. The Berg

GUIDE TO SPECIAL LIBRARY COLLECTIONS 139

also holds related collections of Vita Sackville-West, Leslie Stephen, and others.

Finding aid for the Virginia Woolf collection of papers: http://archives.nypl.org/brg/19159
List of all finding aids in the Berg Collection: http://archives.nypl.org/brg

Name of Collection: The British Library Manuscript Collections

Contact: Manuscripts and Maps Reference Team

Address: 96 Euston Road
London NW1 2DB
England

Telephone: 0207-412-7513
Fax: 0207-412-7745
Email: mss@bl.uk

Hours: Mon. 10 am-5 pm; Tues.-Sat.: 9:30 am-5 pm

Access Requirements: British Library Reader Pass (signed I.D. required and usually proof of post-graduate academic status, or other demonstrable need to use the collections—see www.bl.uk). In addition, access to most literary autograph material only available with letter of recommendation.

Restrictions: Paper Copies, Microfilms, and Photography of selected items available upon receipt of written authorization for photo duplication from the copyright holder.

Holdings Relevant To Woolf: Diaries 1930–1931 (microfilm); *Mrs. Dalloway* and other writings (1923–1925) three volumes (Add MS 51044-51046); letter from Leonard Woolf to H. G. Wells (1941) (Add MS 52553); two letters from Virginia Woolf and three letters from Leonard Woolf to John Lehmann (1941) (Add MS 56234); letters from Virginia Woolf (1923-1927) and one written on behalf of Leonard Woolf to S. S. Koteliansky (1946) (Add MS 48974); notebook of Virginia Stephen (1906–1909) (Add MS 61837); Stephen family papers (Add MS 88954); travel and literary notebook of Virginia Woolf (Add MS 61837); A sketch of the past revised ts (1940) (Add MS 61973); letters from Virginia Woolf in the correspondence files of Lytton and James Strachey (Add MS 60655-60734); letter from Virginia Woolf to Mildred Massingberd (Add MS 61891); letter from Virginia Woolf to Harriet Shaw Weaver(1917) (Add MS 57353); (in the same volume as the letter on behalf of Leonard); letter from Virginia Woolf to Frances Cornford (1929) (Add MS 58422); letter from Virginia Woolf to Ernest Rhys (1930) (Egerton MS 3248); correspondence of Virginia Woolf in the Society of Authors archive (1934–1937) (Add MS 63206-63463); letter and postcard from Virginia Woolf to Bernard Shaw (1940) (Add MS 50522); three letters (suicide notes) from Virginia Woolf (1941) (Add MS 57947). "Hyde Park Gate News" 1891–1892, 1895 (Add. MSS 70725, 70726). Letters of Virginia and Leonard Woolf to Lady Aberconway, 1927–1941 (Add MS 70775). List related to a fund for Desmond MacCarthy, annotated by Virginia Woolf, 1927 (Add MS 70776). Letters from Virginia Woolf to Macmillan Co. 1903, 1908 (Add MS 54786-56035). Letters from Virginia Woolf to P. Strachey, 1935-1937 (Add MS 81956). Letter to Marie Stopes from Adeline Virginia Woolf, 1941 (Add MS 58495). Collection of RPs ("reserved photocopies"–copies of manuscripts exported, some subject to restrictions).

Name of Collection: Harry Ransom Center

Contact: Head, Research Services

Address: Harry Ransom Center
The University of Texas at Austin
P.O. Box 7219
Austin, TX 78713-7219

Telephone: 512-471-9119
Fax: 512-471-2899
Email: reference@hrc.utexas.edu

Hours: See web site for most current information: www.hrc.utexas.edu

Access Requirements:	Completed online research application; current photo identification.
Holdings Relevant To Woolf:	The manuscript collection includes the typed manuscript with autograph revisions of *Kew Gardens*, and the typed manuscript and autograph revisions of "Thoughts on Peace in an Air Raid." The Center holds 571 of Woolf's letters, including correspondence to Elizabeth Bowen, Lady Ottoline Morrell, Mary Hutchinson, William Plomer, Hugh Walpole and others. Further mss. relating to Virginia Woolf include letters to her from T. S. Eliot and reviews of her work. A substantial collection of the first British and American editions of Woolf's published works, as well as 130 volumes from Leonard and Virginia Woolf's library and a collection of books published by the Hogarth Press, is also housed.

An art collection holds a landscape painting of Virginia's garden and a series of Cockney cartoons in a sketch book, signed "V.W." The center also has extensive holdings of materials related to Leonard Woolf, Ottoline Morrell, Mary Hutchinson, Lytton Strachey, Dora Carrington, E. M. Forster, Clive Bell, Roger Fry, Vanessa Bell, Bertrand Russell, Elizabeth Bowen, William Plomer, Stephen Spender and Hugh Walpole. |
Name of Collection:	Houghton Library (Monk's House Photograph Albums)
Contact:	Houghton Public Services
Address:	Harvard Yard Cambridge, MA 02138
Telephone: Fax: Email: URL:	617-495-2440 617-495-1376 houghton_library@harvard.edu http://hcl.harvard.edu/libraries/houghton/
Hours:	Mon, Fri, Sat 9-5 Tue-Thu 9-7

Access Requirements: http://hcl.harvard.edu/info/special_collections/index.cfm

The Monk's House photographs are restricted due to fragility. Users should consult the digital surrogates linked from the finding aids below. Access to originals requires permission from the curator of the Harvard Theatre Collection.

Holdings Relevant To Woolf: Virginia Woolf Monk's House photograph album, MH-1
Virginia Woolf Monk's House photograph album, MH-2
Virginia Woolf Monk's House photograph album, MH-3
Virginia Woolf Monk's House photograph album, MH-4
Virginia Woolf Monk's House photograph album, MH-5
Virginia Woolf Monk's House photograph album, MH-6
Virginia Woolf Monk's House photographs

Users can also page through the albums by following the links on this website (http://press.pace.edu/woolf-studies-annual-wsa/)

Name of Collection: The Lilly Library

Contact: Joel Silver, Director and Curator of Early Books and Manuscripts
Erika Dowell, Associate Director and Curator of Modern Books and Manuscripts

Address: The Lilly Library, Indiana University
1200 East Seventh Street
Bloomington, IN 47405-5500

Telephone: 812-855-2452
Fax: 812-855-3143
Email: liblilly@indiana.edu, silverj@indiana.edu, edowell@indiana.edu
URL https://iub.aeon.atlas-sys.com/ (for registration and requests)

GUIDE TO SPECIAL LIBRARY COLLECTIONS 143

Hours: Mon.-Thurs. 9 am-6 pm; Fri. 9 am-5pm; Sat. 9 am–1 pm; *Closed Sundays and Major Holiday*

Acess Requirements: Valid photo-identification; brief registration procedure.

Restrictions: Closed stacks; material use confined to reading room; wheelchair-accessible reading room, exhibitions, and restroom

Holdings Relevant To Woolf: Corrected page proofs for the American edition of *Mrs. Dalloway*; letters to Woolf from Desmond and Mary (Molly) MacCarthy; 77 letters (published in Letters) from Woolf to correspondents including Donald Clifford Brace, Robert Gathorne-Hardy, Barbara (Strachey) Halpern, Richard Arthur Warren Hughes, Desmond MacCarthy and Molly MacCarthy; "Preliminary Scheme for the formation of a Partnership between Mr Leonard Sidney Woolf and Mr John Lehmann to take over The Hogarth Press" (includes contract signed by Lehmann, Leonard Woolf, and Virginia Woolf and receipt for Lehmann's payment to Virginia Woolf to purchase Virginia Woolf's share in the Hogarth Press); photographs of Virginia Woolf, Leonard Woolf, Lytton Strachey, Strachey family, Roger Fry, and Vanessa Bell (Hannah Whitall Smith mss.); (Richard) Kennedy mss. (four hand-colored lithographs of Virginia Woolf: artist's proofs for RK's portfolio, VIRGINIA WOOLF: "AS I KNEW HER"; Sackville-West, V. mss. (10,529 items: includes the correspondence of Vita Sackville-West, and Harold Nicolson); MacCarthy mss. (ca. 10,000 items: papers of Desmond and Molly MacCarthy); correspondence between LW and Mary Gaither regarding publication of *A Checklist of the Hogarth Press* (1976, repr. 1986); Todd Avery, *Close and Affectionate Friends: Desmond and Molly MacCarthy and the Bloomsbury Group* (The Lilly Library/Indiana University Libraries, 1999).

Name of Collection: Literature & Rare Books, Special Collections, University of Maryland Libraries

Contact: Amber Kohl, Curator of Literature and Rare Books in Special Collections and University Archives

Address: University of Maryland
2208 Hornbake Library
College Park, MD 20742

Telephone: 310-405-9212
Email: askhornbake@umd.edu

Hours: Dates and hours of operation subject to change. Regular hours are Monday-Friday, 10 am to 5 pm. Extended hours are available on select days during the academic school year.
Email askhornbake@umd.edu before planning a research visit

Access Requirements: Photo ID.

Holdings Relevant To Woolf: Papers of Hope Mirrlees contain five autograph letters and postcards (1919–1928) from Virginia Woolf to Mirrlees. Also in the collection are 113 letters from T. S. Eliot to Mirrlees, and three letters from Lady Ottoline Morrell to Mirrlees. A finding aid is available at http://hdl.handle.net/1903.1/1536.

Name of Collection: Monks House Papers/Leonard Woolf Papers/Charleston Papers/Nicolson Papers

Contact: University of Sussex, Special Collections

Address: The Keep
Woollards Way
Brighton & Hove
BN1 9PB

Telephone: 01273 482349
Email: library.specialcoll@sussex.ac.uk
URL http://www.thekeep.info

GUIDE TO SPECIAL LIBRARY COLLECTIONS 145

Access Requirements: By appointment. Identification to be presented on arrival. Registration and material requests can be made through our website.

Restrictions: Photocopying strictly controlled.

Holdings Relevant To Woolf: The University of Sussex holds two large archives relating to Leonard and Virginia Woolf: The Monks House Papers, primarily correspondence and MSS of Virginia Woolf, including the three scrapbooks relating to *Three Guineas*, and Virginia Woolf's engagement diaries from 1930 to her death in 1941; and The Leonard Woolf Papers, primarily correspondence and other papers of Leonard Woolf. (Monks House Papers are available on microfilm in many research libraries.) The Charleston Papers consist in the main of letters written to or by Clive and Vanessa Bell and Duncan Grant which had accumulated in their home; the library houses Quentin Bell's photocopied set; letters from Roger Fry, Maynard Keynes, Lytton Strachey, Virginia Woolf, Vita Sackville-West, E. M. Forster, T. S. Eliot, Frances Partridge and others. The Maria Jackson letters comprise some 900 letters from Maria Jackson to Julia and Leslie Stephen. The Nicolson Papers complement these three Sussex archives relating to the Bloomsbury Group, and consist of Nigel Nicolson's correspondence relating to his editorial work as principal editor of the six-volume *Letters of Virginia Woolf*, published between 1975 and 1980.

The Bell Papers. A. O. Bell's correspondence relating to her editorial work on Virginia Woolf's diaries, a parallel collection to the Nicolson Papers. Collection level description may be accessed at www.archiveshub.ac.uk

Name of Collection: The Morgan Library & Museum

Contact: Reading Room

Address: 225 Madison Avenue
New York, NY 10016

Telephone: 212-590-0315

Email: readingroom@themorgan.org
URL: www.themorgan.org

Access Requirements: Admission to the Reading Room is by application and by appointment. See www.themorgan.org/research/reading.asp for application form.

Recent Acquisitions: Letter from Virginia Woolf, Wells, to Clive Bell, 1908 August 3? : autograph manuscript initialed. 1 item (6 pages) MA 22718. Gift from the estate of Nancy N. Brooker, 2018

Letter from Virginia Woolf, London, to Clive Bell, 1909 July? : autograph manuscript initialed. 1 item (2 pages) MA 22719. Gift from the estate of Nancy N. Brooker, 2018

Holdings Relevant To Woolf: Letter from Virginia Woolf, Cornwall, to Clive Bell, 1909? December 26: autograph manuscript initialed. 1 item (7 pages) MA 22720. Gift from the estate of Nancy N. Brooker, 2018

Letter from Virginia Woolf, London, to Clive Bell, 1909 December 31?: autograph manuscript initialed. 1 item (4 pages) MA 22721. Gift from the estate of Nancy N. Brooker, 2018

Letter from Virginia Woolf, London, to Clive Bell, 1910?: autograph manuscript. 1 item (2 pages) MA 22722. Gift from the estate of Nancy N. Brooker, 2018

Letter from Virginia Woolf, Beddingham, to Clive Bell, 1917 December 22? : autograph manuscript initialed. 1 item (3 pages) MA 22723. Gift from the estate of Nancy N. Brooker, 2018

Letter from Virginia Woolf, London, to Clive Bell, 1922 March 20?: autograph manuscript initialed. 1 item (2 pages) MA 22724. Gift from the estate of Nancy N. Brooker, 2018

Letter from Virginia Woolf, London, to Clive Bell, 1922 November 7? : autograph manuscript initialed. 1 item (1 page) MA 22725. Gift from the estate of Nancy N. Brooker, 2018

Letter from Virginia Woolf, London, to Clive Bell, 1923 February? : autograph manuscript initialed. 1 item (2 pages) MA 22726. Gift from the estate of

Nancy N. Brooker, 2018
Letter from Virginia Woolf, London, to Clive Bell, 1927 November? : autograph manuscript signed. 1 item (2 pages) MA 22727. Gift from the estate of Nancy N. Brooker, 2018
Postcard from Virginia Woolf, London, to Clive Bell, 1931 June 9: autograph manuscript initialed. 1 item (1 page) MA 22728. Gift from the estate of Nancy N. Brooker, 2018
Letter from Virginia Woolf, Rodmell, to Eric Duthie, 1927 October 2: typescript signed. 1 item (1 page). Saying that she is very interested in the series of biographies that he has described, but unfortunately she is too busy to write a volume for it. MA 22729. Gift from the estate of Nancy N. Brooker, 2018
Postcard from Virginia Woolf, London, to A.W. Brickett, 1937 February 17: autograph manuscript signed. 1 item (1 page). Thanking him for sending her a copy of the "Saturday review of literature." MA 22730. Gift from the estate of Nancy N. Brooker, 2018
Virginia Woolf reclining in an armchair [photograph]. Rodmell, England, between 1919 and 1941. Gelatin silver print. 6 15/16 x 4 13/16 inches (17.6 x 12.3 cm) MA 22731. Gift from the estate of Nancy N. Brooker, 2018

Virginia Woolf. Autograph manuscript notebook, 1931 Sept. 24. 1 item (52 p.) ; 265 x 208 mm. Contains drafts of "A Letter to a Young Poet," a brief letter to the press entitled "The Villa Jones" [ff. 3–5] and a monologue by a working-class woman [ff. 44–46]. MA 3333. Purchased on the Fellows Fund with the special assistance of Anne S. Dayton, Enid A. Haupt, Mrs. James H. Ripley, Mr. and Mrs. August H. Schilling, and John S. Thacher, 1979.

Virginia Woolf. Autograph letters signed (2) and typed letter signed, dated London [etc.], to E. McKnight Kauffer, 1931 Apr. 4–23, and undated. 3 items (4 p.). Concerning a drawing of her and a bibliography of her works. MA 1679. Purchased in 1959.

Vanessa Bell. 84 autograph letters, 3 typed letters, 7 postcards, and 3 telegrams. Most, but not all, are written by Vanessa Bell to John Maynard Keynes. Concerning Duncan Grant, Roger Fry, Clive Bell, the Bell children, Leonard and Virginia Woolf, Lytton Strachey, John Maynard and Lydia Lopokova Keynes, David Garnett, Ottoline Morrell, and others. MA 3448. Items in this collection are described in 97 individual records (MA 3448.1-97). Purchased on the Fellows Fund, special gift of the Gramercy Park Foundation (Mrs. Michael Tucker), 1980.

Letter from Virginia Woolf, London to R. W. Chapman, 1930 November 13. 1 item (1 p.). Concerning revisions to the criticism section of a bibliography of Jane Austen. Accompanied by carbon copy of a letter from Chapman to Woolf dated 1930 November 11. MA 8893. Purchased on the Drue Heinz Fund, 2017.

Name of Collection: Jane Marcus Collection

Contact: Mount Holyoke College Archives and Special Collections

Address: Mount Holyoke College
50 College Streeet
8 Dwight Hall
South Hadley MA 01075

Telephone: 413-538-3079
Fax: 413-538-3029
Email: archives@mtholyoke.edu

Hours: Monday-Friday; 9:30am-noon and 1-4:30pm

Access Requirements: Please contact the staff to make an appointment for your visit. Researchers complete a registration form upon arrival.

Restrictions: The Jane Marcus Collection was received in December 2016 and is currently being reviewed.

GUIDE TO SPECIAL LIBRARY COLLECTIONS 149

	Please contact the Archives and Special Collections staff for updated access information
Holdings Relevant To Woolf:	Jane Marcus, who died in May 2015, laid the groundwork for feminist studies to become a mode of inquiry within the academy and her work established Virginia Woolf as a major canonical writer. The collection includes several of Marcus's unpublished manuscripts, as well as her research files and correspondence.
Name of Collection:	1. Katherine Mansfield Papers 2. Arts Club of Chicago Papers
Contact:	Martha Briggs, Lloyd Lewis Curator of Modern Manuscripts Liesl Olson, Director, Scholl Center for American History and Culture
Address:	The Newberry Library, 60 West Walton Street, Chicago, IL, 60610
Telephone:	312-255-3554 (Briggs) 312-255-3665 (Olson)
Email:	briggsm@newberry.org olsonl@newberry.org
Hours:	Tuesday-Friday: 9-5 Saturday: 9-1
Access Requirements:	The Newberry's reading rooms are open to researchers who are at least 16 years old or juniors in high school. Before using the collections, all researchers must apply for and receive a reader's card. Issued in the Reference Center on the third floor, cards require a valid photo ID, proof of current home address, and a research interest that is supported by the Newberry's collections.
Holdings Relevant To Woolf:	The papers of the Arts Club of Chicago—since 1916, a private club and preeminent exhibitor of international art—contain material related to Bloomsbury artists and how they were received in Chicago. The papers of Katherine Mansfield con-

tain manuscript copies of some of Mansfield's most important work, and outgoing correspondence—the bulk to artist Dorothy Brett and Lady Ottoline Morrell. There are a few incoming miscellaneous letters, printed works, photographs and memorabilia.

Name of Collection: University of Reading Special Collections

Contact: Special Collections Service

Address: Special Collections Service
University of Reading
Redlands Road
Reading RG1 5EX

Telephone: 0118-378-8660
Fax: 0118-378-5632
Email: specialcollections@reading.ac.uk
URL: http://www.reading.ac.uk/special-collections/

Access Requirements: Prior appointment suggested to consult material. Permission required to consult or copy material in the Hogarth Press, Jonathan Cape, and Chatto & Windus collections from Random House:

Random House Group Archive & Library
1 Cole Street
Crown Park
Rushden
Northants. NN10 6RZ

Archive@penguinrandomhouse.co.uk

Holdings Relevant To Woolf: Hogarth Press (MS 2750): editorial and production correspondence relating to publications of the Press including Woolf's own titles. Production ledgers 1920s–1950s. Correspondence between Leonard Woolf and Stanley Unwin about progress with his collected edition of the works of Freud. Order books—e.g. lists of booksellers, book clubs and how many books they have ordered for a particular title. Newscuttings—press clippings of advertisements for Hogarth Press books including Virginia Woolf publications. Correspondence files regarding translation rights of Virginia Woolf's publications, 1924-1983 (MS 2750/C).

Chatto & Windus (CW): small number of letters 1915-1925; 1929-1931. Various letters and notes by Leonard Woolf; outgoing letters to Leonard Woolf: 22 November 1927 (CW A/119); outgoing letters to Virginia Woolf: 29 January 1936 (CW A/172), 22 December 1931 (CW A/135), 31 December 1931 (CW A/135), 15 December 1920 (CW A/100), 20 December 1920 (CW A/100).

George Bell & Sons (MS 1640): 5 letters from Leonard Woolf 1930-1966.

Routledge (RKP): Reader's report by Leonard Woolf on George Padmore's "Britannia rules the blacks" (1935); "How Britain rules Africa." 1 letter from Leonard Woolf (June 1941) from Miscellaneous publishing correspondence 1941-1942 Wi-Wy RKP 174/15. Draft introduction by Leonard Woolf to *Letters on India* by Mulk Raj (1942) and 1 letter to Leonard Woolf from Mulk Raj Anand 1942-1943 RKP 178/3. Correspondence concerning the publication of *The War for Peace* by Leonard Woolf, 1939-1940 RKP 160/5. 1 letter from Virginia Woolf declining an invitation from Routledge to write a biography of Margaret Bondfield, 25 May 1940 RKP 160/5.

Megroz (MS 1979/68): 2 letters from Leonard Woolf, 1926.

Allen & Unwin (MS 3282): Correspondence with Leonard Woolf c.1914-1918 (re. his book *International Government*), 1923-1924; 1939-1940; 1943; 1946; 1950-1951; 1953; 1965 (concerning ill-founded rumors about the Hogarth Press); 1967 (concerning a reprint of *Empire and Commerce in Africa*).

Jonathan Cape (MS 2446): All correspondence from file JC A43. Correspondence between Jonathan Cape and Virginia Woolf and Cape and A. C. Gissing concerning Virginia Woolf's introduction to George Gissing's *Ionian Sea* to which A. C.

Gissing objects. 1 postcard (1935), 1 letter (1933), 2 letters (1932) from Virginia Woolf. 1 letter (1932) from Virginia Woolf declining to write an introduction to Jane Austen's *Northanger Abbey*. 4 letters (1931) from Virginia Woolf declining to write an introduction to one of Miss Thackeray's books.

Letters from Vanessa Bell: 1 letter from Bell CW 152/2; 1 letter from Bell CW 171/10; 2 letters from Bell CW 578/1; 1 letter from Bell CW 59/9; 1 letter from Bell (1936) CW 61/10. Artwork by Vanessa Bell for various Virginia Woolf titles.

Artwork by Angelica Garnett, Philippa Bramson and others for various books in the Chatto & Windus archive.

Name of Collection: Frances Hooper Collection of Virginia Woolf Books and Manuscripts.
Elizabeth Power Richardson Bloomsbury Iconography Collection.

Contact: Karen V. Kukil, Associate Curator of Special Collections.

Address: Mortimer Rare Book Collection
Young Library
4 Tyler Drive
Northampton, MA 01063

Telephone: 413-585-2908
Email: kkukil@smith.edu
URL: www.smith.edu/libraries/libs/specialcollections

Hours: Mon.-Fri. 10 am-5 pm

Access Requirements: Appointment to be made with the Curator.

Holdings Relevant To Woolf: The Hooper Collection emphasizes Woolf as an essayist but also includes many Hogarth Press first editions, limited editions of Woolf's works, and translations. The collection includes page proofs of *Orlando*, *To the Lighthouse*, and *The Common Reader*, corrected by Woolf for the first American editions, a proof copy of *The Waves* that Woolf inscribed to Hugh Walpole, and the proof copies of *The Years* and of *Flush*. The Collection also has one of the deluxe editions of *Orlando* that was printed on green paper. Other items include twenty-two pages of reading notes from 1926, three pages of notes on D. H. Lawrence's *Sons and Lovers*, thirty-three pages of notes for Roger Fry, a six-page ms. "As to criticism," a five-page ms. of "The Searchlight," and a fourteen-page ms. of "The Patron and The Crocus." The Hooper Collection also owns 140 letters between Woolf and Lytton Strachey as well as other correspondence, including a 13 February [1921] letter to Katherine Mansfield and ten letters to Mela and Robert Spira.

The Richardson Collection is a working collection of books and materials used by Richardson in preparing her *Bloomsbury Iconography*. It includes Leslie Stephen's photograph album, ninety-eight original exhibition catalogs dating back to 1929, clippings and photocopies of such items as reviews of early Woolf works, and Bloomsbury material from *British Vogue* of the 1920s. The Collection also has three preliminary pencil drawings by Vanessa *Bell for Flush*.

The Mortimer Rare Book Collection also owns Woolf's 1916 Italian ms. notebook and her corrected typescripts of "Reviewing" and "The Searchlight." In addition, there is a 1923 photograph of Woolf at Garsington. Original cover designs for Hogarth Press publications include *The Common Reader*, *On Being Ill*, and *Duncan Grant*. The Mortimer Rare Book Room also has a Sylvia Plath collection that includes eight of Woolf's books from Plath's library, several of which are underlined and annotated, as well as Plath's notes from her undergraduate English 211 class at Smith (1951-1952) in which she studied *To the Lighthouse*. The collection also includes Woolf's 26 February 1939 letter to Vita Sackville-West, a 1931 bronze bust of Virginia Woolf by Stephen Tomlin, a 1923 Hogarth Press edition of T. S. Eliot's *The Waste Land*, a 1919

Hogarth Press edition of *Paris* by Hope Mirrlees and first editions of Vita Sackville-West and Katherine Mansfield publications. Additional Bloomsbury items include *Original Woodcuts* (Omega Workshops, 1918), Vanessa Bell's original woodcut for the cover of *Monday or Tuesday* (1921), and exhibition catalogs for *Manet and the Post-Impressionists* (Grafton Galleries, 1911), *Friday Club Members* (Mansard Gallery, 1921) *Paintings and Drawings* by Vanessa Bell (Independent Gallery, 1922). Additional photographs include the Mary L. S. Bennett (née Fisher) Family Photographs. A recent gift of the Henrietta Worth Bingham Papers (1905-1968) includes her correspondence with Stephen Tomlin and John Houseman, photographs, ephemera, books and research files. Online exhibitions are available on the Mortimer Rare Book Room's website.

The Mortimer Rare Book Collection continues to acquire through gift and purchase first editions of Virginia Woolf titles in their original dust jackets of To the Lighthouse (Hogarth Press) and American editions of *The Voyage Out, Night and Day*, and *Mrs. Dalloway*.

Name of Collection: Woolf/Hogarth Press/Bloomsbury

Contact: Lisa J. Sherlock

Address: Victoria University Library
71 Queens Park Crescent E.
Toronto M5S 1K7
Ontario Canada

Email: victoria.library@utoronto.ca
URL: http://library.vicu.utoronto.ca/special/bloomsbury.htm

Hours: Mon.-Fri. 9 am-5 pm

Access Requirements: Prior notification; identification.

Restrictions: Limited photocopying.

Holdings Relevant
To Woolf: This collection, the most comprehensive of its kind

with nearly 5,700 items, contains all the work of Virginia and Leonard Woolf in various editions, issues, variants and translations; all the books hand-printed by Leonard and Virginia Woolf at the Hogarth Press, including many variant issues and bindings, association copies and page proofs; a nearly comprehensive collection of Hogarth Press machine printed books to 1946 (the year Leonard Woolf and the Press joined Chatto & Windus) including presentation copies, signed limited editions, page proofs, variants as well as substantial amounts of ephemera, such as the *Catalogue of Publications* to 1939 with annotations by Leonard Woolf. The collection is also very strong in Bloomsbury Art and Artists, especially the decorative arts, including important examples of Omega Workshops publications and exhibition catalogues. Materials include the catalogue of the second post-impressionist exhibition, 1912; catalogues relating to Vanessa Bell and Duncan Grant exhibitions; bronze medal of Virginia Woolf by Marta Firlet; oil on canvas portrait of Amaryllis Garnett by Vanessa Bell (c.1958); Portrait sketch of Leonard Woolf by Vanessa Bell; portrait of Leonard Woolf by Duncan Grant; Duncan Grant and Vanessa Bell designed Clarice Cliff dinner plates; original Vanessa Bell and Duncan Grant sketches and designs for dust jackets, novels, and other special projects; Duncan Grant charcoal portrait of Virginia Woolf (1968); Quentin Bell set of five pottery plates based on the novels of Virginia Woolf (ca. 1979); Quentin Bell pottery figurine in aid of Charleston (ca. 1980); a selection of other pottery by Quentin Bell; bronze busts of Lytton Strachey and Virginia Woolf by Stephen Tomlin (1901-1937); as well as the Marcel Gimond bust of Vanessa Bell and the Tomlin bust of Henrietta Bingham. Book hand bound by Virginia Woolf. Wooden plaque from the Hogarth Press at 24 Tavistock. Examples of programmes, posters, and handbills relating to productions of plays, movies, and dance productions with content relating to Bloomsbury group members. Original correspondence and mss. material includes that by Vanessa Bell; Leonard Woolf; Ritchie family re:

Anne Thackeray Ritchie/Stephen family; Duncan Grant; Quentin Bell; S. P. Rosenbaum mss. Letters from E. M. Forster, Bertrand Russell, James Strachey, Raymond Mortimer, David Garnett, Nigel Nicolson and others in the Bloomsbury Circle; as well as biographers, scholars and bibliographers such as Joanne Trautmann, Carolyn Heilbrun, J. Howard Woolmer, Leon Edel, Leila Luedeking, P. N. Furbank, Noel Annan and others. Large Ephemera Collection includes items revealing Virginia Woolf's effect on popular culture.

Name of Collection: Library of Leonard and Virginia Woolf (Washington State University)

Contact: Trevor James Bond
Head, Manuscripts, Archives, and Special Collections

Address: Washington State University Libraries
Pullman, WA 99164-5610

Email: tjbond@wsu.edu
URL: www.wsulibs.wsu.edu/holland/masc/masc.htm

Hours: Mon.-Fri. 8:30 am-4:30 pm

Access Requirements: Letter stating nature of research preferred; student or other identification.

Restrictions: Materials must be used in the MASC area under supervision. Photocopying or photographing is permitted only when it will not harm the materials and is permitted by copyright.

Recent Aquisitions: Correspondence to Clive and Vanessa Bell (approximately 30 items), with most items addressed to Clive. Correspondents include Stephen Tallant, Eric MacLagan, John Pollock, H. J. Norton, Lyn Irvine (including one letter mentioning Mrs. Raven Hill), Sir George Grahame, Karen Costelloe, John Alford, Ivor Churchill, the Earl of Sandwich, George Lansbury, Clifford Sharp, F. H. S. Shepherd, Gilbert Seldes, Lord Evan Tredegar, C. E. Stuart, Max Eastman, E. Hilton Young, Col. Heward Bell.

GUIDE TO SPECIAL LIBRARY COLLECTIONS 157

Holdings Relevant To Woolf: WSU has the Woolfs' basic working library including many works which belonged to Woolf's father, Sir Leslie Stephen, and other family members. Over 800 titles came from their Sussex home, Monks House, including some works bought at auction soon after Leonard Woolf died in 1969. Later additions include: 1,875 titles from his house in Victoria Square, London; 400 titles from his nephew Cecil Woolf; and over 60 titles from Quentin and Anne Olivier Bell. WSU has been actively collecting: all works in all editions by Virginia Woolf; all titles by Leonard Woolf; dust jackets; works published by the Woolfs at the Hogarth Press through 1946; books by their friends and associates, especially those by Bloomsbury authors and about Bloomsbury artists; relevant correspondence and original works of art. Original artwork by Vanessa Bell; scattered letters by Vanessa Bell, E. M. Forster, Roger Fry, Leslie Stephen, Lytton Strachey, and Leonard Woolf. Original artwork by Richard Kennedy for illustrations in his book *A Boy at the Hogarth Press*; scattered letters by Roger Fry, Leslie Stephen, Ethel Smyth, and Leonard Woolf. Virginia Woolf's initialed copy of *Cornishiana*; Leonard Woolf's annotated copy of *An Anatomy of Poetry* by A. Williams-Ellis; Leslie Stephen's copy of *Lapsus Calami and Other Verses*, inscribed by James Kenneth Stephen. Several letters from Virginia Woolf, including two written in 1939 to Ronald Heffer, and a letter to Edward McKnight Kauffer. New in the Hogarth Press Collection are a copy of E. M. Forster's Anonymity, an Enquiry, bound in cream paper boards, and what Woolmer calls the third label state of Forster's *The Story of the Siren*. The Library of Leonard and Virginia Woolf is once again shelved separately so that scholars visiting Pullman may see the collection apart from the other rare book collections.visiting Pullman may see the collection apart from the other rare book collections.

Name of Collection: Yale Center for British Art

Contact: Elisabeth Fairman, Senior Curator of Rare Books and Manuscripts

Address: 1080 Chapel Street
P.O. Box 208280
New Haven, CT 06520-8280

Telephone: elisabeth.fairman@yale.edu
Fax: 203-432-2814
Email: 203-432-2814
URL: https://britishart.yale.edu/collections

Hours: Tue.-Fri. 10 am-4:30 pm

Access Requirements: Patron registration required to visit Study Room. Can provide images upon request but cannot grant permissions.

Holdings Relevant To Woolf: Rare Books & Mss Department: 94 letters from Vanessa Bell and Duncan Grant to Sir Kenneth Clark; 6 letters from Lytton Strachey (to Clive Bell, Siegfried Sassoon, et al.).
Prints & Drawings Department: 7 drawings by Vanessa Bell; 6 drawings by Duncan Grant; 16 drawings by Wyndham Lewis; 1 drawing by Frederick Etchells; 2 photographs by Julia Margaret Cameron.
Paintings Department: 3 paintings by Vanessa Bell, 7 paintings by Duncan Grant (including 2 portraits of Vanessa Bell); 4 paintings by Roger Fry.

Reviews

Orlando: A Biography. Suzanne Raitt and Ian Blyth, eds. (Cambridge UP, 2018) cxviii + 654 pp.

"Many friends have helped me in writing this book. Some are dead and so illustrious that I scarcely dare name them... Others are alive" (*O* 5). Thus Woolf begins *Orlando,* establishing the novel as a parody of the Victorian biography in a Preface that includes seemingly spurious acknowledgements of canonical writers, scholars, friends and associates. Paired with a (sketchy and faulty) Index, this would seem to establish the novel as an "escapade" (*D*3 131). However, as Suzanne Raitt and Ian Blyth demonstrate in this edition, the accreditations have a serious dimension too, for they are the first indications that *Orlando* is based on serious and detailed research. As this edition amply shows, *Orlando* is shaped by Woolf's skills as a historian, which Leena Kore-Schröder and Melba Cuddy-Keane first drew to our attention.

In their introduction, Raitt and Blyth note that "*Orlando* is one of her most ambitious and complex texts. In it, Virginia experiments with a new form for the novel; she tells a playful version of Vita [Sackville-West]'s life-story; she re-writes the history of the Sackville family; she re-imagines the genre of biography; she offers a detailed social history of England; she recreates some of the golden moments of British literature; and she sketches a detailed geographical history of the city of London" (*O* xxxvii). These layers are unpacked over the course of the Introduction and the Explanatory Notes (EN). The latter are extensive (akin to Anna Snaith's edition of *The Years,* and more detailed than Michael Herbert and Susan Sellers's edition of *The Waves* in the same series), presenting original research as well as extending insights from other editions. The notes on the history of the Sackville family history cement the case that Orlando in his early years is closely based on Thomas Sackville, First Earl of Dorset (1536-1608), whose portrait appeared on the dust jacket for the first edition (*O* 326, EN11:11), and that Woolf changes her ancestral model to match the passing years, later taking in the poet and patron Charles Sackville, the Sixth Earl (1636/7-1706) (*O* 390, EN 103:2/6), before correspondences are followed "more loosely" after Orlando's sex-change (*O* 434, EN 179:17). This edition also provides superb detail on the extent to which Woolf's descriptions of Orlando's home incorporate acute observations of the Sackville ancestral home at Knole, reflecting its evolving architecture, the layout of individual rooms, and details of the paintings, stained glass, and especially the arras which, along with its Ovidian theme, becomes a motif across the novel. The edition also shows how closely Orlando is modelled on Vita Sackville-West: the Introduction shows how the gestation of the novel was influenced by the vicissitudes of Woolf's relationship with Sackville-West, including changes of heart during the redrafting process, while the EN show how closely Sackville-West's works are woven into the fabric of Woolf's prose. The point is amply demonstrated with extensive quotations from Sackville-West's own works including, enchantingly, the lesser-known miniature book she wrote for Queen Mary's dolls' house, first displayed at the Empire Exhibition in Wembley in 1924 (*O* xliii-iv). Likewise, the Edition shows how Woolf uses direct and covert literary allusions to reflect the changes in English literature over the centuries, from Ariosto's *Orlando Furioso* and a wide range of Shakespearean texts at the start, through to a parody of the stream-of-consciousness technique in the present day. Again, these allusions are addressed in greater detail, with more extensive use of quotation and closer engagement with Woolf scholarship than in previous editions.

One critic of earlier volumes in the Cambridge Edition found fault with the extent to which minor details were explained (Stape 412), in line with the Cambridge policy of paying attention to "every character's name, shop name and place name, however passing" (*O* xxi). However, no EN in this volume seems gratuitous, for the smallest detail is ripe with potential significance: for example, the editors' explanations of locations within London and Kent show Woolf's attention to topographical detail; this edition pays particular attention to the "shifting patterns of everyday life" (*O* lxxxvi), showing Woolf's interest in the ways in which changing fashions in clothes, eating, transport, or lighting did indeed impact upon life as it was lived. Servants' names bear out Woolf's principle that the lives of ordinary people are important, as many of these share their names with past and contemporary employees of the Knole estate and the Woolf household. Even the formidable Nelly Boxall is mentioned more than once, albeit with her name misspelled.

This volume, like all those in the Cambridge Edition (with the exception of *Between the Acts*), uses the first UK edition as its copy text. In the case of *Orlando,* the rationale is that this was a "published version Woolf herself oversaw," incorporating later corrections than the first US trade edition, and is therefore "the closest we are likely to get to the novel Woolf 'intended' to publish" (*O* lxxxiv). Nonetheless, other editions are represented in the thorough Textual Apparatus and Textual Notes, and in the publication history set out in the Introduction (*O* lxi-lxxii). References to other editions are often enlightening, such as the observation that the first proof of the American edition has Orlando "attend the Queen at court. The Queen was at Whitehall," which, the editors suggest, explains to American readers that the royal court moved with the sovereign, rather than being based in a fixed place (*O* 341, EN 23:10).

Lest we are tempted by some of the Explanatory Notes to equate details in the novel too closely with elements of Sackville history (in the way that Mr. Ramsay, for example, is sometimes reduced to a cipher for Leslie Stephen), the

Introduction offers an important counter-balance by reminding us how Woolf in *Orlando,* as elsewhere, got at the truth by fictional means. She experimented with fiction to write and critique biography, as "readers were invited to speculate about the factual foundations of the text, while delighting in its mockery of the genre after which it was named" (*O* xlviii). Fantasy likewise helped Woolf manage highly dangerous truths, not least through the sex change which was "the image she needed to unleash her imagination and to allay her fears about 'writing the memories of one's own times during peoples lifetimes' [*D3* 157]" (*O* lv).

This volume will provide Woolf scholars, textual scholars, and students with rich resources for papers, articles and dissertation topics for years to come, by usefully presenting references to Woolf's other works, quotations from or citations of key critical interventions, and details of the sources of allusions, often supported by substantial quotations. *Orlando* is a complex novel that deserves painstaking editorial attention: this fine volume provides it admirably.

—Jane de Gay, *Leeds Trinity University*

Works Cited

Cuddy-Keane, Melba. "Virginia Woolf and the Varieties of Historicist Experience." *Virginia Woolf and the Essay,* edited by Beth Carole Rosenberg and Jeanne Dubino, Macmillan, 1997, pp. 59-77.

Kore-Schröder, Leena. "'Who's Afraid of Rosamond Merridew?': Reading Medieval History in 'The Journal of Mistress Joan Martyn.'" *Journal of the Short Story in English,* vol. 50, Spring 2008. https://journals.openedition.org/jsse/719. Accessed 5 November 2018.

Stape, J. H. "The Cambridge Woolf." *English Literature in Transition 1880-1920,* vol. 55, no. 3, 2012, pp. 409-18.

Woolf, Virginia. *The Diary of Virginia Woolf: Volume 3 1925-30,* edited by Anne Olivier Bell, assisted by Andrew McNeillie. Penguin, 1982.

———. *The Years,* edited by Anna Snaith. Cambridge UP, 2012.

———. *The Waves,* edited by Michael Herbert and Susan Sellers. Cambridge UP, 2011.

The Handbook to the Bloomsbury Group. Derek Ryan and Stephen Ross, eds. (Bloomsbury Academic, 2018) x + 315 pp.

Presented as "the most comprehensive available survey of contemporary scholarship on the Bloomsbury Group," this new anthology edited by Derek Ryan and Stephen Ross provides an intriguing sampling of some of the latest approaches in Woolf and associated studies. A platform for writing by new scholars bolstered by key essays from experienced scholars, it aims to place conversations about Bloomsbury in a wider intersectional social, political, and historical landscape. The collection is particularly attentive to a more global concept of modernism which opens up "hitherto ignored or marginalized figures, texts, and contexts" (8) and is, in structure as well as content, a lively and thought-provoking contribution to the field.

The book is organized around ten decentered rubrics which interpenetrate each other, each topic being explicated by two essays: one a general overview, the other a more tightly focused case study. Helpful in outlining previous critical perspectives, all of the overviews are notable for going beyond placid summary to include new insights or theoretical slants and for their use of archival or hitherto unexamined primary materials; the case studies raise provocative new issues while generously widening the scope of the Bloomsbury canon. The ten thematic threads—sexuality, the arts, Empire, feminism, philosophy, class, Jewishness, nature, politics, and war, in that (only seemingly arbitrary) order—create an intermeshed crisscrossing of topics which is in itself a theoretical statement about the inevitable necessity of interdisciplinary approaches. Running through the volume is a consistent thread of attention to the details of political contexts, not only those enlivening Bloomsbury at the time, but also those influencing critical assessments of its influence and importance ever since.

Beginning with Todd Avery's survey of the personal sexual choices among the members of the group and Jesse Wolfe's more detailed tracing of the influence of Edward Carpenter on E. M. Forster, the first chapter on "Bloomsbury and Sexuality" establishes initial connections between queerness and the artistic experiments of Post-Impressionism. These are picked up next in Maggie Humm's discussion of "relational aesthetics" in her masterful introduction to "Bloomsbury and the Arts," and then extended many sections later in Peter Adkins's fascinating attempt to link art theory and ecofeminism in a discussion of "queer nature" in Woolf and Sackville-West's writings. Connections between queer sexuality and the politics of race and Empire resurface in Anna Snaith's case study in "Bloomsbury and Empire," in Vicki Tromanhauser's rendering of the metaphors of meat, as well as in David Ayers's overview of "Bloomsbury and Politics."

Chapter Two, "Bloomsbury and the Arts," features Maggie Humm's brilliantly comprehensive overview, emphasizing the "relational aesthetics" by which the origins of artistic practices are examined in terms of "human relations and their social context" (46), a theme pursued throughout the entire volume. Also attentive to relational context, Mark Hussey's admirably systematic case study of the evolution and influence of Clive Bell's concept of "significant form" begins a discussion of the epistemological challenges to realism mounted by the aesthetics of the Bloomsbury Group which extends through Benjamin Hagen's remarkably clear and cogent overview of "Bloomsbury and Philosophy" and Peter Adkins's discussion of "Bloomsbury and Nature."

Widening the scope of social concerns, Chapter Three on "Bloomsbury and Empire" anticipates later sections on class and Jewishness. Sonita Sarker's introductory overview ranges widely across topics, including how the definition of Britishness is founded on racial/racist assumptions accepted by figures in the Bloomsbury Group, interrogating the many contradictions and hypocrisies which undercut its members' critiques of Empire. Anna Snaith's case study of Bunny Garnett's homoerotic connections to the radical Indian activist Madan Lal Dhingra, who assassinated Sir Curzon Wylie, adds welcome contingencies to the canonical account of the Dreadnought Hoax.

The fourth chapter on "Bloomsbury and Feminism" folds back to the previous concerns of "Bloomsbury and the Arts." Concentrating on conversations between women in the contemporaneous women's movement in Woolf's short fiction, and in Vanessa Bell's painting *A Conversation,* Lauren Elkin's overview essay carries on the volume's interest in "relational aesthetics" and significant form, as does Claire Battershill's case study on Bloomsbury as a site for feminist activism and the Hogarth Press as a platform for women's voices. Bell's painting reappears in several subsequent essays as well as on the cover of the volume, carrying one of many threads weaving the whole collection tightly together.

"Bloomsbury and Philosophy," Chapter Five, reaches back to the essays on the arts and feminism as well as forward to sections on Jewishness, Politics, and War. Hagen's corrective reading of Bloomsbury figures not as professional philosophers (excepting Bertrand Russell) but as thinkers asking philosophical questions casts a clarifying new light on accounts of G. E. Moore's influence, and is one of several essays in the volume to suggest new ways of and reasons for reading John Maynard Keynes more fully and closely. His discussion of the philosophical implications of Lytton Strachey's *Eminent Victorians,* Vanessa Bell's *A Conversation,* and Woolf's *To the Lighthouse* and *Roger Fry* recontextualizes these oft-studied works as part of a shared philosophical inquiry. In the same chapter, Laci Mattison's case study of "Bloomsbury, Mulk Raj Anand, and Henri Bergson" harkens back to the section on Empire while also anticipating several other essays in offering detailed, contextualized treatment of a figure on the margins of the Bloomsbury group both racially and geographically. Her exploration of parallels between Hinduism and the idea of *elan vital* involves helpful readings of several of Anand's works as well as adding new insight to how Bergsonian ideas are diffused in Virginia Woolf's thought.

Beginning with the section on "Bloomsbury and Class," the second half of the volume focuses on topics more social than aesthetic. Returning to issues of group identity and to an analysis of the politics of varying critical and class perspectives brought up in the Introduction, as well as to assessments of the contributions of the Omega Workshop and the Hogarth Press previously discussed in the sections on art and feminism, Kathryn Simpson's overview essay is an exemplary review of previous scholarship. Clara Jones's case study of cross-class encounters in Bloomsbury's rural precincts examines ephemeral village records and combs through sketches and letters published and unpublished to add engaging new detail to our understanding of daily life at Charleston farmhouse and Monk's House in Rodmell.

Returning to topics first broached in "Bloomsbury and Empire," Chapter Seven, on "Bloomsbury and Jewishness," refuses to excuse the persistent anti-Semitism by which most members of the Bloomsbury group defined their cultural identity as English, while also tracing possible modulations of its severity. Susan Wegener's overview catalogues the careless stereotypes employed by everyone from Vanessa Bell and Strachey to Virginia Woolf herself, calculating the effects of such casual cruelty on Leonard Woolf, suggesting that by the writing of *The Years*, Virginia had become more conscious of the moral effects of such prejudice. Steven Putzel's exhaustive case study of Keynes and Leonard Woolf's attitudes to the establishment of Israel offers a detailed look into how complicated Bloomsbury attitudes towards race could be, analyzing contradictory assessments of Keynes as an anti-Semitic Zionist and of Woolf as a Jew against extreme Zionism who was aware of the claims of Palestine.

The next section, Chapter Eight on "Bloomsbury and Nature," exhibits the progressively widening scope of the volume. As earlier mentioned, Adkins's overview essay, one of the most exciting and provocative in the collection, provides a complex nexus of associations among issues of art theory, philosophy, queer theory, and eco-feminism while offering new interpretive insights into Woolf's *To the Lighthouse* and Sackville-West's poem, *The Land*. Vicki Tromanhauser's case study of the "Aesthetics of Meat" in *The Years* dovetails nicely with Wegener's previous treatment of the novel; while continuing to expand the contextual relevance of queer viewpoints, her explication of carnivorous patriarchy anticipates concerns with politics and war taken up by the remaining essays.

One of the more contentious pieces in the collection, David Ayers's overview of "Bloomsbury and Politics" in Chapter Nine lays out an account of the changing climate of Woolf Studies from "economic to cultural leftism" (254). In light of the intersectionality of the rest of the volume, his tendency to downplay both queerness and feminism as mere fashions of identity politics seems rather incongruous. In the same chapter, Michaela Bronstein offers a thought-provoking look at the political intentions behind the Garnetts' Russian translations, how not only word choice, but also the selection of materials to translate and the crafting of accompanying prefaces helped create Bloomsbury's somewhat romanticized view of Russian literature.

The tenth chapter on "Bloomsbury and War," completes the volume's arc from the personal to the political. J. Ashley Foster's ambitious overview, an argument for an expanded concept of pacifism that incorporates a wide "variety of intersectional visions for peace" (277), traces Bloomsbury pro-peace projects from the First World War through the Spanish Civil War and World War Two. Returning to the aesthetic concerns of the opening chapters, she carries on the collection's emphasis on fugitive and archival sources by analyzing little known manuscripts documenting Roger Fry's volunteer work in France as well as Duncan Grant's recently uncovered designs for Spanish Civil War posters.

The last essay, Jane Goldman's meditation on the classical concept of *otium*, continues and extends Foster's argument for Bloomsbury's contribution to a pacifist aesthetics, examining the work of Virginia Woolf, Keynes, and Jewish novelist, editor, and publisher John Rodker in order to trace a developing suspicion of the concept of "peace" after the manipulated negotiations at Versailles. From her detailed textual analysis of Woolf's revisions of essays on Dorothy Wordsworth to her recovery of Rodker's little-known "phantasmagoric" prose piece, *Adolphe 1920*, Goldman provides a fitting coda to a collection whose elegantly complex unity is unusual among critical anthologies.

The volume would be improved by more illustrations; what few there are are small and rather low contrast, but it is easy enough to Google most of the visual references. It is unfortunate that the readership for this useful and topical marker of the current state of Bloomsbury scholarship will be confined to those who have access to university library systems that can afford to purchase it, given its present very high cost. The prospect of a paperback edition is eagerly anticipated.

—Elisa Kay Sparks, *Clemson University*, Emerita

Woolf's Ambiguities: Tonal Modernism, Narrative Strategy, Feminist Precursors. Molly Hite (Ithaca: Cornell UP, 2018) xvi + 186pp.

Woolf's experiments in narrative style—and especially her representations of human consciousness—have long fascinated modernist theorists. Dorrit Cohn's *Transparent Minds* (1978) and Ann Banfield's *Unspeakable Sentences* (1982), most notably, take a linguistic approach to these innovations. The ethicoaesthetic vision of the novels, in contrast, has only recently been the focus of book length studies, for instance in Lorraine Sim's *Virginia Woolf: The Patterns of Ordinary Experience*

(2010). Hence, the study under review is groundbreaking in that it closely attends both to Woolf's formal experiments and to how these illuminate her ethical praxis.

Hite's argument is two-fold: first, she makes a compelling case that Woolf's "tonal ambiguity" is the greatest innovation of her major modernist writing, and second, she posits that Woolf's relationship to her feminist precursors—in the form of her aversion to those suffrage and post-suffrage era feminists' fiction that "pled a cause"—has been overlooked, in part due to her own success in suppressing them in her role as a creator of the modernist literary canon.

In her first two chapters, Hite focuses on Woolf's tonal ambiguity in *Mrs. Dalloway*, *Jacob's Room*, *To the Lighthouse*, and *The Waves*. Her discussion of tonal ambiguity, which also appeared in an article titled "Tonal Cues and Uncertain Values: Affect and Ethics in *Mrs. Dalloway*" in *Narrative* in October 2010, is an invaluable contribution to Woolf studies and has the potential to shift how critics interpret key characters and scenes in Woolf's novels. Hite's meticulous study of drafts of Woolf's novels uncovers a deliberate "complicating, muting, or effacing" of tonal cues (on which more later), already few and far between, as she revises her work (ix). Moreover, Woolf's decisions to eliminate tonal cues represent a "deliberate strategy to blur or withhold grounds for authorially sanctioned opinions" (ix). In one of the most striking sections of the book, "What good is ethical uncertainty?" Hite rejects both contentions that this strategy is ethically unengaged or a "deliberately open exercise" (56). Rather, she maintains that affective and evaluative uncertainty have "far-reaching positive ethical value" because they "provoke[e] readers to notice and consider norms that might otherwise be taken for granted," "encourage engagement in readers," and represent the reality of our everyday interactions with other minds (57).

Hite defines "tone" as the quality of narrative voice that indicates a narrator's attitude toward a given subject, often made explicit in the form of overt "tonal cues." These cues function as signs guiding the reader about how she should feel about, or "take," certain characters and events in the novel. Thus, the quality of the writing that produces affective as well as intellectual responses from the reader is tone. These tonal cues are usually voiced by a third-person narrator, who functions as the dominant voice in the narrative. Hence, these cues are authoritative, taking on the valence of both the implied narrator's and the implied author's authority.

Women writing polemical fiction in the late nineteenth and early twentieth century used these authoritative cues to communicate their values and, if possible, to convert readers to their worldviews. In contrast, "[b]ecause Virginia Woolf carefully muted or perplexed tonal cues when revising the drafts of her novels," the question of how to take the major characters, and even the famous climax, is an open one (14). Hite builds her case for the characteristic tonal ambiguity of *Mrs. Dalloway* most compellingly by way of Septimus Smith. His tonal presentation veers between the "ludicrous and the profound" (27). He can at once be understood as a paranoid war veteran who is haunted by delusions of persecution and as a sacrificial victim who is practically hunted by other characters and institutions in the novel.

Hite's arguments about the tonal indeterminacy of *Jacob's Room*, *To the Lighthouse*, and especially *The Waves* have great explanatory power. Her claim that the near absence of tonal cues in *The Waves* makes it the "most revolutionary of all Woolf's textual experiments" is especially compelling (44). In the farewell dinner scene, Bernard and Rhoda praise Percival using hyperbole and the clichés of patriotic literature. Hite demonstrates that Woolf revised scenes such as this one to complicate or eliminate clear tonal cues, rendering unclear how the reader should "take" these scenes—is this hyperbole meant to be sincere, joking, satirical? Rather than read Woolf's "publicly voiced antipathy to imperialism" into passages that are tonally indeterminate, as many scholars have done, Hite maintains that it is impossible to finally "assign tone in the absence of the authority of a third-person narrator" (56). How, then, should one read Bernard's "summing up" in the ninth section? Although there is no authorially-sanctioned third-person narration, Bernard "takes over" the narrative to deliver a fifty-page soliloquy at the end of this otherwise heteroglossic novel. Why end the novel this way, in a move that seemingly privileges Bernard's voice above all the others?

Hite's claim that Woolf revised her drafts strategically in order to mute tonal cues is especially apt in her discussion of *The Voyage Out* and *The Pargiters*. Though the earlier *Melymbrosia* manuscripts are clearer in their sanctioning of authorial values via the third-person narrator and though she deliberately muted these tonal cues in later drafts of what would become *The Voyage Out*, Hite argues that this does not mean Woolf engaged in self-censorship. Instead, Hite reads these revisions as "part of Woolf's modernist turn" (112). Hite's discussion of *The Pargiters* in her epilogue builds on her argument about Woolf's turn toward tonal ambiguity and presents a convincing case for the possibilities of this experimental form. Though many critics consider Woolf's initial plan to alternate between "essays" and fictional narration flawed and doomed to aesthetic failure, Hite argues that "*The Pargiters* was an intensely promising experiment for Woolf because it offered her a way of writing a novel 'of fact' in which she could express her own deeply held opinions without resorting to the kind of fiction she dismissed" as too polemical (168).

The second strand of Hite's argument—that Woolf's feminist literary precursors have been overlooked though they provide great insight into what Woolf's modernist turn was away *from*—is central in two chapters, one devoted to Elizabeth Robins and the feminist polemical novel (provocatively titled "Not Thinking Back Through Our Mothers"), and another to *A Room of One's Own*. In her careful analysis of Woolf's version of literary history, Hite points out the irony that *Room* is a "feminist argument that requires women *not* to make feminist arguments when writing fiction" (63). Woolf's ambivalence toward her literary foremothers is especially telling in the list of Edwardian novelists she uses to define her own modernist writings against in her famous manifestoes "Modern Fiction" and "Mr. Bennett and Mrs. Brown." Hite notes that Woolf might have included any number of women writers of polemical fiction and names Sara Grand, Mary St.-Leger Kingsley, Mona Caird, May Sinclair, and Elizabeth Robins as among the most important. Instead, she focuses on Arnold Bennett, H.G. Wells, and John Galsworthy, essentially writing the women in this tradition out of the literary canon.

In the next two chapters, Hite pairs a novel by Robins with one by Woolf; Chapter Five pairs *My Little Sister* with *The Voyage Out* while Chapter Six pairs *A Dark Lantern* with *Mrs. Dalloway*. The first pairing is the much more illuminating of the two, as it conducts the thought experiment: what kind of book might Woolf have written had she followed the precedent of her literary foremothers? In both novels, the young female protagonists fall prey to their culturally mandated denial of sexual education and experience. While Robins deliberately sought to expose forced child prostitution, however, Woolf does not use her third-person narrator to advocate any feminist positions, instead offering a "range of complicated social, environmental, and perhaps even developmental reasons—some mutually exclusive—for the death of a young woman" (133). From the evidence of the uncharacteristically unambiguous tonal cues in the third-person narrator's characterization of Drs. Holmes and Bradshaw in *Mrs. Dalloway*, however, it is clear that Woolf would definitely *not* have glorified the rest cure had she chosen to write a polemical rest cure novel, as does Robins in *A Dark Lantern*. Woolf's insertion of such clear tonal cues in this instance is very intriguing. Why openly condemn only these two characters in what marks such a decided shift away from her deliberate tonal ambiguity? Did Woolf "stop to curse," thereby failing her own standard in this obvious eruption of personal hostility?

Overall, *Woolf's Ambiguities* is an invaluable contribution to Woolf studies, offering provocative insights of specific texts and a way to read her formal experiments and revisions as part of an ethicoaesthetic strategy that she deployed across her entire *oeuvre*.

—Annalee Sellers, *Independent Scholar*

Modernist Physics: Waves, Particles, and Relativities in the Writings of Virginia Woolf and D.H. Lawrence. Rachel Crossland, (Oxford: Oxford UP, 2018) xii + 193 pp.

1905 was to physics what 1922 was to Anglo-American literary modernism. That year, Einstein published his four *Annus Mirabilis* papers that would shape modern physics and inflect the culture that his discoveries emerged from and into. A century after Einstein became a household name, Rachel Crossland channels the perennially strange insights of his 1905 papers into new readings of works by Virginia Woolf and D.H. Lawrence. In her assessment "of three scientific papers, of three intellectual figures, and, most importantly, of three sets of related ideas" (15), Crossland offers an alluring literary account of what is "modernist" about both Einstein's theories and the interdisciplinary terrain that shaped, received, and transformed them.

Above all, *Modernist Physics* is devoted to articulating and testing a method to bring together science and literature within a larger multidisciplinary context. This is a welcome entry point into a subfield that attempts to balance attention to scientific explication, a cultural history of science, and literary form. Crossland intervenes in a century-long attempt to connect the new physics and literature that originated with modernist writers themselves. This line of inquiry swelled in professional literary criticism in the 1980s and 1990s, bookended by studies like Alan J. Friedman and Carol C. Donley's *Einstein as Myth and Muse* (1985) and Michael Whitworth's *Einstein's Wake* (2001; Whitworth was Crossland's dissertation advisor at Oxford). Crossland identifies and attempts to bridge the two approaches the field has taken: the direct influence model and the zeitgeist model. The influence model is precise but risks imposing a disciplinary hierarchy that suggests knowledge travels unidirectionally from science to its beholden interpreters in other disciplines. The zeitgeist model, in contrast, operates on the compelling if vague sense that "the wider cultural atmosphere of a particular period" leads a host of disciplines to take up similar ideas (5). In short, the zeitgeist model yields expansive results but is methodologically hazy, while the influence model is clean but limited.

In order to keep in play the undeniable role of influence while explaining how Einstein-flavored ideas turn up in the works of Woolf and Lawrence before those ideas were popularized, Crossland must address the influence-zeitgeist standoff. To do so, she turns to Gillian Beer's argument that "ways of viewing the world are not constructed separately by scientists and poets; they share the moment's discourse" (qtd. p. 8). Because "shared discourse" accounts for multidirectional routes of influence, as well as a "cultural matrix" through which ideas travel, Beer's approach "allows us to think about *both* direct influence between literature and science *and* a broader cultural setting for both disciplines" (8). It would be useful at this point to know more about what Crossland means by "discourse." (Does she invoke, for instance, "discourse" in Foucault's sense of how power shapes the constitution of knowledge, which might also help her to critique the disciplinary hierarchy assumed in the influence model?) Even so, the term is useful shorthand for what Crossland is after: an account of how literary ideas consonant with the new physics operate before and after Einstein's 1905 work took hold.

Crossland's organization is brilliantly designed to target this issue. She focuses each of her three sections on one of Einstein's four *Annus Mirabilis* papers. The first chapter in each section explicates the paper and contextualizes it within a longer interdisciplinary conversation, testing the extent to which this conversation inflects modernist literature, painting, psychology, and sociology before ideas of the new physics became more mainstream in the 1920s. The second chapter of each section turns to works that post-date Einstein's celebrity status and engage the new physics directly, allowing Crossland to investigate how (and how much) nascent ideas change as a result of direct influence.

Section One, which will give Woolf scholars the most to work with, pairs Einstein's first 1905 paper on light quanta with Woolf's use of light from *The Voyage Out* (1915) to *The Waves* (1931). In challenging the nineteenth-century conviction that light is a wave, Einstein's postulation of light quanta paved the way for two mind-boggling notions that, Crossland suggests, spoke from and to the era's larger preoccupation with dualities. The first was Louis de Broglie's discovery that light is both a wave *and* a particle. The second, which Crossland argues is even more important to understanding Woolf, was Niels Bohr's assertion that wave-particle duality works according to his principle of complementarity: observers will perceive light as either a particle *or* a wave, depending on which they set out to see, but they will never catch it behaving as both at once. Crossland argues that complementarity "provided a sense of liberation for twentieth-century science and thought, a freedom from opposites in the development of an inclusive 'and' which was able to overwrite, *while still expressing*, difference" (44). Over two chapters, she reads Woolf first as a dualistic writer (as many critics have) and later as a complementary writer (as other critics have not). By examining the complementary presentation of gender in *Orlando*, extending critical interest in the behavior of light in *The Waves*, and analyzing key passages from Woolf's diaries, Crossland demonstrates how Woolf grapples with physics as "her efforts to balance opposites, as well as to accept their simultaneous coexistence, become both more frequent and more urgent" (45).

Sections Two and Three follow the same basic structure in vacillating between zeitgeist and influence. Section Two pairs Einstein's special relativity with Lawrence, who engaged Einstein directly in his attempt to develop "a theory of human relativity" in *Fantasia of the Unconscious* (1921). Crossland qualifies the influence model by delineating a proto-theory of human relativity in Lawrence's early work that intensifies following his encounters with Einstein. Section Three is the most ambitious in its scope and its contribution to intellectual history: here Crossland examines intersections in molecular physics and crowd psychology. Einstein's attempt to resolve the problem of Brownian motion—the bewildering observation that particles move when suspended in an apparently still substance—led to increased interest in molecular movement. Crossland demonstrates how crowd psychologists and physicists trade language and insights in describing the behaviors of individuals in crowds and particles in substances. In tracing the "key terms" of "individuals and masses, particles and molecules" (151) through the early twentieth century, Crossland draws from a packed archive in this final section, offering fly-by readings of city crowds in Woolf, Lawrence, James Joyce, and T. S. Eliot. Like physicists and crowd psychologists, Crossland claims, modernist writers were concerned with how "to write the mass without completely losing the individual" (150). This final section also suggests an organizing concern of modernism brought into relief by physics: "the nature and significance of the individual within, and with respect to, the larger whole" (178), be it a particle within a wave, relativistic positions of individual observers within a universe governed by indiscernible constant laws, or a particle suspended in a substance.

Modernist Physics may seem belated. In the context of the Anthropocene, modernist scholars are turning to the seemingly more urgent sciences of biology and geology. But Crossland's book attests not only to the ongoing generative power of the new physics but also to the continued need for scholarship that is internally elegant and surprising. Moreover, in foregrounding and testing a process of inquiry, Crossland models methodological responsibility for an increasingly interdisciplinary field. To assess the book in the terms it offers, *Modernist Physics* thoroughly engages several disciplines in order "to overwrite, *while still expressing*, [their] difference" (44). While this book would be worth reading just for its clear explanations and historical framing of concepts that reimagined the universe, Crossland has also made an enthralling contribution to modernist studies and Woolf scholarship.

—Margaret Greaves, *Skidmore College*

Virginia Woolf and Christian Culture. Jane de Gay, (Edinburgh UP, 2018) 245 pp.

Virginia Woolf features prominently in accounts of modernism as a Godless literature. Indeed, her work is often considered the paradigm of a literature that substitutes art, technique or the act of writing itself for a Christian God in whom no one believes anymore. James Wood gives Woolf a central place in *The Broken Estate: Essays in Belief and Literature* where he argues that she trusts in writing to "hazily" do the work the work of religion (102). Woolf is also a key figure in Pericles Lewis's influential account of "religious experience" in the modernist novel, and she is the single female author to feature in Stephen Kern's recent discussion of unity in form as the modernist answer to the loss of God in *Modernism After the Death of God*.

Going against the grain of this criticism, Jane de Gay's *Virginia Woolf and Christian Culture* describes a writer and an oeuvre embedded in the Christian culture that was her heritage and, in one of the book's most original contributions, still significant in Woolf's own time. This does not amount to an argument that Woolf had "secret leanings" toward Christianity (2). De Gay is careful to note Woolf's hostility towards the faith and towards the Established Church in particular, as well as the anger she expresses towards a "God" who if imagined to be omniscient or omnipotent must also be imagined to be thoroughly malevolent. But de Gay's intent is not to claim Woolf for Christianity so much as to present an altogether more nuanced account of her attitudes to Christianity than seen in previous versions, and in this respect her book is altogether persuasive. In one of the strongest arguments of the book, de Gay notes Woolf's sympathy towards and willingness to engage in theological discussion with female believers from Caroline Emelia Stephen and Violet Dickinson to Vita Sackville-West. This is in sharp contrast, she points out, to Woolf's snippy dismissal of Eliot's conversion to Anglo-Catholicism as "obscene" (*L3* 458). While de Gay notes the difficulty in knowing exactly what Woolf took from Caroline Emelia she offers some suggestive ideas based in readings of the latter's theological works and Woolf's biography. De Gay notes in particular the influence that Woolf's stay at her Aunt's house, The Porch, a celibate Quaker female community, might have had on her niece's understanding of gendered space and the security that comes with a having a space of one's own.

De Gay explains that she selected "Christian culture" rather than "tradition" for the title of her book to signal the fact that Woolf had contact with a number of different Christian traditions and denominations. As might be expected, the book gives a detailed account of Woolf's family background in the Clapham Sect especially as regards the links between her evangelical predecessors and the campaign against slavery. But in an advance on previous work, de Gay does not stop here as though Christianity (for good and ill) were entirely a thing of the past. As noted above, one of the original contributions this book makes to scholarship on Woolf is its alignment of her career with the contemporary history of the Christian churches in Britain. This provides some telling context for what de Gay persuasively presents as Woolf's changing position on Christianity over the course of her career. The increased hostility that Woolf expresses in the 1930s, for example, is helpfully seen as a reaction to the resurgence of religion in this period and to the conservatism of the Anglican Church hierarchy under the leadership of Archbishop Cosmo Lang. De Gay refers in particular to the failure of a commission set up to consider the prospect of women's ministry as well as to the unwillingness of the Church to speak out against Fascism. *Three Guineas*, she points out, is concerned with the possibility of women's ministry and the unnamed photograph of the Archbishop that appears at its center is in fact a photograph of Cosmo Lang. Woolf is productively seen here as part of a wider conversation as to how the Christian churches should respond to political and economic crisis. De Gay notes that the Woolfs' library contained a book published by Gollancz titled *Christianity and the Crisis* (1933) in which a range of public figures and prominent clergymen discuss the possibility of a Christian solution to contemporary problems. De Gay's research into the contents of the Woolfs' library and the significance of now long-forgotten titles such as this one is a key strength of the book.

Virginia Woolf and Christian Culture begins with two chapters that focus loosely on the past and present contexts for Woolf's understanding of Christianity. Chapter One offers a short history of the Stephen family beginning with Henry Venn and working towards the generation immediately before Woolf's own—Leslie Stephen, Julia Stephen, Fitzjames Stephen, and Caroline Emelia Stephen. De Gay offers a useful and accessible introduction to the theology Venn espoused as well as to evangelical codes of conduct and morality that impacted Woolf's upbringing, even in the absence of formal religious belief or education. De Gay is careful not to romanticize Woolf's Nonconformist background pointing out that by the mid-nineteenth century Clapham Sect dissent was thoroughly of the establishment and that, while in some respects Caroline Emelia's Quakerism might be seen as alternative or radical, Caroline Emelia herself viewed Quakerism as primarily another Nonconformist denomination. Chapter Two suggests ways in which Woolf's views on Christianity intersect with those of contemporaries and peers, notably Jane Harrison who saw her research into archaic religion as unavoidably part of a conversation about the relevance and nature of religion in the present. This chapter also shows Woolf engaged both with and against the representatives of the Church in their response to current affairs. De Gay discerns a certain pragmatism in Woolf's approach that took each action and response on its own merits. Quick to blame God for the hypocrisy of the Women's Co-operative Guild following a discussion of Peace, for example, she nonetheless joined Leonard in his support for Archbishop Randall Davidson's call for an end to the general strike on terms favorable to the miners.

Subsequent chapters adopt a thematic approach to Woolf's writing. Chapter Three considers the representation of clergymen and Christian worship in Woolf's fiction before considering women's "ministry" in *To the Lighthouse* and *Three Guineas*. Chapters Four and Five explore the significance Woolf gives to sacred space which de Gay understands both in terms of consecrated buildings—Hagia Sophia and St. Paul's which feature prominently in Woolf's writing—as well as domestic spaces which offer a form of "sanctuary" to her female protagonists. In designating secular sites as places in which women can find spiritual solace or transcendence, de Gay perhaps risks losing her specific focus on Christianity and moving towards the loose definition of the sacred that she critiques in other accounts. But here as elsewhere the book's close attention to Christian registers and intertexts in episodes such as Mrs. Dalloway's "retreat" to her bedroom fully justifies their inclusion as part of Woolf's ambivalent response to the religion. The fourth chapter in this sequence of thematic studies considers Woolf's representation of religious art, specifically pictures of the Madonna and child.

The final chapter takes a slightly different turn towards the material culture of Christianity as manifest in the multiple copies of the Bible the Woolfs owned. The ownership of these books and the altogether unremarkable fact of their presence, *even in the home of unbelievers*, provides a striking demonstration of the book's central argument that Christianity is part of the very fabric of Woolf's culture. De Gay ends the chapter with a reading of *Mrs. Dalloway, To the Lighthouse*, and *The Waves* as Woolf's "passion" trilogy. To some this reading may seem too schematic, especially as regards *The Waves*, which offers a scaled-up view of time and space in which the Christian story of human origins and ends is radically diminished. Yet, as with all of the close readings in this book, de Gay is meticulous in her presentation of textual evidence and cautious in her conclusions. *Virginia Woolf and Christianity* does not assume a readership sympathetic to de Gay's position on the significance of Christianity to Woolf, and is all the stronger for not doing so. This book gives substance and context to Woolf's ambivalent relationship to Christianity, a relationship that given her situation and class she could hardly have avoided, and offers an important corrective to accounts that have minimized this aspect of her work in pursuing the chimera of a fully secularized Anglophone modernism.

—Suzanne Hobson, *Queen Mary, University of London*

Works Cited

Kern, Stephen. *Modernism After the Death of God*. Routledge, 2017.

Lewis, Pericles. *Religious Experience and the Modernist Novel*. Cambridge UP, 2010.

Wood, James. *The Broken Estate: Essays on Belief and Literature*. Jonathan Cape, 1999.

Trans-Woolf: Thinking Across Borders. Claire Davison and Anne-Marie Smith-Di Biasio, eds. (Morlacchi Editore UP, 2017) 297 pp.

Published in the *European Modernism* series, *Trans-Woolf: Thinking Across Borders* is the fruit of long-term research by the Société d'Etudes Woolfiennes (14). Albeit with different perspectives, approaches and aims, all eleven essays in the collection focus on Woolf's writing by extensively exploring its multiple relationships with the semiotic practice of *trans*lation, whose Latin prefix—i.e. "trans"—emblematically appears in the book's title.

The volume's investigative approach is highlighted by its structure, with the essays organized into six major sections. Whereas some of them take a new look at intertextual dialogues in Woolf's works, on both the artistic/disciplinary and contextual/social levels, others focus on their inter- and intra-linguistic sharing, adaptation, manipulation and creation. *Transmedial, transmission, transgression* and *transfixation* are just some of the terms used in the section titles to convey the significance of "trans" as it is applied and researched in each part of the volume. In their brief but persuasive introduction, the editors Claire Davison and Anne-Marie Smith-Di Biasio insist on the twofold essence of the trans-tension that pervades the entire volume, as being both a premise to any act of translation and truly constitutive of Woolf's own philosophy (14). On the basis of this dualism, the figure of the translator provides the editors with a good meta-textual instance of what *Trans-Woolf* intends to achieve in terms of criticism. Indeed, just as the translator's work consists of "thinking outside familiar mappings, crossing borders, and thereby imagining survival" (13), the collected essays appear to act as "translational encounters" (13) that convert the dynamics of translation into a fruitful object of investigation concerning Woolf's writings.

The first section, "*Translational ethics*," immediately provides the reader with some interesting ways of conceiving translation as it relates to Woolf's writing, such as the "untranslatability" of Flush's experience abroad (30) that Catherine Bernard notes in *Flush: A Biography*. Moreover, while discussing the factual and tropic value of *trans*port (30), Bernard stresses the double encounter between languages and spaces in the act of translating and travelling respectively: in both cases, contact of some kind—although oriented in opposite directions—is enabled by the subject's own movement (33). Indeed, as Bernard further observes, the English noun "translation" conveys "displacement" (24), which was also manifested during modernism in both an "imaginary" and a bodily kind of "dislocation" (26).

Another significant movement emerges especially in Woolf's late works. Elsa Högberg points to a backward tendency (51–52), which is further mirrored in the varying relationship between individualism and community (58). This idea is strengthened by the subtle process of "reverse translation" that Högberg envisages in the novel *Between the Acts* (52, 57), where the "modern Anon" who is Miss La Trobe acts as a sort of "cultural translator" (48).

The following section, "*Intra-scriptural dialogues*," starts with Claire Davison's essay. Here, Davison explores the "soundscape" (80) that Woolf was able to create in *The Voyage Out*, by analyzing the drafts of "Melymbrosia" that she wrote before 1909. Davison links Woolf's known familiarity with certain musical discourses to the evolutionary theories that were circulating at that time. Such links become evident in the interpretation of Woolf's drafts in the light of Charles Darwin's *The Voyage of the Beagle* (1839).

In the same section, Jane Goldman unveils certain "*scriptural*" encounters she has while wandering through the empty house in "Time Passes" in search of any sign that has been traced and then erased in "the corridor of text" (105) formed by the central section. Goldman moves from "Time Passes" in *To the Lighthouse* to Kath Swarbrick's "uncanny restoration" in English (105) of Charles Mauron's "Le Temps Passe," i.e. the French translation of an earlier draft of "Time Passes" published in *Commerce* in 1926. Through her painstaking analysis of the two English texts, Goldman reveals which changes originate from the intermediate version, i.e. Mauron's lyrical translation, while simultaneously highlighting poetical echoes recalling French symbolism.

Lyrical vibrations in *To the Lighthouse*, attributed this time to Federico García Lorca (125), are also noted by Anne-Marie Smith-Di Biasio, whose essay appears together with Adèle Cassigneul's paper in the volume's third section, "*Words of light; transmedial spectrality.*" Smith-Di Biasio writes of her experience in Port Bou in Spain, on the border with France, the "contact zone between frontiers, languages and texts" (128). She was returning from Madrid, where she had discovered Antonio Marichalar's Spanish translation of *To the Lighthouse*. She read it, but left it there. It was still speaking in her mind though, "with all the original hallucinatory quality" it had kept in Spanish (126). The meeting of two countries, symbolized by the chromatic confluence of the sky and sea, gave her experience in Port Bou an imprint of foreignness in the simultaneous annihilation of any geographical and cultural borders. Another encounter meanwhile occurred in her mind between Woolf's *To the Lighthouse* and its Spanish translation, both reread through her memory, giving rise to the emblem of a "'reading through' to remembrance" (121).

Memories and journeys also play a key role in Cassigneul's reading of Woolf's *Jacob's Room*, which develops through the lens of multiple connections. Cassigneul relates Woolf's personal experience in Greece to the depiction, in the character of Jacob Flanders, of a phantasmagoric Thoby Stephen, who was re-awakened in Woolf's mind especially after she heard of Walter Lamb's dream of him (141). Woolf's journey and her memories, Thoby's death and oneiric re-appearance, and the photographic (and cinematic) essence of the novel are brilliantly combined in Cassigneul's essay.

"*Transmission and transgression in the present*," which is the volume's fourth section, focuses on the contemporary reception, modulation and translation of Woolf's writings. Anne-Laure Rigeade chooses *Three Guineas* to discuss translation as a dialogic process. Analyzing certain evident changes appearing in two French translations, for example regarding the noun "outsiders" (176–77) and the strategic omission of gender specification (178–79), Rigeade is able to link the issue of communication as it is tackled in *Three Guineas* with the same issue as it pertains to the act of translating it into French. Caroline Marie's essay is concerned with the ways in which Woolf's works and especially her figure as a writer have been both disseminated and inherited over the years. The existence—and creation—of both a highbrow and a popular Woolf exemplifies how the writer has been the object of a concomitant process of appropriation and transgression ("appropriation autant que transgression") (186).

Annalisa Volpone's and Elisa Bolchi's essays are in the volume's closing section, "*Transfixation and embodiment*," both focusing on the linguistic difficulties that can be encountered when rendering Woolf's works into Italian. Volpone sheds light on a crucial issue that any Italian translator has to face, i.e. the lack of any Italian equivalent of the tense most frequently used by Woolf to reference time—namely the present perfect, as well as the past perfect (218). Hence, she focuses on the ways in which certain words—e.g. "'transfix' and 'moment'"—that Woolf employed in *To the Lighthouse* and *Mrs. Dalloway* in relation to time (217) have been rendered into Italian. After analyzing all the available Italian versions—both translations and "re-translations" (237)—of passages from *Mrs. Dalloway* and *The Years*, Bolchi demonstrates that "a search for refined lexical constructions and complicated syntax" has unfortunately prevented some Italian translators from conserving Woolf's rhythms and musicality (256). She argues that "a search for the right rhythm" should be instead the guiding principle of any translation of Woolf's writings (256).

This section naturally accompanies the reader to the "*Epilogue and afterlife*" of *Trans-Woolf*, where, as both a scholar and a translator, Nadia Fusini reflects on her own personal experience of modulating Woolf's writing in Italian. Among the structural features she admires while translating Woolf's works are "the movement of her sentence" and "her punctuation" (272). Fusini's conclusion to the volume exemplifies how, while providing several lenses through which to look at translation in accordance with distinct theoretical frameworks, sometimes the authors' own *trans*portation to the semiotic arena of translation regarding Woolf's œuvre may itself become the focus of discussion. In addition, by lamenting previous Italian versions, where "Woolf had in fact not been *tràdita* (translated), but *tradìta* (betrayed)" (266), Fusini's "Virginia Woolf, Lost in Translation" also foregrounds the authors' mournful awareness of potential losses and gains in and through translation, a theme which emerges throughout *Trans-Woolf*.

This volume demonstrates the continuing desire on the part of scholars to rediscover what has apparently been lost during the numberless inter-textual encounters that Woolf's writing has given rise to over the years (and is still giving rise to today), as well as attempting to grasp its fascinating complexity. *Trans-Woolf: Thinking Across Borders* thus itself represents the forum for yet another encounter, experienced by several women researchers who, from various European countries, have been brought together by the editors Davison and Smith-Di Biasio to explore the *becoming* of Woolf's own works, both beyond and against all borders and limitations.

—Cristina Carluccio, *Università del Salento*

Sentencing Orlando: Virginia Woolf and the Morphology of the Modernist Sentence. Elsa Högberg and Amy Bromley, eds. (Edinburgh UP, 2018) ix + 225 pp..

Orlando: A Biography is equally remarkable for its fantastic conceit and its documenting of Vita Sackville-West's life and ancestry. Critics have swooned over the rainbow of its subversive queering of sex, history, time, and biography itself, just as they have mined the granitic reality of the friend and lover who inspired Virginia Woolf to write the book. Until this collection of essays, however, we have not attended to just how radical Woolf's fictional biography is at the level of the sentence. Comprised of sixteen chapters by a stellar international line-up of scholars, expertly curated by Elsa Högberg and Amy Bromley, *Sentencing Orlando* demonstrates the myriad ways that Woolf's sweeping themes are explored through sentences every bit as allusive, innovative, and suggestive as her more celebrated modernist novels. In the process, the book offers a surprising new vocabulary to describe what is distinct about Woolf's formal experimentation in her 1928 text, from "bubbly" (Bahun 76) to "chaotic" (Putzel 139), "freakish" (Koppen 196) to "analeptic" (de Gay 60), "eruptive" (Bellamy 84) to "orgasmic" (Goldman 29). In doing so, each chapter illustrates what the editors call the "morphological variations" of Woolf's sentences as the building blocks of the "architecture" of her text (1). *Orlando*, as Högberg and Bromley underline in their lively introduction, proves itself especially well-suited to this critical methodology of close sentence-by-sentence reading. Not only do "fantasy, parody[,] and satire combine to produce a wide spectrum of different sentence types" (2), but the word's "legal and discursive" meanings are themselves examined "through Woolf's subversive treatment of material property, declarations, verdicts, censorship, sexuality and gender" (5). It is this finely conceptualized and consistently executed approach that sets the volume apart from many edited collections, rendering it exemplary of how an often undervalued genre of academic publication can produce original and exciting work.

Each contributor has chosen a single sentence to build an argument around, with detailed textual analysis informed by careful historicizing and insightful theorizing. Unsurprisingly, topics concerning gender and sexuality feature prominently (Goldman, Frøsig), but they are related more to the politics of the sentence than to well-worn arguments over identity politics. The array of other themes covered include Woolf and Greece (Kolocotroni), fame (Spiropoulou), the everyday (Randall), spirituality (Avery), and colonialism (Koppen); it is through discussion of these topics, and many more besides, that the volume showcases the radical aesthetics and intertextual resonances embedded in *Orlando*. The latter—intertextuality—is one of the greatest strengths of the volume, and its complexity is captured in Sanja Bahun's remark that "the *Orlando* edifice is comprised of differently valued and deliberately mixed intertextual material, where quotations, self-quotations, paraphrases, allusions[,] and writerly gestures interact irreverently" (71). Contributors explain how Woolf writes through, with, or against the likes of Michel de Montaigne (Allen), William Wordsworth (de Gay), Thomas Browne (Hagen), Laurence Sterne (Bellamy), Thomas De Quincey (Högberg), and T. S. Eliot (Bahun). Woolf is also read alongside contemporary women writers as different as Vita Sackville-West and Gertrude Stein, though the predominantly masculine list of interlocutors explored in most of the essays will not pass readers unnoticed. In her compelling chapter, Högberg astutely ties Woolf's engagement with male sentences to questions of inheritance, and specifically the fact that Vita as a woman could not inherit Knole: "Woolf takes aesthetic property that is not fully hers—the male sentences of De Quincey and others—and transforms it in order to make a symbolic gift for her female lover of material property that she cannot inherit" (46). Sentences in *Orlando* also lead back to Woolf's earlier texts, such as "Kew Gardens" (Staveley), while "The New Biography" and *A Room of One's Own* are touchstones throughout. Indeed, it is the volume's attention to the densely allusive nature of Woolf's fictional biography—whether to her own writing or those of other literary figures—that makes it a perfect companion to the weighty Cambridge Edition of *Orlando*, edited by Suzanne Raitt and Ian Blyth, also published last year (see review in this volume).

It is impossible with a collection as full of treasures as the one assembled by Högberg and Bromley to do justice to all its contributors, and a key feature of the book is the sustained quality of its scholarship; it does not succumb to the unevenness so often apparent in edited volumes. But the space here does allow me to provide a few examples of how the microscopic focus on sentences opens up larger questions. Jane Goldman, amid her riveting analysis of the short spurt, "The

Queen had come," draws our attention to the textual "mischief" of *Orlando* when she notes that Rosina Pepita (second name shared with Vita's grandmother) in the first British edition becomes Rosina Lolita in the second and third impressions. For Goldman, this subtle but significant alteration can be understood as distancing the text from the "granite-like factual link" to Vita's genealogy and possibly as a swipe at Vita's mother (Pepita's daughter) following an unkind letter about *Orlando* (27-8). Amy Bromley's analysis of her chosen sentence— "But now and again a single phrase would come to him over the ice which was as if torn from the depths of his heart"—demonstrates how ambiguity and contradiction are structuring principles of Woolf's poetic prose and discourse of love. Bromley explains: "It begins with a contradiction—'But'; situates a complex temporality with 'now and again'; and constructs semblance through simile, turning the whole sentence upon a figure 'as if.' This sentence performs the lover's creation of mental and linguistic figures relating to the beloved and the love-plot." She goes on to note how lack of punctuation leaves meaning open-ended: "is it the 'single phrase' or 'the ice' which is 'as if torn from the depths of his heart'? Is it Orlando's heart or that of the actor/character on stage?" (153). Judith Allen shows how form and content collude by zooming in on the use of the word "vast" in her chosen sentence (itself too lengthy to quote here) and its repeated deployment throughout *Orlando*. "Like the other words that reflect inconclusiveness," she argues, "the word 'vast'—in its spatial openness—is a call for freedom as it provokes the imagination, creativity and risk" (207). Abundantly clear in these and other essays is just how diverse Woolf's sentences are in terms of syntax, punctuation, rhythm, and length (from four words in Goldman's case to seventeen lines in Allen's)—and that is before we add variations in content and theme. What unites the readings of Woolf's sentences in this volume is that they are all shimmering with multiple forms and meanings, and only rarely does it feel as though too much weight is being hung on a particular clause, phrase, or word. Far from exhausting these sentences, if anything the essays occasionally feel a little too compressed, where the wealth of information and interpretation squeezed into (roughly) ten pages may have benefitted from expansion and elaboration.

Sentencing Orlando is, then, an overwhelming success: creative, rigorous, timely, and fun! Summing up the volume in her dazzling "Aftersentence," Rachel Bowlby appraises that "these new critical sentences, the sentences about Woolf's sentences, are models of precision and elegance in their own right"; she predicts that "many will surely be quoted on other pages, in other textual places, in the future" (215). I can only add to this that in gathering and shaping the material the work of the editors also provides a model for future collaborative projects. Their decision, for example, to eschew the temptation to order chapters based on the chronological appearance of each sentence in Woolf's text ensures a fluent transition from one chapter to the next, allowing rich nodes of connection and contrast to emerge.

Moreover, limiting each essay's central focus to just one of Woolf's sentences not only undergirds the collection's efforts "to recuperate the text as one of her most aesthetically dynamic novels" (3), but also creates the conditions for the art of close reading to be revitalized. Crucially, this methodology is not one that results in a backward step towards an apolitical formalism but is rather one that reignites the text as "an aesthetically as well as historically and politically charged entity" (1). All of which is to say that Högberg and Bromley have provided an invaluable resource for both research and pedagogy, perfectly captured in Benjamin Hagen's reflection that "Woolf's sentences prompt us—indeed, they train us with continued engagement—to become more agile, creative and discerning readers" (175). So impressive is this book on these different levels that its publisher would do well to consider an entire series inspired by it: might now be the time to sentence modernism?

—Derek Ryan, *University of Kent*

Walking Virginia Woolf's London: An investigation in Literary Geography. Lisbeth Larsson (Palgrave MacMillan, 2017) xi + 247 pp.

Ever since Rachel Bowlby's groundbreaking study of "Walking, Women and Writing: Virginia Woolf as flâneuse" (1992), scholars have recognized the importance of walking in both Virginia Woolf's personal life and in the lived environment of the characters in her books. A meticulous and comprehensive addition to studies of Woolf's walking, Lisbeth Larsson's book sets out to trace all of the London walks by all of the characters in Woolf's major works. A theoretically informed update of such classic handbooks as Dorothy Brewster's *Virginia Woolf's London* (1960) and Jean Moorcroft Wilson's *Virginia Woolf: Life and London: A Biography of Place* (1987), it is an extension of points first made by Susan Merrill Squier in *Virginia Woolf and London: The Sexual Politics of the City* (1985), which also presents a sustained and intelligent argument about the gendering of space and place in Woolf. While enriched by a firm foundation in space/place theory, the book is not an attempt to apply Michel de Certeau et al.'s theories to Woolf as much as it is an inductive survey of the actual walks taken by various characters which uses the tools of literary geography to draw insightful conclusions about Woolf's political demarcations of London and her critiques of class, patriarchy, and colonialism. Unlike earlier studies, Larsson's comprehensive coverage of all the walks of all the characters in all the novels allows her to trace the arc of Woolf's changing attitudes towards the city, including her later doubts about its utopian promise for women.

Not as biographical as earlier treatments, Larsson's book focuses instead on the importance of walking as a manifestation of and trope for female independence. Her second chapter on *The Voyage Out* establishes the prominence of central London—the area of The City encompassing Fleet Street and The Strand—throughout Woolf's writing, analyzing its dual significance as a symbol of both patriarchal entrapment in social conventions and utopian freedom from them.

The next chapter on *Night and Day*, one of the two longest in the book, provides a thoroughgoing interpretation of the novel, based around a total of seven maps illustrating the individual walks of each character. This level of detail allows Larsson to explore the relations between class, gender and geographical location as she traces the character's travels from Katherine's home in Cheyne Walk in Chelsea to Mary Datchet and William Rodney's apartments in Central London to other London locations such as the British Museum, the Embankment, and the open spaces of Regent's Park and Kew Gardens, uncovering Woolf's "map method" by which "movement in space also involves a movement in feeling and thought" (54).

While much shorter, the next chapter, on *Jacob's Room*, displays a deft and thorough marshaling of a range of critical insights, again radiating from observations about characters' London locations. With fewer walks, the characters appear as a series of scattered dots popping up at Kensington, St. Paul's, Leicester Square, the British Museum, and Hyde Park. Typical of Larsson's commonsense insights is the realization that, for the most part, only Jacob moves from place to place; the various women are confined to their situations.

More has been written about London in *Mrs. Dalloway* than in any other Woolf novel, and Larsson's next chapter shows a firm grasp of this critical tradition. Widening her purview from Clarissa's ramble to include every other walk in the novel allows her to map the interconnections and transections of all the various characters. Examining the time spans involved in various walks adds another dimension to our spatial awareness and complicates the tight pattern within which most of the characters are bound, despite the novel's celebration of the city's utopian promise.

Having traced the pinnacle of Woolf's London mapping in *Mrs. Dalloway*, Chapter Six is a kind of omnibus chapter, sketching the attitudes towards London in the next major books written by Woolf. Shifting from space to place, Larsson introduces the prominence of the house as central motif in Woolf's fiction from *To the Lighthouse* on, noting the continued centrality of London in *Orlando* and *The Waves* while testing the tension between house and walking in Woolf's essays "Street Haunting" and *A Room of One's Own*. The chapter ends with an analysis of the dialectic between rural liberty and urban enclosure in *Flush* that prepares for Woolf's intensified critique of the city as a site for the imposed hierarchies of patriarchy.

Turning again to a novel almost entirely located in London, Chapter seven on *The Years* is nearly as long and detailed as that on the earlier realistic London novel, *Night and Day*. Beginning with an encyclopedic map of all walks, bus, and car rides in the entire book, the chapter's four maps combine character movement with the location of key houses to enhance the sense that London is deteriorating. Although the map of London has expanded and the novel breaks crucially with the tradition of family chronicles in following the women of the family, the city it circumnavigates is increasingly dirty, dangerous, and rotten at its core.

Concluding Larsson's argument, Chapter Eight, on *Between the Acts*, is a parallel bookend to the opening chapter on *The Voyage Out,* returning to Rachel's nightmare dream of London as the hub of patriarchy, made violently oppressive by its role as war machine. As Larsson cogently points out, the dream of walking arm in arm down narrow streets has disappeared; Woolf's characters can only access London by reading newspapers.

This chapter-by-chapter synopsis hits only a few of the high points of Larsson's book, leaving out much of its subtlety and many of its commonsense insights. Particularly useful to readers are the meticulous maps of all the London walks in the five main novels (*VO, ND, JR, MD, TY*). In the book, these maps have been printed at a frustratingly tiny resolution, with key numbers often so small that these aging eyes could not make them out, even with a magnifying glass. I found myself repeatedly trying to zoom the printed pages with my fingers, wanting to trace the tantalizing information. There is, however, a cure—Palgrave Macmillan has a web site that provides links to all twenty-one maps, zoom-able and color-coded. Go to www.palgrave.com/in/book/9783319556710 to experience this contribution to digital Virginia Woolf scholarship.

—Elisa Kay Sparks, *Clemson University, Emerita*

Virginia Woolf's Influential Forebears: Julia Margaret Cameron, Anny Thackeray Ritchie and Julia Prinsep Stephen. Marion Dell (Palgrave Macmillan, 2015) xiv + 200 pp.

Matrilineal descent defines and animates Marion Dell's notion of the ways Virginia Woolf was "shaped as a woman and a writer." From the outset, Dell promises to examine how "the work of Cameron, Ritchie and Stephen is textually, artistically, biographically, and genealogically embedded in Woolf's" (1). Dell devotes separate chapters to the work of Julia Margaret Cameron, Woolf's great-aunt; Julia Prinsep Stephen, her mother; and Anny Thackeray Ritchie, her aunt, in order to create a picture of a complex artistic inheritance. This is not a feminist book, Dell cautions her readers early on, nor does it provide a social and political context; the book title should also not be misread as "intellectual forebears." Rather, Dell's analysis "is informed by genetic theory" which "challenges the authority of any one text or version," because it anticipates "the constant reworking and recycling" (2) of Woolf's biographical source material, broadly speaking.

Dell uses the term "genetic instability" (3) to describe Woolf's modern condition. Because she regards Woolf's novels as texts that reveal elements of her genetic legacy, Dell is committed to showing readers how Woolf constantly "rewrites and reinvents her ancestors" (9) through her own autobiographical writing. As an example, Dell's biological impressions of artistic inheritance define her understanding of what she calls Woolf's "aesthetic transformations" (3, 17), by which Dell means Woolf's insertion or excision of family history in her fiction and other prose. What Dell then calls Woolf's "ambivalence" is informed exclusively by the extent to which she believes Woolf intentionally or accidentally borrowed, obscured, misrepresented, or denied the life and work of her predecessors. In short, by "ambivalence" Dell means psychologically-conflicted, as in unsettled and unresolved; not contrary, as in oppositional or rebellious. Dell's use of ambivalence is therefore strikingly unlike the conventional postmodern use of the term, since neither epistemology nor political reckoning is the object of her investigation, nor is she interested in Woolf's attraction to or repulsion from the social realities, gender politics, or class dynamics of her day.

Rather, Dell wants to convince readers of Woolf's "desire to identify with her forebears, to imaginatively 'become the people that we were two or three generations ago', to 'be our great grandmothers'" (134). As a result, Dell constructs Cameron, Ritchie, and Stephen as "invisible presences" (158) that periodically haunt Woolf's creative life: Woolf's ancestors are constantly "knocking at the door" (20) for her attention; they are the unseen forces that urge her to explore "fluidities" (25, 36, 73) and "border-crossings" (20) between her writing and the women of her biological past. Because of their unavoidable influence, Woolf is inspired, even compelled, to "blur the boundaries" (87) and "bridge the gap" (73) between her Victorian past and her modern present. Dell confirms her own method reflexively whenever she perceives Woolf's exploration of identity is fractured or unstable; whenever Woolf's syntax is intentionally ruptured or her characters' roles are reversed or destabilized; whenever a forebear's character is overtly fictionalized, distorted, or denied; whenever repeated tropes (e.g. cycles of time, the searchlight, the door, the frame, the caravan, the telescope) and matriarchal myths recur to define opportunities or close down options for Woolf's characters.

Dell's chapters on the individual impact of Cameron, Ritchie, and Stephen are bookended in the front by a chapter on the "genetic legacies" that inform Woolf's *Night and Day* (1919), and in the back by a chapter that draws upon the fictional but "recreated family histories" that define *The Years* (1937). Dell's close reading of *Night and Day* finds Woolf's metaphoric oppositions expunged as she steers her central character to find a "liminal space" (4, 8, 21). In that uncertain zone, Dell claims Woolf, like her character, hovers on the threshold, enamored of her family's ancient tangled roots and tendrils, ultimately becoming immaterial: "a shape of light, the light itself" (37). Similarly, Dell regards *The Years* as an opportunity for Woolf to interrogate her past and "play her life over again" (7). In this chapter, Dell finds confirmation of her associations of the telescope with Cameron, the street musicians with Ritchie, the caravan and the "Angel in the House" with Stephen.

In fact, Dell's chapters on the three "influential forebears" draw upon simplifications of the achievements of these three women. For example, Dell finds that Ritchie "employs a first person digressive narrative voice" that "combines autobiography with biography, not only of the overt subjects, but also of her father who is almost always inserted anecdotally" (56-57). Although Dell believes Ritchie "refuses to play the role of Angel in the House" (57), she notes how Ritchie represents her work as the result of chance rather than hard work. Dell agrees that Ritchie explores a wide range of narrative styles and voices, but she nevertheless finds that Ritchie cannot escape her own biography and "child's-eye view" (56) of the world. Ritchie's so-called *espièglerie* (mischievous playfulness) establishes a defining model for Dell, as she interprets Ritchie's use of irony, for example, as "deceptively non-threatening" (45). Yet Dell's insistence that Ritchie's *espièglerie* influenced Woolf has the effect of blunting Woolf's sometimes acidic, angry, or subversive prose.

Julia Margaret Cameron, too, is defined narrowly, in terms of soft-focus, "beauty," and idealization. To Dell, Cameron bequeaths to Woolf her interest in lighting, framing, and unconventional positioning of the subject. Not once does Dell consider what Cameron was trying to say with her allegorical photographs, which Woolf and her sister Vanessa Bell collected and wrote about as inferior to her portraits of the "great men" (*E4* 382). And Julia Stephen is handled the most reductively of the three ancestors, condensed to an abstraction of an idealized femininity. Dell finds Stephen bestowing upon Woolf both the bereaved mother trope and the fantasy of matricide and resurrection. But Dell never considers what poor Julia Stephen did to deserve this in Woolf's eyes, as nothing in Stephen's biography or writing is brought forward as "evidence" for why Woolf should be so haunted by her mother, as if by "spirit photographs," or by nostalgia, a powerful sentiment that is unconvincing when Dell employs it at the end of the book (176-77), no doubt because nostalgia has always been a social and political interpretation of the world and not genetically-derived.

Politics and history largely elude *Virginia Woolf's Influential Forebears*, yet Dell acknowledges that Cameron, Ritchie, and Stephen all possessed an Anglo-Indian past. It does not seem that Dell is interested in this history, however, using it as Woolf does in *Night and Day* (34), more as a situational device rather than as an opportunity to explore the legacy of empire on the Pattle/Jackson/Stephen family or in the modern world that Woolf inherited. Like Mia Jackson (Stephen's mother), Cameron was married to an official of the East India Company, as were their sisters, Sara Prinsep and Sophia Dalrymple; another sister, Virginia, apparently infatuated Thackeray before she married Lord Somers. Yet, Thackeray's attachment to the Pattle sisters, his writings in *Punch*, or his *Notes on a Journey from Cornhill to Cairo* (1846) never come up as possible influences on Ritchie. Similarly, Dell reduces Thérèse de l'Étang, (Mia Jackson and Julia Margaret Cameron's mother) to "a diamond and ruby ring and a sapphire brooch" (160). And while Dell acknowledges Julia Stephen's skills in nursing her mother Mia and sister Adeline, she overlooks possible causes for her declared agnosticism and interest in higher education, denying their connection to the "reform movement" in England, a cause shared by Leslie Stephen.

Dell's genetic theory does not offer readers insight into Woolf's awkward relationship to "not knowing Greek," nor does she use her biological approach to make sense of Woolf's decision to wear blackface and a beard as part of the *Dreadnought* hoax. Dell does not ask why Woolf gave Colonel Pargiter a mangled hand from the Indian Mutiny (as it was called then) in *The Years*, nor does she question why India or colonialism inform the background to her final novel, *Between the Acts*. In her diary entry of 18 January 1918, however, Woolf wrote sympathetically of Lady Strachey's "rumination" over her own past in which she shared their interrelated Indian legacy with the young Virginia. Woolf recorded the old woman's words: "Splendid men they were, the [East India] Company servants. Your Prinsep relations among the finest" (*D1* 108). *Virginia Woolf's Influential Forebears* would have profited from at least some consideration of this important social, political, and historical heritage, for without it, Dell only tells part of the story.

—Jeff Rosen, *Higher Learning Commission*

Virginia Woolf and Being-in-the-world: A Heideggerian Study. Emma Simone (Edinburgh UP, 2017) viii + 256 pp.

Emma Simone's ambitious effort to bring Virginia Woolf and Martin Heidegger into sustained dialogue aims to unveil "a mostly unexamined understanding of [Woolf's] approach to the relationship between self and world" (24). The approach, *Virginia Woolf and Being-in-the-world* contends, comes into focus by attending to the affinities Woolf and Heidegger share, specifically their "sustained critique of Cartesian dualism"; "an understanding of the individual as a temporal being"; "the emphasis upon intersubjective relations, insofar as Being-in-the-world is defined by Being-with-Others"; and "a consistent emphasis upon average everydayness as both determinative and representative of the individual's relationship to and with the world" (1). There has been no shortage of criticism concerning itself with

Woolf's nuanced treatment of self and world, "intersubjective relations," "everydayness," etc., which raises the question of the value of recasting her literary output in terms of *Being and Time*. Simone is to be commended for drawing on a wide range of writings, from novels and manuscripts to short stories, letters, and diaries, to elucidate Woolf's attitudes toward "Being-in-the-world"; more often than not, though, Woolf ends up sounding uncomfortably like Heidegger, and it never becomes clear that applying his phenomenological vocabulary to her works actually produces novel insights. While wishing for more strenuous readings of Woolf's writings, on their own terms, I was also frustrated by the insufficient articulation of how Simone's project revises or extends earlier investigations into the filiations of Woolf and Heidegger.

The first chapter considers the relationship of self and world in light of Woolf's social commitments, her stance toward "those expectations, prescriptions and hierarchal structures of the prevailing milieu and social order," which "define the individual's view of the world" (25). For Woolf and Heidegger, Simone explains, it is average everydayness that determines one's relation to the world, a connection generating the statement: "Arguably, Woolf's writings explore, from a literary perspective, the phenomenology of everyday Being-in-the-world that is represented throughout Heidegger's text" (26). Here, as elsewhere, the case for meaningful points of connection, or reciprocal illumination, is weakened by the hedge "arguably," which frequently stands in for more persuasive, in-depth analysis. At the same time, long quotes from *Being and Time* tend to be left unparsed, followed by unconvincing slides into Woolf; for instance, a point about Heidegger's anti-dualistic conception of Being-in-the-world eventuates in Clarissa Dalloway, riding a London bus, recast as Heideggerian protagonist. Overall, the arguments for Woolf's Heideggerian sense of the intersubjective, embodied nature of being come to feel formulaic: in *The Waves*, sunlight and darkness "demonstrate Woolf's sense of the inherent and inescapable unity of self and world," while pollution in *Orlando* "provides a material measure of the sense that Being-in-the-world consists of Being-with-Others" (34, 36). Clearly, both Woolf and Heidegger are keenly concerned with the individual's everyday engagements, how her existence in the world and with others shapes subjectivity. But even as Simone suggestively links them to Woolf's politics, it remains uncertain why we need Heidegger to recognize, in her texts, that "reality and truth come to be understood as multi-faceted, fluid and inclusive" (62).

The next chapter examines the role of place for the two, asserting that "place is a primordial and integral element of what it means to be human," while Woolf's works disclose the "inherent connection between the individual, experience and place" (64). These generic points are seconded by the observation that everyday engagements determine one's relationship to place. Woolf undoubtedly understands the question of being as inextricable from one's social existence and spatial awareness, and her critics have frequently investigated the relationship; what plagues Simone's attempt to rehearse it in Heideggerian terms is that we often lose sight of the singularity of Woolf's writing. Considering *Between the Acts*, for instance, Simone argues that "the land signifies the temporal interpenetration and co-existence of the past, present and future"; this is paired with the remark that, for Heidegger, "authentic time is understood as the interpenetration of past present and future, rather than a linear sequence that privileges the present" (77). These are fair points, but they don't appear to contribute to a more discerning appreciation of either Woolf or Heidegger. Later, Simone suggests an interesting connection between Woolf's sense of place and patriarchal, social, and imperial hierarchies; once Heidegger is brought to bear on it, though, we are left with the underwhelming conclusion: Woolf "repeatedly emphasizes the essential connection that exists between the individual and the places that he or she inhabits, remembers and imagines" (98).

The third chapter opens with another seeming commonplace: "the notion of home is arguably one of the more significant expressions of place" (102). Here, Simone wishes to track the tension in Woolf's writing "between the discomfort of authentic homelessness, and the comfortable, yet tranquilised, state of Being-at-home in the world" (104). For Woolf, she argues, "authentic homelessness" emerges when characters, like *The Waves*'s Louis and Rhoda, register and resist prevailing social codes. Louis "spends all his life vacillating between a desperate desire to achieve a sense of Being-at-home within English middle-class society, and disgust at the ways in which the social order constricts the individuality and agency of the self"; Rhoda, then, enacts the "unsuccessful desire to mask her homelessness through a conscious and desperate attempt to conform to socially accepted norms and expectations" (110, 111). While there seems little to quibble with here, the interpretations are fairly orthodox, contributing to the suspicion that Heidegger is superfluous to adequately perceiving the Woolfian struggle between authenticity and inauthenticity. Moreover, the explicit effort to recast it as Heideggerian drama can feel forced and incongruous: "Arguably, for Woolf, one of the more significant manifestations of thrownness is the facticity of the lived body, due to its impact upon, and determination of, the average everyday lived experience of the individual" (115). The intersections of embodiment and everydayness are crucial for Woolf, but the lack of sustained argument unpacking the particulars of Woolfian "thrownness" or "facticity" undermines the case for repackaging her in such alien terms. Lastly, some efforts to link Woolf and Heidegger simply seem facile; Woolf's insistence upon the need for a room of one's own "in which to think, work and write," for instance, accords with Heidegger's "personal desire for a place of his own in which to carry out philosophical work" (128).

The next chapter takes on Woolf's and Heidegger's views of time, or "the essential connectedness and interpenetration of the past, present and future" (140). In

Simone's reading of Woolf, "traditional historical discourse" is a force that fosters "the exclusion and marginalisation of certain social groups, particularly women"; her writings, then, seek to disrupt "the typical focus of historical discourse upon the deeds of 'great men' and events such as war" (141). While the chapter offers a competent overview of Heideggerian temporality, the question remains unanswered: Why is Heidegger necessary to reveal what relatively straightforward readings of *Mrs. Dalloway* and *A Room of One's Own* already tell us? The final, most interesting chapter turns to the relationship between moods and the world. Like Heidegger, Simone says, Woolf demonstrates that moods "consistently colour and inform the individual's state of Being-in-the-world" (183). Of particular interest is how anxiety and moods experienced in times of illness trigger Woolf's epiphanic moments, breaking with the "cotton wool" of everyday experience. While Simone's attention to the revelatory power of death in Woolf is well-considered, the epiphanies that emerge from it are reduced to a "recognition of the inherent thrownness that defines Being-in-the-world" (207). The application of Heidegger to Woolf becomes more vexing when Simone turns to boredom; here, a dense quote concerning the temporal awareness induced by moments of profound boredom—in which past, present, and future achieve an "*unarticulated unity* in the simplicity of this unity of their horizon all at once" (Heidegger 148)—is presented as self-explanatory. In lieu of critical distillation, Simone writes: "The propensity of profound boredom to disturb the individual's captivation by the present is reflected in Woolf's aforementioned 1926 diary entries" (211). Certainly, past, present, and future intensely coexist in Woolf's heightened moments, but we might expect a more fulsome description of where and how we encounter "the simplicity of this unity of their horizon all at once." The sense of Heidegger's irrelevance is amplified in the chapter's conclusion, that Woolf's "moments of being" "define and reveal the individual's inextricable connection to the world" (225).

In closing, Simone reiterates that reading Heidegger and Woolf side-by-side opens a heretofore unsuspected perspective on Woolf's treatment of self and world, while indicating future inquiries attending to the philosopher's later writings. One of these involves his emphasis on art as "both site and source for the disclosure of the truth of Being," which, she writes, "is arguably reflected through Woolf's capacity to convey her particular vision of the relationship between self and world" (232). After reading *Virginia Woolf and Being-in-the-world*, we may, arguably, find ourselves longing for an unmediated return to the particularities of that vision.

—Kelly S. Walsh, *Yonsei University*

Works Cited

Heidegger, Martin. *The Fundamental Concepts of Metaphysics: World, Finitude, Solitude*. Translated by William McNeill and Nicholas Walker, Indiana UP, 1995.

Homes and Haunts: Touring Writers' Shrines and Countries.
Alison Booth (Oxford UP, 2016) xii + 333 pp.

Virginia Woolf's first-accepted essay, "Haworth, November 1904," is an extended meditation on the biographical ethics of author museums, written in the heyday of the popular homes and haunts genre. Homes and haunts essays, collected in books and periodicals, describe acts of literary tourism and record visits to the homes, birthplaces, graves, and countries of authors. Despite her ambivalence about literary tourism and its impact on authors' legacies, and her skepticism about whether a visit to an author museum might yield insights into their literature or lived experience, Woolf finds herself taken in almost against her will. Touring the Brontë Museum at Haworth, she is moved by "the little personal relics…of the dead woman," Charlotte Brontë (*E*1 7). But emotional connection comes at a cost. In the presence of her assembled shoes, dresses, and letters, "Charlotte Brontë the woman comes to life," but as Woolf acknowledges, it is at the expense of her writerly persona, for "one forgets the chiefly memorable fact that she was a great writer. Her shoes and her thin muslin dress have outlived her" (*E*1 7). The literary biographical museum poses a risk to the woman of letters: if her personal effects have the power to humanize and resurrect her, they might also deaden the visitor's sense of her literary accomplishment. Woolf ends the essay still unable to resolve these difficulties, merely observing that "An effort ought to be made to keep things out of these mausoleums, but the choice often lies between them and destruction, so that we must be grateful for the care which has preserved much that is, under any circumstances, of deep interest" (*E*1 7). Throughout her career, Woolf continued to pursue authors at home in her essays and reviews, while her fiction and drama similarly demonstrate a fascination with the domestic sites of literary production, as evidenced in *Orlando*, *Flush*, and *Freshwater*.

Unsurprisingly, Alison Booth's *Homes and Haunts: Touring Writers' Shrines and Countries*, a meticulously researched study of the development of the interrelated texts and practices that comprise homes and haunts from the mid-nineteenth century to the first decades of the twentieth, is itself haunted by Woolf's presence. Throughout, Booth draws on Woolf's analyses of how material remains, including houses, relics, graves, and landscapes, mediate relationships between author, text, and reader. Chapter Five, "The Sage, his Wife, the Maid, and her Lover: Reconstructing a Literary House Museum with Virginia Woolf," offers an extended consideration of Woolf's lifelong engagement with the domestic circumstances of Thomas and Jane Welsh Carlyle at 24 Cheyne Row in Chelsea. The Carlyles' home was the stage for their tempestuous and controversial marriage as well as for the composition of the Sage's great works and his wife's now celebrated letters. Like many homes memorialized in topo-biographical literature, it was a site of hospitality for eminent Victorians and literary pilgrims eager to meet Carlyle, and in 1895 it became, with the help of Leslie Stephen, a biographical museum. Booth perceptively traces Woolf's evolving understanding of what is most significant about this site, beginning with her diary commentary on Carlyle's writing instruments in 1897, when she was fifteen and visiting for the first time with her father, to her mature observations about the feminist implications of water provision and the domestic labor carried out by Jane and her maid(s). Booth builds on existing scholarship on Woolf's engagement with literary homes but plots it as part of a larger history of transatlantic writing and visiting that occurred throughout the long nineteenth century. This book will be especially useful to scholars interested in Woolf's engagement with literary geography and material culture.

Homes and Haunts joins a number of recent studies that recover multimodal reception histories in the long nineteenth century, including Nicola Watson's *The Literary Tourist: Readers and Places in Romantic & Victorian Britain* (2006), and *Literary Tourism and Nineteenth-Century Culture* (2009, to which Booth contributed a chapter on Dickens), Paul Westover's *Necromanticism: Traveling to Meet the Dead, 1750-1860* (2012), and Alexis Easley's *Literary Celebrity, Gender, and Victorian Authorship, 1850-1914* (2011). Booth's book is unique, however, in offering a sustained analysis of the development of homes and haunts literature alongside author museums, which, like their textual counterparts, are read as prosopographies, or collective biographies. Although Booth focuses on predictable sites, such as the Brontës' Haworth and Irving's Sunnyside, her meticulously researched history of the transatlantic exchanges of hospitality and reception between nineteenth-century authors, professional and amateur biographers and critics, collectors, fans, and conservators, sheds new light on the complex and nonlinear ways in which canons are formed and reputations are made—often outside of the academy. One of the most delightful elements of *Homes and Haunts*, itself a prosopography, is Booth's Woolfian approach; modeling personal pilgrimage, often in the company of her sister, Booth betrays both the scholar's skepticism and her capacity to be charmed by the places where authors were born, lived, and died.

Conceiving of homes and haunts texts and visiting as practical reader response, Booth, in the introduction, stresses the importance of hospitality and reception as metaphors that help us understand the "structured social exchange between host and guest [...] underlying the practices of literature as a profession as well as the histories we write about literature" (1). Booth argues for the interconnectedness of homes and haunts literature and house museums, which she reads narratively as assembling collective biographies of authors through relics, signage, and official guidebooks. Tracing the origins of homes and haunts visits and texts to Christian pilgrimage, the Grand Tour, country house visiting, and Gothic literature, Booth also emphasizes the importance of expanded rail networks and the increased affordability of print by the mid-nineteenth century. Justifying her focus on old England and New England, she explains that not only do the two areas contain the highest concentration of literary house museums but that homes and haunts narratives—most of which were written by men about visits to men—were part of a racial and nationalist discourse that asserted the superiority of literature written in the Anglo-Saxon tradition. She also begins to sketch some of the complex motivations of literary pilgrims and the rhetoric used to narrate visits. These threads are carried through in the chapters that follow.

Chapter One continues the discussion of homes and haunts antecedents, and provides a history of the blue plaque scheme, undertaken in 1867, and the establishment of a number of author museums toward the end of the nineteenth century. Touristic motivations and rhetoric are further explored, and Booth stresses the seriality of these texts, which often collect visits to more than one author in a geographical area. Homes and haunts texts respond to, adapt, and build on one another; although these texts encompass diverse literary modes, including poetry, fiction, letters, interviews, and ethnography, they tend to share many distinctive characteristics, such as images of the writer in their study. Chapter Two expands on the theme of belatedness. Pilgrims who set out in search of a deceased author's literary remains, which might include portable relics or a visitable location, are often disappointed; they arrive to find the author gone, the relics dispersed, and the aura disrupted by the pilgrims who proceeded them. Booth illustrates this disappointment in her account of Washington Irving's visit to Stratford in pursuit of Shakespeare. Demonstrating the frequently reciprocal nature of hospitality and reception, Irving not only establishes Sunnyside as a site for the reception of men of letters and pilgrims, the inn at which he stayed in Stratford also became a site of pilgrimage for those in pursuit of Geoffrey Crayon. This chapter also introduces the Howitts, married authors who collaborated on topo-biographical and homes and haunts collections that represented England as a country of literary landscapes and associations. Chapter Three concerns the uniformity of the ways in which women authors and their homes have been envisioned, among pets and flowers. Booth focuses on Mary Russell Mitford, Elizabeth Gaskell, and the Brontës, and includes extended commentary on Woolf's catalogue of women authors in *A Room of One's Own*. Chapter Four considers authors' houses in the Lake District, comparing the ease with which Wordsworth's Dove Cottage and Rydal Mount became pilgrimage destinations while Martineau was unable to establish her home, the Knoll, on the same footing. It also introduces the homes and literary landscapes of Longfellow, Hawthorne, and James. Chapter Five, as mentioned, concerns the establishment of a biographical museum at 24 Cheyne Row and Woolf's ongoing engagement with the Carlyles, exploring marriage, desire between women, and the Victorian domestic realities that limited the exercise of women's abilities. Booth also recounts her

visit to Monk's House and the history of its transformation into an author museum. Finally, Chapter Six considers Dickens Country, Dickens World, and Dickens as a metonym for a host of Victorian associations. Booth's journeys to the homes and haunts of nineteenth-century authors illuminate the significance of an often overlooked and undervalued kinetic mode of literary reception that continues to impact literary studies in the twenty-first century, and in the process unseats simplistic distinctions between academic and amateur engagement with authors in place.
—Amber Pouliot, *Independent scholar*

Virginia Woolf: The War Without, the War Within: Her Final Diaries & the Diaries She Read.
Barbara Lounsberry (Gainesville: UP of Florida, 2018) vii + 397 pp.

War—both literal and figurative—haunts the pages of Virginia Woolf's diaries of the 1930s, and Barbara Lounsberry's *Virginia Woolf: The War Without, the War Within: Her Final Diaries & the Diaries She Read*, the final volume of a three-volume study, astutely examines the ways in which Woolf assessed, assimilated, fought, and accepted the many forms of violence, oppression, and horror she found during the years of these diaries' composition—1930-1941. Lounsberry's study of Woolf's diary began with *Becoming Virginia Woolf: Her Early Diaries & the Diaries She Read* (2014), which covers the years of Woolf's "passionate apprenticeship" and the beginnings of her literary career, and continued in *Virginia Woolf's Modernist Path: Her Middle Diaries & the Diaries She Read* (2016), which illustrates Woolf's burgeoning modernism and her growing confidence and fame as a writer. I argued in my review of the latter (in *Woolf Studies Annual* 24) that the middle installment of any trilogy is where the action happens, which implies that the final volume—the final act of the play, as it were—is where the threads come together and the story resolves, in this case with Woolf's death. Woolf's diary ends with ellipses; her life ends in suicide. It is to Lounsberry's credit that her book is not remotely gloomy: despite the oppressive nature of much that Woolf writes about in the years covered by these diaries—and Lounsberry herself acknowledges that "[m]elancholy hovers" (vii) as she concludes her work—her approach is clean, light, and life-affirming, highlighting Woolf's curiosity, love of language and literature, and joy and pleasure in art.

The final volume of Lounsberry's project is a welcome addition to Woolf studies, for it completes what is the most thorough examination of Woolf's diary to date. As I wrote of the second volume, it has been a peculiarity of Woolf studies that her diary has, until recently, received little critical attention and has been used largely as a biographical aid or a supplement to criticism of the novels, essays and stories. Throughout the three volumes, Lounsberry posits a three-part structure to Woolf's diaries that is rather at odds with the received opinion of the diaries' editors, Mitchell Leaska and Anne Olivier Bell. Rather than viewing Woolf's "apprenticeship" as ending with the 1909 diary as suggested by Leaska in *A Passionate Apprentice*, Lounsberry places the apprenticeship's end in 1918, thus including the first volumes of what Bell referred to as the "main series." Woolf's "middle period," for Lounsberry, runs from 1918 to 1929, the years in which Woolf establishes her modernist aesthetic and reaches what is arguably a career peak. In this final period, from 1930 until her death, Lounsberry discerns a change in Woolf's diaristic approach: she writes more frequently, fills more volumes, and comes to regard herself as something of a witness to global events while never forgetting the diary's personal benefits: "Her *own* diary now must be her parachute, her 'life,' her raft, her outlet. Woolf's diary now moves subtly toward public form" (314). Lounsberry's approach is in keeping with current trends in Woolf studies "that see Woolf's whole body of work [...] as one interrelated, yet multiform foray against tyranny and war" (3). Thus, it seems that she sees Woolf's diaries as proof against victimhood, a place in which she can assert her own being, speak in her own voice, and claim a place in the world in the face of approaching annihilation.

In *Virginia Woolf: The War Without, the War Within*, Lounsberry continues using the structure she established in the first two volumes. Each chapter begins with a description of each diary volume's physical characteristics—type of cover, color of pages and ink—gleaned from firsthand examination of the manuscripts in the Berg Collection of the New York Public Library (and she takes note of the occasional dramatic alteration to the diary's form, as when Woolf switches to a loose-leaf, two-ring notebook in 1937 [223]), and continues with an assessment of the volume's content, concluding with a discussion of the diarists Woolf read at the time of the volume's composition, with speculation as to how each diarist influenced Woolf's own writing, both in and out of the diary. For instance, the diary of Ellen Weeton, a governess, directly influences *Three Guineas* (198), and "[t]he Amberley diaries [...] revive the England of 1854 to 1876" (179) and refer directly to Woolf's relatives, including her father, Sir Leslie Stephen, which may have affected her thinking about the late-Victorian family dynamic at the time she was formulating her thoughts on *The Pargiters*. Woolf's diary reading during this period is typically broad and eclectic, and among the diarists cited here are Alice James, André Gide, Guy de Maupassant, Dr. John Salter, James Woodford, Leo and Countess Tolstoy, and Lord and Lady Amberley. As with the diaries Woolf read in the other periods of her life, there is little of the Harold Bloom "anxiety of influence" in Woolf's reading; rather, she finds inspiration and camaraderie in the diaries of others, and values them for what they can teach her, for the doors they open into other lives, for the mirrors they hold up to her. She finds comfort in Stephen MacKenna's love of the Greeks and in Dr. John Salter's depiction of the early loss of a parent and his long but childless marriage. Lounsberry's juxtaposition of analysis of Woolf's diary with discussion of the diarists she read provides further confirmation of Woolf's sensitivity as a reader.

From the outset, Lounsberry positions Woolf as a political animal, as someone who has so internalized the coming global conflict that it can be deemed, as Chapter One is titled, "the war within": "The *outer* world touches profoundly Virginia Woolf's *inner* life in 1929" (5). As the 1930s progress, Woolf's diary begins to incorporate more news, more headlines. As early as 1930, when she is writing *The Waves*, Woolf includes headlines of international events ("Lord Willingdon appointed Viceroy of India," "Gandhi set free") and more local stories, often on the topic of death ("Suicide of Peter Warlock" 30). This back and forth between the personal and the political, the global and the local, the sweeping and the quotidian, the large and small, is a hallmark for Lounsberry of Woolf's diary writing during these years. She argues that Woolf "attacks her fears" (103) squarely in the pages of the diary, fears both personal and global: her shyness, her "dress mania," and Hitler's rise to power and the progress of Oswald Mosley's British Union of Fascists (101).

Lounsberry presents a diary—and thus a life—that becomes less insular and more politically engaged, and which shows an awareness of the pressures of the outer world. There is a gradual sense in which Woolf begins to see her diary as something of a war chronicle, and Lounsberry suggests that the "weightier" (303) diary of 1940 is intended to interest Woolf's older self (at the moment that self is beginning to write her memoirs), so that she may look back later and more vividly recall the war years. Lounsberry's reading of the months leading up to Woolf's death in March 1941 is refreshingly free of gloom, and she chooses, in fact, to read Woolf's last entries as life-affirming, as when Woolf thinks of Vanessa Bell and wishes they could "infuse souls" (322) and, in the diary's last line, when she ends this life's work with the image of Leonard Woolf tending flowers. Nowhere is there a whiff of victimhood. It's difficult to imagine such a reading of Woolf's diaries in the 1980s, when the prevailing view of Woolf seemed to devolve into what Jane Marcus called "pathographies."

Barbara Lounsberry has achieved something remarkable with the completion of her project. She has given Woolf scholars a road-map through the text of Woolf's diaries, a text that is often so all-encompassing that it is difficult to get a foothold. By using the lens of Woolf's diaristic influences, Lounsberry provides readers with a clear focus for examining the diaries as a whole. As someone who is immersed in Woolf's diaries myself, I find Lounsberry's contribution invaluable, and it is a pleasure to salute her at the end of her endeavor.

—Drew Patrick Shannon, *Mount St. Joseph University*

Notes on Contributors

Erica Gene Delsandro is an Assistant Professor in the Department of Women's and Gender Studies at Bucknell University. Her research interests include modernist women writers, the gender politics of authorship, gender and lifewriting, as well as the gender politics of literary studies. She has published in *Soundings*, *Woolf Studies Annual*, *Clio*, and *Pedagogy* as well as in several of the *Selected Papers* volumes from the Annual Conference on Virginia Woolf. She was the guest editor of the Spring 2015 issue of *Virginia Woolf Miscellany*. Delsandro is currently working on a co-edited collection about affiliations among modernist women writers (UP of Florida) and on a monograph, *Modernism on the Margins: Misfits, Mongrels, and Mistresses.*

Diane F. Gillespie is Professor Emerita of English at Washington State University. Her research interests include early twentieth-century British women novelists, dramatists, and painters; relationships between visual and verbal art forms; and Hogarth Press publications. She is author of *The Sisters' Arts: The Writing and Painting of Virginia Woolf and Vanessa Bell* (1988, 1991 ppr.); co-editor of *Julia Duckworth Stephen: Stories for Children, Essays for Adults* (1987, 1990 ppr.), *Virginia Woolf and the Arts* (1997), and Cicely Hamilton's play *Diana of Dobsons* (2003); as well as editor of *The Multiple Muses of Virginia Woolf* (1993) and Woolf's *Roger Fry: A Biography* (1995) for the Shakespeare Head Press. In addition, she has published numerous journal articles and book chapters in, for example, Maggie Humm's *Edinburgh Companion to Woolf and the Arts* (2010), Helen Southworth's *Leonard and Virginia Woolf: The Hogarth Press and the Networks of Modernism* (2010), and *Virginia Woolf: Twenty-First-Century Approaches* edited by Jeanne Dubino et al. (2015).

Theodore Koulouris is senior lecturer in media and literary theory in the School of Media, University of Brighton. He is the author of *Hellenism and Loss in the Work of Virginia Woolf* (2011) and, in addition to the transcription of the "Greek Notebook," he has also recently published a political re-reading of Sophocles' *Antigone* through the prism of what he calls the neoliberal law: "Neither Sensible, Nor Moderate: Revisiting the Antigone" (2018), available here: www.mdpi.com/2076-0787/7/2/60. He is currently working on digital ontology through Jacques Derrida's work on the archive.

Submission Guidelines

Woolf Studies Annual invites articles on the work and life of Virginia Woolf and her milieu. The *Annual* intends to represent the breadth and eclecticism of critical approaches to Woolf and particularly welcomes new perspectives and contexts of inquiry. Articles discussing relations between Woolf and other writers and artists are also welcome.

Articles are sent for review anonymously to a member of the Editorial Board and at least one other reader. Manuscripts should not be under consideration elsewhere or have been previously published. It is strongly advised that those submitting work to *WSA* be familiar with the journal's content. Among criteria on which evaluation of submissions depends are whether an article demonstrates familiarity with scholarship already published in the field, whether the article is written clearly and effectively, and whether it makes a genuine contribution to Woolf studies.

Preparation of Copy

1. Articles are typically between 25 and 30 pages, and do not exceed 8,000 words. This is a guide rather than a stipulation, and inquiries about significantly shorter or longer submissions should be sent to the Editor at woolfstudiesannual@gmail.com.

2. A separate file should include the article's title, author's name, address, phone number, and email address. The author's name and any other identifying references should not appear on the manuscript to preserve anonymity for our readers.

3. All submissions must include an abstract of no more than 250 words.

4. Manuscripts should conform to the most recent MLA style.

5. Submissions should be sent as Word files by email to woolfstudiesannual@gmail.com.

6. Authors of accepted manuscripts are responsible for any necessary permissions fees and for securing any necessary permissions.

All editorial inquiries should be addressed to woolfstudiesannual@gmail.com.

Inquiries concerning orders, advertising, reviews, etc. should be addressed to PaceUP@pace.edu.

Mississippi
~ *Quarterly*
The Journal of Southern Cultures

Since 1948, the *Mississippi Quarterly* has published refereed articles on the life and culture of the South, past and present. Recent issues include essays on Toni Morrison, Kate Chopin, George Washington Cable, James Meredith, William Faulkner, Johnson Jones Hooper, Augusta Jane Evans, Ernest J. Gaines, Ron Rash, and Karen Russell. Recent special issues are devoted to William Styron's *The Confessions of Nat Turner* and The Twenty-First-Century Southern Novel.

Mississippi State University
College of Arts & Sciences

missq.msstate.edu

LEGACY
A Journal of American Women Writers

Edited by Susan Tomlinson,
Jennifer Putzi, and Jennifer S. Tuttle

The only journal to focus exclusively on American women's writing from the seventeenth through the early twentieth centuries.

The official journal of the
Society for the Study of American Women Writers

Legacy is available online through Project MUSE and JSTOR.

Both offer free access via library subscriptions.

Read it at
bit.ly/LEG_MUSE
or *bit.ly/LEG_JSTOR*

There are additional resources and information about publishing in *Legacy* at **legacywomenwriters.org**

Follow *Legacy* on Twitter:
@LegacyWmenWrite

For information on membership in the Society for the Study of American Women Writers, visit *ssawwnew.wordpress.com*.

For subscriptions or back issues:
Visit nebraskapress.unl.edu
or call 402-472-8536

Tulsa Studies in Women's Literature

A special forum on Latin American Women Authors

Spring 38, No. 1

@TSWLJournal   tswl.utulsa.edu   Find us on Facebook!

Mosaic
an interdisciplinary critical journal

51.3 (September 2018): Scale

Given the scale of such issues as climate change and of factors contributing to it, must theory, too, undergo a transition from local and individual to global perspectives? In what might a global imaginary consist, and how might it relate to existing critiques of globalization as but a label for the hegemony of Western culture? This issue considers "greening" theory, ecocriticism, the Anthropocene, climate change, and environmental and animal ethics.

51.4 (December 2018): Living On Symposium Proceedings

This issue brings together papers presented at *Mosaic's* 50th-anniversary *Living On* Symposium, held at the University of Manitoba on March 9-11, 2017. Taking its theme and title from Jacques Derrida's "Living On/Borderlines" (1979), the Symposium brought together participants from diverse disciplines to reflect on the continuing life of their fields into the next 50 years.

Call for General Submissions

Mosaic, an interdisciplinary critical journal is a quarterly journal that brings insights from a wide variety of disciplines to bear on the theoretical, practical, and cultural dimensions of literary works. We accept submissions for our general issues year-round. Please see our website for complete submission guidelines. All enquiries can be directed to:

Dr. Shep Steiner, Editor
Mosaic, an interdisciplinary critical journal
Email: mosasub@umanitoba.ca
Website: https://mosaic.umanitoba.ca
Submit Online Now: https://mosaic.umanitoba.ca/common/submit

Twentieth-Century Literature

Focusing on literary-cultural production emerging from or responding to the twentieth century, *Twentieth-Century Literature* offers essays, grounded in a variety of approaches, that interrogate and enrich the ways we understand the literary cultures of the times. This includes work considering how those cultures are bound up with the crucial intellectual, social, aesthetic, political, economic, and environmental developments that have shaped the early twenty-first century as well.

Lee Zimmerman, editor

Sign up for new issue alerts at **dukeu.press/alerts**.

Subscribe today.

Quarterly
Online access is included with a print subscription.

Individuals $40
Students $28
Single issues $12

dukeupress.edu/twentieth-century-literature

The twenty-fifth volume of *Woolf Studies Annual*
was published in Spring 2019
by Pace University Press

Cover and Interior Layout by Alicia Hughes
The journal was typeset in Times New Roman and Arial
and printed by Lightning Source in La Vergne, Tennessee

Pace University Press

Director: Manuela Soares
Associate Director: Sephanie Hsu
Marketing Manager: Patricia Hinds

Graduate Assistants: Jessica Estrella and Alicia Hughes
Graduate Student Aide: Daren J. Fleming

www.ingramcontent.com/pod-product-compliance
Lightning Source LLC
Chambersburg PA
CBHW061445300426
44114CB00014B/1851